LOOKING IN
SEEING OUT

To Lori
with respect
& universal Love

Menas

Dr. Menas Kafatos holds a Ph.D. in physics from M.I.T. He teaches and researches theoretical astrophysics and quantum theory at George Mason University, Fairfax, Virginia. Author of *The Conscious Universe: Part and Whole in Modern Physical Theory,* he has published seven books and over 100 articles. A student of many philosophical systems, he is also a Reiki Master.

Dr. Thalia Kafatou holds a Ph.D. in computer science and management information systems. She has taught computer science at three universities and has held management posts at M.I.T. and DuPont. A longtime student of Kashmir Shaivism, she is also a Reiki Master.

Cover art by Lifesmith, Classic Fractals
Cover design by Pam Norpell

LOOKING IN SEEING OUT

Consciousness and Cosmos

Menas Kafatos and Thalia Kafatou

This publication made possible with the assistance of the Kern Foundation

QUEST BOOKS
The Theosophical Publishing House
Wheaton, Ill. U.S.A.
Madras, India/London, England

The Theosophical Publishing House
P.O. Box 270
Wheaton, IL 60189-0270
A publication of the Theosophical Publishing House,
a department of the Theosophical Society in America

Library of Congress Cataloging-in Publication Data
Kafatos, Menas C.
    Looking in, seeing out : consciousness and cosmos / Menas
Kafatos, Thalia Kafatou.
        p. cm.
    Includes bibliographical references.
    ISBN 0-8356-0674-0 (pbk.)
    1. Consciousness. 2. Cosmology. 3. Mysticism. 4. Quantum
theory. I. Kafatou, Thalia. II. Title.
B105.C477K34 1991
126—dc20   91-50275
                                                                    CIP

Printed in the United States of America
by Versa Press

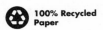 **100% Recycled Paper**

Contents

List of Illustrations

Acknowledgments

The authors would like to express thanks to their editor, John White, for his assistance and encouragement.

We thank SYDA Foundation for permission to refer to Swami Muktananda's writings and his and Swami Chidvilasananda's sayings.

Introduction
Undivided Wholeness

This work is a treatise on wholeness: the wholeness implied by modern physical theory and the intrinsic wholeness of consciousness. Quantum phenomena exhibit a wholeness which is usually absent or at least imperceptible in the world of everyday experience, the world where the mind and the senses rule supreme. Wholeness and union of opposites along with complementarity and indeterminacy constitute the foundation of the quantum view of the world. The peculiar union of opposites postulated by quantum theory is not merely a philosophical principle. The very phenomena of the microcosm demand the union of opposites. If it turns out that this peculiar union of opposites applies not just to the world of the quantum but to universal phenomena at all levels, it would have profound implications for our views of the universe. *It would constitute the beginning of scientifically establishing that undivided wholeness is the fundamental property of the cosmos.* That is precisely what we demonstrate in this book.

Using the terms "undivided" with "wholeness" is not being redundant. Even though they are related, the terms are not a grammatical tautology. The reason is, quite simply, that until recently natural sciences proceeded under the assumption that what is whole—namely the universe—can be studied by dividing it into parts, and that the subsequent study of these constituent parts will eventually disclose the whole. If, however the universe is truly an undivided whole, this reductionist approach to science is bound to fail. The whole is more than the sum of its parts. The parts do not imply the whole: on the contrary, the undivided whole implies the parts.

In this book we deal with the microcosm, the macrocosm and the underlying consciousness which, we believe, gives substance as well as meaning to both. Obviously the very large and the very small are related; after all the same physics is used to study both. But what about consciousness? How is it related? What is consciousness after all? We know we are conscious, and we think that at least the most advanced animals possess some sort of consciousness. As one ponders the question of how to define consciousness, one realizes that it is much easier to talk about the characteristics of something or someone who is conscious than to give a precise definition of consciousness. Typical definitions of consciousness found in a common dictionary such as *Webster's* are:

1. The quality or state of being aware, especially of something within oneself. (This would constitute the "looking in" quality of consciousness.)
2. The state or fact of being conscious of an external object, state, or fact. (This would constitute the "seeing out" quality of consciousness.)
3. Awareness.
4. The state of being characterized by sensation, emotion, volition and thought (i.e., the properties of mind).
5. The totality of conscious states of an individual.
6. The normal state of conscious life.
7. The upper level of mental life of which the person is aware as contrasted with unconscious processes.

These definitions are not entirely satisfactory. Many, like the second definition, contain the very word they are to define. The first and third definitions substitute the terms "aware" or "awareness," which are as difficult to define as "consciousness." The fourth definition equates consciousness with the mind. Animals possess sensation, emotion and probably volition, but it is not clear what the term "thought" implies in the case of animals: probably most scientists as well as lay people would hesitate to attribute mind to animals. Yet animals are conscious, and as a result any definition which makes mind a prerequisite for consciousness is necessarily incomplete. The problem with any attempt to define "consciousness" or other equivalent terms such as awareness is that one runs into circular logic. We all know we are conscious and suspect that most, or even all, living beings are conscious, yet we cannot define consciousness in words.

Rather than attempting to define consciousness, one can be more successful at describing its functions. Perhaps no system of thought has come closer to dealing as completely as possible with consciousness than Eastern metaphysics. The ancient sage-philosophers of the East—especially of India, Kashmir, Tibet, Japan and China—wrote extensively about consciousness. Their writings reflect general principles which emerged from their own experiences and yet had universal validity. In the East we find a wonderful interweaving of subjectivity and objectivity, of everyday world and transcendence, of practical life and metaphysics. In the East looking in and seeing out are not considered irreconcilable opposites but rather complementary aspects of the human capacity. The eastern sages found it easier to talk about the functions of consciousness. They called these functions the five-fold act. These five acts are creation, sustenance, reabsorption, concealment and revelation. These same five acts can be seen operating in all processes in the universe, even those involving "inanimate" quanta. We elaborate on this in Chapter 3. This set of correspondences makes it plausible that consciousness itself may be fundamental not just to sentient beings but to the entire cosmos.

The operational definitions of consciousness found in various philosophical traditions of the world can be better understood as a state that is personally experienced rather than as intellectual statements. Various philosophers/sages of both the East and the West have talked about consciousness as nothing more than existence, the awareness of existence and the completeness or contentment that arises from that awareness. They arrived at those definitions from their own experiences, experiences so consistently universal that they must be considered to reveal a timeless objective state beyond the narrow confines of human history, tradition, religion or language. It is then possible that matters pertaining to consciousness can be scientific in the sense that conclusions can be verified objectively and even experimentally, so long as the experimentation involves one's entire being, not just the intellect, as is the case in scientific inquiry. Such work would seek to understand our whole undivided consciousness.

Returning to the significance of consciousness for the physical universe, we must keep in mind that consciousness constitutes awareness of outside objects of perception (seeing out) or internal states of existence (looking in). It seems fundamental that any systems of knowledge which seek an understanding of the universe involve consciousness in a fundamental way. The operational definitions of consciousness from the East imply that consciousness is that underlying glue which keeps everything in the universe together. Its very nature must be undivided wholeness because consciousness itself cannot be divided, cannot be experienced as a separate object apart from the agency of awareness, since *it is* that very agency of awareness. Consciousness itself divides but it also synthesizes. To put it in other terms, consciousness is the means through which one attempts to know consciousness. Consciousness thus cannot be known as an object of perception because it is the very light by which knowledge is illumined. The *contents of consciousness* are secondary to *consciousness* itself. Consciousness is also the end; for once realized, consciousness constitutes the union of the individual with the underlying reality of everything: undivided wholeness—the union of looking in and seeing out.

If indeed consciousness constitutes undivided wholeness, then hints of such wholeness should be prevalent in the universe. Nevertheless, those hints cannot be proven scientifically because science itself is based on the division between object and subject, while consciousness is fundamentally indivisible. It is here that Western science and its most advanced guard, quantum physics, play an important role. Quantum theory implies the underlying wholeness and yet cannot prove it, since any science or system of knowledge which is based on the division between object and subject cannot prove wholeness.

A quantum is a very small bit of physical energy. As the most successful scientific theory of the physical world, quantum physics provided a profound new paradigm or system of our view of the world with staggering implications for science, philosophy and our understanding of the nature of reality. The predictions and experimental verifications of quantum theory have demonstrated that our everyday "commonsense" views of the world are decidedly limited.

Quantum theory is based on the *principle of indeterminacy,* or uncertainty, formulated by the German physicist Werner Heisenberg. It states that one cannot possibly know simultaneously with limitless accuracy all the physical parameters of a quantum system. It follows that today we understand that the universe is so immensely intricate because, ironically, nature itself imposes definite limits to our knowledge of the universe.

The world of the phenomena "out there" is intricately interwoven with our knowledge and its limitations. Were it not for the fundamental limitation of the uncertainty principle encountered in quantum phenomena, we would know nothing of radioactivity, nuclear reactions and, therefore, energy generation in the interior of the stars and the sun. Without the sun, of course, there would be no life. The cosmos would be easier to explain and yet it simply would not be what it is, a cosmos of structure, evolution and life.

Not only are there fundamental limits to our knowledge of the physical universe; a pervasive duality complicates reality even further. Quantum phenomena exhibit what appears at first glance to be a prevalent dualistic nature. This tendency, called the *principle of complementarity* was formulated by the Danish physicist Niels Bohr. The significance of complementarity cannot be grasped by appealing to everyday experience. Even though life is full of dualities, opposites do not seem to get reconciled in our everyday world. In the world of the quantum, however, they do. In simple terms, quanta behave in two ways, sometimes as particles, sometimes as waves. These two constructs, particle and wave, are diametrically opposite. A particle is a localized "something" in space and time; a wave extends non-locally over large regions of space and time. In other words, quantum theory states that one thing sometimes becomes its opposite, its *antithesis*.

Another intriguing consequence of quantum theory is that it entails *non-locality*. Non-locality provides the most direct connection to the general metaphysical principle of wholeness and is prevalent in quantum phenomena. Particles are not just localizable entities; when they are not observed, they imply a wave-like, non-local existence. The very "limitation" of the uncertainty principle allows then for the non-local nature of quantum phenomena and hints not only that the universe cannot be completely known but also that it cannot be fundamentally divided. To put it differently, what is whole cannot be known completely as an external object of perception. How could it be otherwise, since wholeness must also include all observers and all instruments of perception? Quantum theory has substantiated the metaphysical belief that since the universe is an undivided unity, science will not ultimately achieve complete knowledge of the universe as an external object of perception. *It is in this important aspect that Western science and Eastern philosophy seem to agree,* even though the first concerns itself with the universe (seeing out) while the second concerns itself primarily with the individual (looking in). In an ultimate sense, from both universal and individual perspectives, consciousness and its objects of perception constitute an undivided whole.

To bring the point home, let's look at the nature of quanta in relation to the universe. As we saw, the term "quantum" means a very small increment or parcel of energy. On the other hand, energy is defined in physics as the capacity to do work. In other words a quantum is a small, individual parcel of capacity to do work. Since Einstein showed in his special theory of relativity that matter and energy are equivalent, a quantum could really refer to a parcel of energy, like a photon of light, or to a parcel of matter, like an electron. We will use the term "quantum" to refer both to constituents of matter and bits of energy. These two concepts, matter and energy, are complementary; they are both needed to define a greater whole, even though in our everyday experience energy and matter are not the same. That greater whole is what we term, for a lack of a better term, *quantum reality*. And this is what complementarity conveys—the notion that pairs of opposites are needed to understand the greater whole which the opposites constitute.

At the other end of the scale of physical sizes lies the macrocosm, the physical universe. A working definition of the term "universe" involves the totality of things and phenomena observed or postulated to exist. A synonymous term for our purposes is "cosmos," an ancient Greek term, allegedly invented by Pythagoras, which means ornament. The fundamental beauty and intricacy of the universe, like a beautiful ornament, leaves the spectator with a sense of awe. The universe constitutes the macrocosm, the whole, the large, in juxtaposition to the small, the individual quantum. These two, the microcosm of the quantum and the macrocosm of the universe, constitute the limits of what we can perceive. In the middle of this range, lies the comfortable "everyday" world of human experience.

Examining the quantum and the cosmos raises questions about ultimate order in the universe, the ultimate capacity of the human intellect to comprehend rationally everything there is. Here the issue needs to be generalized beyond Einstein's specific concerns about the validity of quantum theory. The issues that Einstein and Niels Bohr debated for so many years seem to have been settled in the laboratory in accordance more with Bohr's views than Einstein's: the probabilistic interpretation of quantum phenomena and the associated uncertainty principle (to which Einstein objected) are a great triumph of the human mind and have been confirmed again and again in the laboratory, most recently with the experiments testing Bell's theorem (explained below). Yet Einstein's concern is also valid. He held that in principle the scientist can understand the universe rationally and completely. The study of the universe reveals a great paradox. The universe is knowable through the language of mathematics. Human intellect concludes that there is great order, great rationality in the universe. Yet, quantum theory demands that knowledge of the physical world is inherently probabilistic, inherently not completely determinable.

The issue of reality bothered Einstein even more than the issue of knowledge based on probabilities. Upon closer examination one realizes that the two issues are closely related. For if the universe is inherently indeterminable, then what is "real"? If we cannot achieve complete knowledge of reality, how can we know what is real in an absolute sense? Can something be real if we cannot know it? These are metaphysical issues that touch the very foundation of science. Precisely because they are metaphysical issues, they cannot be answered through the scientific method alone.

Modern physics is based on foundations which are radically different from the philosophical underpinnings of classical physics. The latter provided a view for a world which, in principle at least, was completely knowable and real—real in the sense that the world and the mathematical and physical description of it were assumed to exist independently of what the observer did to find out about the world. However, there is nothing in either modern physics or classical physics that can define or describe what is "real." Somehow the issue of reality, as well as the issue of existence to which it is closely related, remain outside the machinery of science. The great difference between classical physics and quantum physics is that the former presumed a set of metaphysical principles about reality and knowledgeability based on the assumption that the observer and the observing process are completely divorced from the cosmos, while the latter recognizes from the outset that the observer and the observing process are intricately interwoven with what is being studied. Quantum theory recognizes the interweaving of the observer and the observed and yet can provide no explanation of how to introduce the observer formally into the theory. The situation is like trying to measure the temperature of water: inserting a thermometer into a container of water alters even so slightly the temperature of the water. For quantum theory, the observing process is a necessity and also a mystery. For classical physics the observing process was totally irrelevant because it presumed that the universe and the mathematical tools used to study the universe were both real. In other words, classical physics presumed that the universe was real in the physical domain and that the mathematics used to study it were real in a transcendent mental domain outside the physical world. Classical metaphysics entailed a two-domain division that was put into a system of thought most eloquently by Descartes. Metaphysical dualism is a prevalent, almost unchallenged view followed to this day by most practicing scientists. The issue of reality, though, is glossed over by the still popular insistence that the language of mathematical physics is fundamentally real and complete in the sense of existing outside the human intellect that invented the language.

Upon examination, one realizes that the issue of reality is the same as the issue of existence. For example, do quanta really exist? Science cannot *prove* the reality of something, nor its existence. These issues can be addressed but never resolved, once the foundations of science, or the general principles which form metaphysics, have been established and once consciousness itself is addressed. The word "metaphysics" contains the prefix *meta*, which denotes that which is beyond or higher than. Ultimately reality, existence and consciousness are terms which cannot be defined even though everyone knows intuitively what they mean. After all, it is only our interactions with the sense objects of which we are aware, not the inner essence of objects.

In the first part of this book we examine what modern science has to say about the nature of the universe. We follow the great triumphs of classical Newtonian physics and the Age of Reason to the beginning of the twentieth century when the roof collapsed, and the classical way of looking at the universe was shown to be an inadequate description of the universe. Within a few years a profound revolution in the way of perceiving the universe was ushered in by the development of quantum theory. This new way of perceiving the universe brought about a wholeness, a synthesis that did not exist in classical physics. The role of the observer was shown to be of paramount importance in formulating our perceptions of the universe. No longer could one talk about a physical universe and be totally oblivious to the existence of observers. The theories of relativity and quantum theory, the greatest intellectual scientific achievements of our time, both emphasize this point.

In pursuing a new vision of the universe, the foundations for a synthesis between physical science and metaphysics are laid. A generalized principle of complementarity, applied to cosmology as well as other fields, such as mathematics, biology and psychology, is likely to be a very important component of the emergent scientific paradigm. Such a generalized principle of complementarity serves to demonstrate how consciousness works, how the universe is projected out, how we perceive the universe and how we obtain a coherent picture of the outside world.

Since contemporary science says little about consciousness, one must switch to philosophies that have more to say. The sages have insisted that consciousness itself—not mere human consciousness but a primal field of cosmic extent—is the cause of the universe as well as the only Existence after everything else has been dissolved. Even though the language used by these "perennial" philosophies is sometimes difficult for Westerners to understand, what they say is nevertheless profound: the primal and final cause of the universe is nothing other than consciousness, and in truth the universe itself is nothing other than the same consciousness. Consciousness is indeed an integral part of the universe present since creation, rather than a mere afterthought of evolution. In a sense, the great field from which the cosmos springs is universal Consciousness, which as it vibrates creates everything. In human terms a vibration of consciousness is thought. In this context, the statement that everything sprang from Thought, or *Logos* as the ancients termed it, acquires profound meaning.

The universal creative process expounded in the ancient philosophy of Shaivism can be experienced in the individual as the unfoldment of sound from the depths of one's being.

The creative process assumes many steps which result in the final earth level, the level of the everyday world. However, the ancient sages did not intend to formulate a philosophical theory of the creative process that could be followed by the intellect alone. The mind is important, but the creative process has to be experienced in one's entire being. Transcending the mind leads to direct mystical experiences, experiences beyond the ordinary, which reinforce whatever intellectual understanding one has of the identity between individual and universal consciousness.

Moreover, the mystical experience is a universal phenomenon. The remarkable fact one discovers when one studies the phenomenon of mysticism, as described in all perennial traditions, is how common it is. Mystical experience is nothing more than the union of the individual with the universal, the merging of the two, the rediscovery of one's own true nature. This experience is not limited to a particular country, culture, religion or school of thought. The tendency to assume that a single culture, religion or philosophical system has a monopoly on Truth goes counter to the universal message that all great sages, philosophers and religious thinkers of all traditions promulgated.

The second part of the book deals with this *perennial philosophy*, or what we may term the metaphysical science of consciousness. The founders of this science, in both East and West, emphasized the universality of their teachings. This is the experience of countless humans who embarked on the task to find out their true nature. It is a science because, like physical science, it is a complete body of knowledge that can be taught. Unlike physical science, though, which is concerned only with phenomena outside of one's own being (seeing out), metaphysical science involves experience at the most fundamental human level (looking in). And as such it predates ordinary science and will probably last as long as humans last. The metaphysical thinkers of the great philosophical schools of Vedanta and Shaivism were concerned with the origin and evolution of the universe as well as with the origin and evolution of the individual. In their view, one could approach either and understand the other because, at the most fundamental level, universal principles are at work. *Sound*, or vibration, for them was fundamental in the process of creation of both the universe and the individual.

To the great metaphysical thinkers the nature of the mind was of paramount importance to understanding human nature. Like sound, the mind is nothing other than vibration. Whereas gross sound is a vibration of matter, the mind is a subtle vibration of consciousness. As one begins to explore one's own inner nature, one experiences subtler and subtler vibrations of the mind below the thinking process. However, the foundation of our being cannot ultimately be understood by the mind, because that foundation provides the very light of consciousness which allows the mind to function.

The last part of the book deals with a synthesis between physical science and metaphysical science. Such a synthesis cannot ignore the individual human being and his or her place in the universe. The words and experiences of the great sages and metaphysical thinkers can guide us in the process of experiencing the undivided wholeness which includes us as an integral part. One then goes, in full circle, back to understanding and experiencing one's own true nature from which in reality all philosophies start. All great philosophers and sages have urged humans to look within themselves in order to discover a vast hidden treasure. On this internal level the synthesis is consummated: everything one is looking for is within. The outer universe is then seen to be what it really is—a projection of consciousness (looking in seeing out). Moreover, individual consciousness is seen as identical to universal Consciousness. We can look through our telescopes at the farthest reaches of space or through our microscopes to the smallest atoms. Or we can close our eyes and experience the vast universe within ourselves, as a grain of sand can be experienced within one's hand. Human consciousness is part of universal Consciousness in the same way that a drop is part of the ocean. The stuff of the drop *is* the stuff of the ocean; they are identical. The reason we search for the origins of the cosmos is because we are really searching to find out who we are. The search for the outer is no different from the search for the inner reality. Looking in and seeing out are ultimately two sides of the same process. It is here that the ancient philosophical urging "Know Thyself" acquires its true meaning.

The present work can be distinguished from many popular books which attempt to prove fundamental connections between modern physics and philosophical, religious systems. Quantum theory says nothing about consciousness. It only shows the inadequacy of the scientific paradigm to obtain a complete picture of the universe which must include the role of the consciousness of the observers. Modern physics shows the need for synthesis but does not accomplish that synthesis. We do not attempt to show that quantum physics is evolving toward Eastern philosophies or that Eastern philosophies are becoming more valid because of the findings of Western science. Our position is that physics does not need mysticism for support, and neither does mysticism need physics for validation. Rather, the two are complementary.

This book represents a synthesis. It synthesizes our training as two physicists and technical people with our study of metaphysics and Eastern philosophies and with our practice and experiences of Siddha meditation and other systems which expose one to other dimensions, such as Reiki, the Usui system of natural healing.[1] It is our deepest belief that both science and philosophy, both physics and metaphysics, both everyday experiences and transcendent experiences are essential to our search for the truth about ourselves and our place in the vast, beautiful cosmos.

1
The Universe of Newton and Einstein

I cannot believe that God plays dice.
Albert Einstein

Today many people believe that the natural sciences hold the key to all the mysteries of the universe. Yet the sciences are a fairly recent human intellectual product. Barely four hundred years ago, scientific methodology was in its infancy. Scientists answer questions in their field by formulating theories and testing these theories in the laboratory. Scientific theory and experimentation go hand in hand. Armed with this dual weapon, the sciences have achieved truly impressive successes. Natural sciences, particularly physics, chemistry and astronomy, are viewed by many people as rational systems of knowledge which possess ultimate objectivity based on the rules of logic, since their language is mathematics. Although scientists know better, in many people's minds there is no limit to scientific knowledge. However, the scientific method has been so successful precisely because scientific knowledge is by its very nature in constant flux. What we consider scientifically correct today is likely to be shown to be at least limited if not wrong a few years down the road.

The new physics accepts quite clearly that there are fundamental and inherent limits to our knowledge of nature. Also, quantum theory implies profound truths that run counter to common sense. For example, it questions the independent reality of objects and suggests that reality has to be non-local. And yet, despite the great revolution in physics brought about by the theories of relativity and quantum physics, science is still viewed today as if it were an all-powerful, complete system of knowledge, with answers to everything. This opinion is a vestige of the way seventeenth to nineteenth century mathematicians and physicists saw their fields. What quantum physics says about the world has not yet filtered down to the common person or even to the other physical sciences. It is even fair to say that physicists themselves do not worry in their everyday work about the limits of scientific knowledge or about the profound implications of what quantum theory says about how we should view the universe.

Revolutions in science are not written in blood but in ink. Over time they bring about profound shifts in the outlook of scientists and, ultimately, of society at large—what Thomas Kuhn termed a shift in the dominant paradigm (Kuhn, 1962), or a shift in the dominant view of the world. The worldview implied in the profound paradigm shift which occurred during the Renaissance (between the sixteenth and seventeenth centuries) was fundamentally different from the paradigm shift that occurred at the beginning of the twentieth century. In what follows we will provide the reader with a brief introduction to the worldviews associated with these two shifts—the shift to the paradigm of classical physics and the shift from this to the paradigm of modern physics. We start here because, to make sense of metaphysical views of reality and to attempt a synthesis between science and metaphysics, we first have to examine what science says about physical reality. The interested reader can find more detailed accounts of modern physics elsewhere (see, for example, Herbert, 1987; Zukav, 1979; Kafatos and Nadeau, 1990, and references therein) and this discussion is not intended as a crash course in quantum theory or the theory of relativity. Rather it is an introduction to the salient points of these great theories and their consequences.

Renaissance

The life and teaching of Jesus of Nazareth brought about a profound change in European history. The Western world became more humane. Christ's vision coupled with the ideals of the ancient Greek philosophers transformed the Roman world. With the fall of the Roman Empire in the West and the survival of the Eastern Empire in Constantinople, European civilization's dominant paradigm was a religious outlook. Throughout the Middle Ages the chain of continuity linking the Divine with human life and with nature remained intact. However, this chain was severed by the new vision brought about by the Renaissance and by the emergence of the paradigm of classical physics.

In the two centuries between the fall of Constantinople and the birth of Isaac Newton on Christmas Day, 1642, Western Europe experienced far-reaching changes. In late medieval times a new class of merchants became prosperous and powerful throughout Europe. Sparked by the new wealth and the concentration of power in the hands of the merchants, medieval feudalism disappeared, and nobility and royalty began to lose their absolute control of society. These changes affected society's basic philosophical outlook. Religious life and God were not the central concern of the average person anymore; instead the individual gradually became the center of the universe. As a result, people began to question the authority of Christian theology.

Along with the shift in the West away from God, a dualistic conception of reality, which implied a split between human beings and nature and a split between the individual and society, became legitimated in people's minds, as the authority of science became more established. For centuries, the Christian churches had provided an unchallenged authority that was comforting to medieval people because it provided answers to basic questions, such as the purpose of human birth and the role of each person in society. However, the new scientific paradigm proved incapable, perhaps by its very nature, of answering such questions. Despite the excesses of medieval religion in the West, the loss of God eventually damaged the very ideals of Western societies: With the loss of a sense of divine purpose in the life of the average person, the freedom, rights and betterment of the individual did not harmonize with the rights and betterment of society at large.

It is often stated that the Renaissance was brought about by the rediscovery of ancient Greek writings. However, the work of Renaissance thinkers such as Copernicus, Kepler and Galileo was in fact more a reaction to the Aristotelian outlook of the Catholic Church than a result of the adoption of an ancient Greek philosophical system. It is undoubtedly true that in their quest for a new system that would account for physical phenomena, Renaissance thinkers were strongly influenced by the mathematics of Pythagoras and the philosophy of Plato regarding the eternal, immutable truths and used these ideas in their polemics against Aristotelian physics and astronomy. However, Renaissance thinkers certainly did not adopt uniformly either the Pythagorean or Platonic systems of living. It is, therefore, an exaggeration to claim that the Renaissance signaled a return to ancient ideals, because the Greek philosophical ideals entailed a complete way of living. Renaissance Europe did not resemble the ancient Greek city-states in any way, and it would be naive to assume that the new conceptual system of the world was identical to that of the ancient Greeks. In fact, the work of Archimedes, the ancient Greek who perhaps came closest to thinking and working like a modern scientist, remained relatively unknown until modern times.

The rise of modern science is usually traced to the work of five Renaissance figures: Copernicus, Kepler, Galileo, Descartes and Newton. These men should not be called "scientists," at least in the modern sense. They were interested not only in purely scientific concerns such as the structure of the solar system but also in metaphysical questions. In Renaissance terminology, they were "natural philosophers." Nicolaus Copernicus (1473-1543), for example, would have been described by his contemporaries as an administrator, diplomat, student of economics and classical literature and, foremost, church dignitary. The ideal Renaissance scholar was concerned with general principles and, unlike most modern scientists, did not specialize in a particular discipline. Natural philosophers drew no clear dichotomy between religion and science, between individuals and God. Most Renaissance scholars were either devoutly religious or did not easily dismiss the spiritual.

Copernicus' bold step consisted in realizing that the established Aristotelian/Ptolemaic geocentric system of the universe was cumbersome and could be replaced by a simpler system, in which the sun was the center of the universe. His work was probably influenced by the Neo-Pythagorean belief systems, widespread during the Renaissance, which held that a "central fire" was the center of everything. Similarly, Johannes Kepler (1571-1630), who formulated famous laws of planetary motion, was probably motivated by the mystical, Pythagorean-like belief in the existence of geometrical symmetries in the universe (Burtt, 1954).

Galileo Galilei (1564-1642) constructed a telescope with which he observed the planets, sun and moon. His observations dealt a mortal blow to the Aristotelian belief that the heavens are perfect and totally different from the earth. Galileo was the first to weld together experimentation and mathematical reasoning into what is known today as scientific methodology (Drake, 1957, 1970). Despite his clash with the hierarchy of the Catholic Church and with Aristotelian scholars, Galileo still had a role for God in his philosophy. Whereas in medieval philosophy, God, human beings and nature formed a continuous chain, in Galileo's view humans stood apart from nature, which was essentially mathematical, and which was set in motion by God who provided the first cause (Crombie et al., 1961). The methodology of Galileo eventually proved superior to that of Aristotelian scholars. It includes the process of experimentation and allowed Galileo to formulate important physical principles, such as the law of inertia and the relativity of motion, according to which the laws of physics are independent of the motion of the observer. As long as one deals only with the physical realm, religion cannot account for observed phenomena as well as science, because scientific methodology is precisely suited for the physical realm. Yet, in a strange sense, Galileo, Descartes and Newton were unabashed idealists, who were responsible for the establishment of the scientific idealism that has recently been questioned by quantum theory. They deeply believed that mathematical and geometrical ideas mirror the essences of physical reality and that nature is mathematical in its essence (Kafatos and Nadeau, 1990). In this idealistic view of a universal, mathematical perfection, they did not differ from their intellectual opponents, Catholic scholars, who were likewise idealists who believed in a perfect metaphysical order, albeit a different one—a divine perfection.

The Emergence of Newtonian Physics

Isaac Newton (1642-1727) is considered by many people to be the greatest scientist who ever lived. His genius opened the path that is still followed by the majority of scientists. By combining observation and deductive reasoning— reasoning from the general to the particular—he demonstrated that the universe could be understood in terms of the language of mathematics. In his *Philosophiae Naturalis Principia Mathematica* (1687) Newton provided a grand synthesis of what we now call classical mechanics and the application of his physics to the motions of planets around the sun. His famous law of gravity applied everywhere and was thus rightly termed universal by Newton. His three laws of motion accounted for Kepler's planetary laws. Moreover, Newton provided a physical basis to justify the Copernican system, previously only a mathematical model. After Newton, theories in physics would be formulated in terms of statements called "laws," expressible in the symbolic language of mathematics. Newton assumed—as every classical physicist after him has also assumed—that these laws are eternal and that they transcend the physical world which they describe. Despite his brilliance, Newton and his successors completely ignored the role of the observer-physicist who is formulating these laws. As we have noted, quantum theory eventually questioned Newton's conclusions and the entire classical paradigm, including the very meaning of physical laws.

It took Newton only a few years to develop his physics, but it took the next two hundred years for the paradigm based on his work to become fully developed and for its implications to be appreciated. To be sure, a number of serious problems in Newtonian physics were never resolved. Newton assumed that space is absolute—in Newton's own words "similar and unmovable"—although this concept was rejected by his contemporary, German natural philosopher Gottfried Wilhelm Leibniz, and was continually debated by philosophers over the next two centuries. Newton also assumed that space is infinite in extent. But how then could the effects of gravity be felt by distant objects? Also implicit in Newton's dynamics was the assumption of instantaneous propagation of the effects of forces, the so-called "action at a distance." The followers of Descartes and Leibniz would term the concept of action at a distance "obscure," and Newton himself was not happy with it. In the conclusion of his *Principia* Newton opted instead for the concept of a field, to be examined shortly.

It was not until the theories of relativity and quantum electrodynamics were developed that these problems were resolved. We now know that in physical interactions there is no instantaneous propagation of the effects of forces. The maximum speed of propagation is the speed of light; the effects of gravity, like light, propagate with the maximum speed of light. We now also assume that space and time are finite rather than infinite; in other words, the universe had a definite beginning and may well be finite and bound in space. Finally, the very concept of Newtonian force was done away with by Einstein's theory of general relativity. These limitations of Newtonian physics in no way diminish the significance of Newton's contributions. After all, classical physics is widely applicable in most scientific situations even today, as it adequately describes everyday physical experience.

In addition to his pioneering work in physics, Newton wrote extensively on metaphysics—more than a million words of theological writings. Newton speculated about what were then metaphysical questions like the age of the universe. Newtonian physicists thought it possible that the universe was infinitely old, although Newton himself believed the biblical version of cosmogony and held that the universe had existed for 6000 years. In his *General Scholium* appended to the second edition of *Principia*, Newton describes his belief in God:

> This most beautiful system of the sun, planets and comets, could only proceed from the counsel and dominion of an intelligent and powerful Being.

Newton called this Being the "Lord God or Universal Ruler" and, in the third edition of *Principia*, "the God of Israel, God of Gods, Lord of Lords."

Newton and future scientists regarded rational inquiry as a valuable tool for discovering the divine plan of the world. To conduct rational inquiry was, in a sense, to attempt to comprehend this divine plan, and Newton believed in a divine plan. He held in principle that the universe is understandable and predictable through rational inquiry, and that the tools of the inquiry were physics, astronomy and the language of mathematics. Confidence in scientific rationalism reached a peak in the eighteenth century, the period known as the Enlightenment. Newton's system was incorporated into a precise philosophical system of the world by the followers of the philosophers Descartes and Spinoza and of the mathematician Laplace.

The Metaphysics of Classical Physics

René Descartes (1596-1650), is usually credited with the dualistic concept of reality, the basic split between mind and matter. Even though he expressed the perceived dualism more eloquently than others, one person alone could not have been totally responsible for a shift in the dominant paradigm. A perception of duality between mind and matter was already present in the outlook of the ancient Greek philosophers, particularly Pythagoras and Plato. However, because of Descartes' work, dualism took on a new dynamism and emerged as the main focus of thought in the Renaissance and the Age of Reason which followed it.

Descartes argues for a mechanistic universe from purely geometrical reasoning. He imagined that real space is marked by intersecting straight lines of rectangular—or what we now call Cartesian—coordinates. Descartes claimed that he had a vision which revealed to him the basic geometric structure of space. Perhaps this claim should not easily be dismissed. Often deep states of trance are perceived in geometrical forms. It may very well be that Pythagoras, Plato and Descartes all had direct experiences of the causal plane and thus attributed so much importance to a basic mathematical-geometrical structure of reality.

Like Aristotle and Plato before him, Descartes' physics was secondary to his metaphysics. He insisted that there could be no possible connection between mind and matter: the essence of matter is extension into space, and the essence of mind is thought (Burtt, 1954). He concluded that there are two distinct worlds, one of mind and another of matter, and that the two never meet. From the perspective of this book, this is partially true, but it is not absolutely true. The duality between matter and mind should really be perceived as a *complementary relationship* and, as we argue below, like all complementarities, this duality is ultimately consumed in the Light of Consciousness which supports the existence of all relationships. Descartes stated, "I think therefore I exist." This philosophical statement caused more problems than it resolved, since it implied a system of metaphysics which is not clearly stated. A slightly different way of expressing Descartes' statement would make a significant difference. If Descartes had said, "I exist, therefore I think," his statement would refer to the underlying reality of existence, to which all thought ultimately refers.

Descartes' own formulation, was however, right with respect to the ordinary reality of our everyday lives. We think, and our thoughts shape our experience, which we then identify as our existence.

It is probably because Descartes did not express clearly that he was referring to the relative existence of our everyday lives and not to ultimate existence that Berkeley and the idealist philosophers disagreed with him and his philosophical school. The idealists insisted instead that mind and matter do interact and, therefore, that matter must be of the same nature as mind—in other words, that the essence of matter is thought. The belief of the idealists makes Descartes' famous statement more meaningful, although it is not known if Descartes himself would have agreed with them.

The mechanistic system of the Cartesians implied a perfect determinism. The universe is ruled by impersonal physical laws and follows an order that is in principle determinable. Descartes himself described the world as a "cosmic hydraulic system." While Plato and Aristotle had rejected the deterministic world of Democritus as unthinkably regular, Descartes, Leibniz and Spinoza found that complete determinism implied security, not oppression (Drake, 1957). The clockwork mechanistic universe of Descartes is implied in the term "Newtonian physics," although Newton himself never accepted a fully mechanistic universe. In this clockwork universe, the observer only observes. Unlike the observer-participant of quantum physics, the classical physicist can in principle understand all workings of nature as long as he or she has knowledge of the initial conditions. The universe ticks away under the action of immutable, eternal laws (see Figure 1). The implication for humans is that we are passive observers of the workings of nature, standing behind a thick, unbreakable wall of glass separating us from the universe, separating mind from matter, unable to influence events in the universe in any meaningful way. It may be that this view of the universe gives us a feeling of security; yet it ironically assigns a completely incidental role to human beings. One cannot but feel glad that this rather oppressive and pessimistic view was finally abandoned when quantum theory became fully developed in the twentieth century.

The great watchword of the seventeenth and eighteenth centuries was reason (Wheeler, 1981). The concept of reason occupied a central role in the writings of Benedictus de Spinoza and the philosophy of the rationalists. Spinoza imagined that the mathematical mode of reasoning applied to all problems, metaphysical, oral or scientific. The cult of reason suggested belief in a rational universe and as a

View of the Universe According to Classical Physics

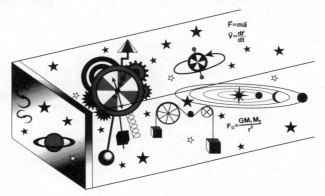

Figure 1. The clockwork universe of classical physics. The observer just observes, never participates, behind a thick wall separating mind from matter. The universe is ultimately determinable but at the expense of an ultimate total isolation of the observer.

result created the conditions in which science could develop and thrive. Spinoza's deterministic outlook found its way into the twentieth century. It was the main reason Einstein resisted the indeterminate character of certain quantum phenomena, and why he tried so hard to prove that quantum mechanics is not a complete theory. Einstein's famous statement "God does not play dice" can be traced back to his approval of the rationalists and Spinoza.

Whereas Newton strongly believed in God as the Prime Mover without whom the universe could not start (Durham and Purrington, 1983), the new rationalists, exemplified by the French mathematician Pierre Simon Marquis de Laplace, found that they could dispense with the idea of the Prime Mover. In their new rational universe there was no room for a personal relationship with a supreme Being. All that mattered were the perfect, divine if you like, mathematical principles of a completely determinable universe. Adherence to causality, determinism and reason is best summarized by Laplace (Gleick, 1988):

We may regard the present state of the universe as the effect of its past and the cause of its future. An intelligence which at a given moment knew all the forces that animate nature, and the respective positions of the beings that compose it, and further possessing the scope to analyze these data, could condense into a single formula the movement of the greatest bodies of the universe and that of the least atom: for such an intelligence nothing could be uncertain, and past and future alike would be before its eyes.

Belief in transcendent, eternal and immutable laws of physics and its mathematics would form an integral part of the classical scientific paradigm. The famous nineteenth-century German physicist Heinrich Hertz stated (Holton and Brush, 1985):

One cannot escape the feeling that these mathematical formulas have an independent existence and intelligence of their own, that they are wiser than we, wiser than their discoveries, that we get more out of them than was originally put into them.

Plato himself could not have put it better. A few decades later the revolution unleashed by quantum theory rendered these statements by Laplace and Hertz meaningless. But in the two centuries following Newton's death, Newtonian mechanics, the electromagnetic field theory developed by nineteenth-century physicist James C. Maxwell and the new sciences of thermodynamics and statistical mechanics were together a remarkably successful system for describing the world. They comprise the system we know as classical physics. Yet, even in the atmosphere of utter confidence which prevailed during the Age of Reason, the foundation of new ideas was laid, such as the first hint about complementarity formulated by German philosopher Immanuel Kant. Kant's work ultimately undermined the confidence of the determinists and influenced the thinking of quantum physicists like Bohr (Folse, 1985).

Nevertheless, the mechanistic, rational and deterministic world system still guides the practical way most physicists work and think every day, and its influence is felt not only in other physical sciences but also in the political and social sciences. Classical physics was, and still is easily accepted, because it deals with the tangible objects of our everyday experience. Before we describe the profoundly different quantum paradigm, let us summarize the metaphysical foundations of classical, Newtonian physics (Hooker, 1972):

1. There is an independently existing physical reality which is eternal. Time is absolute, the same for everyone.

2. A physical system exists in a well-defined state in which changes occur continuously.

3. For this reason, a classical system is determinate and is subject to causality. In other words, the future state of the system can be predicted based on complete knowledge of the initial conditions by applying the correct laws of physics.

4. Physical systems exist and evolve independently of the act of observation and the presence of observers. Knowledge of the state of a physical system is obtained by making measurements. A measurement is a straightforward physical process of interaction between the measuring apparatus and the system that is being measured, the outcome of which is related to the feature under investigation in a known way.

5. A successful scientific theory mirrors the world in the sense that every relevant element of reality and every relevant physical attribute of these elements has a corresponding counterpart in the theory.

6. The universe can be divided into constituent parts which can be prepared so that no interaction occurs between them. In other words, the universe is local at every level.

These principles seem self-evident and obvious. Nevertheless each was modified or completely rejected by quantum physics. It is still true that we use measurements to find out about the state of physical systems, although science cannot really reveal reality in its entirety. In quantum phenomena, as noted, one cannot ignore the role of the observing process.

Despite the quantum revolution, in practice most physicists still adhere to these classical principles, as Einstein did, because they have been ingrained in our minds from the world of everyday experience. Einstein's statement "God does not play dice" seems self-evident, and yet quantum phenomena have revealed a remarkable reality which is indeterminate at the physical level. Until the late 1800s, physicists felt that the main theories to account for all physical phenomena were already established and that any future scientific work would involve only fine tuning the existing theories to fit better data. The prevailing optimism of Victorian times is perhaps best summarized by the arrogant attitude of the nineteenth-century physicist Lord Kelvin, who declared that physicists had formulated all the fundamental theories and that only "two small clouds" remained on the horizon (Bohm, 1980)—the negative results of the Michelson-Morley experiment and the mystery of black body radiation. It turned out that Kelvin's "two small clouds" signaled the arrival of the two great storms that swept away classical physics—the theory of relativity and quantum theory, respectively. Lord Kelvin certainly chose his clouds well! The resultant crisis in classical physics turned out to be very deep. It took the critical thinking of the great mind of Einstein to see beyond what appeared to be absolute truths and to develop the theory of relativity. Nevertheless, Einsteinian relativity in a deep sense duplicated the Newtonian dream of ultimate determinism, in principle if not in practice.

The Emergence of Relativity

James C. Maxwell's electromagnetic theory treated light as propagating waves. Many experiments in the eighteenth and nineteenth centuries demonstrated that light behaves as waves; even light's wave speed was known. Newton had argued that light is made of corpuscles. The ensuing debate between holders of Newton's view and that of his contemporary Christian Huygens, who insisted that light is made of waves, marks the beginning of the great quantum paradox of the dual nature of light. At the beginning of the nineteenth century Newton's views were discarded, until Einstein made the particle theory of light fashionable again when he explained the photoelectric effect.

Physicists have identified two types of waves, transverse and longitudinal. Light is a transverse wave, in contrast to sound, which is longitudinal (Figure 2).[1] Maxwell proved that light arises when electric and magnetic fields vibrate. A field in classical physics represents the distribution of forces in space. Early physicists theorized that a material medium was needed for electromagnetic vibrations to propagate. They called this hypothetical medium the "ether." When American experimenters Albert A. Michelson and Edward W. Morley searched for the ether in 1887 using a new device called the interferometer, they found no evidence of the effects of ether on the propagation of light at different directions.[2] Their experiments demonstrated that one could not measure velocities in reference to the

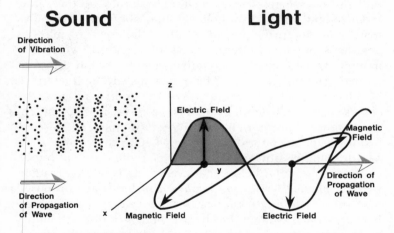

Figure 2. Light is transverse in the sense that the vibrating electric and magnetic fields are perpendicular to the direction of propagation of the wave and to each other. In sound, the vibration of air molecules is in the same direction as the propagation of sound.

ether. These experiments—the first cloud of Kelvin— indicated that no medium was needed for the propagation of light.

Kelvin's cloud loomed on the horizon until it was resolved by Albert Einstein. In formulating his theories, Einstein

devised many ingenious *gedanken* or "thought experiments."
In one of these, he showed that classical mechanics and
Maxwell's electromagnetic theory could not be reconciled.
Einstein identified the difficulty as lying in the Newtonian
assumption of absolute space. To Einstein it seemed clear
that one could not catch up with light. Thus one could
not find a unique frame of reference in which the laws of
physics would behave differently compared to any other
stationary frame. In other words, like absolute space,
absolute motion is impossible. In a single bold step, Einstein
reasoned that Newtonian mechanics had to be revised, even
though this seemed to go counter to common sense.

Einstein expanded the so-called Galilean relativity
principle, formulated by classical physicists, which stated
that the laws of classical mechanics should be the same,
independent of the motion of the observer. Einstein's
new relativity principle stated that the laws of physics
are the same in different frames of reference which are
moving with a constant relative velocity—what Einstein
termed "inertial frames." These systems are characterized
by observers who measure space by rulers and time by
clocks. In the Einsteinian universe, physics is independent
of motion, a point well exemplified in passengers' confusion inside a smooth train as to whether they or the train
next to them is moving. Einstein's relativity does not imply,
contrary to popular belief, that everything is relative; rather,
views of physical events are relative. Einstein later proposed
a second postulate to the special theory of relativity, published in 1905, namely that light propagates through empty
space with a speed equal to 300,000 kilometers per second,
or more than 180,000 miles per second. This speed is independent of the state of motion of the emitting body.
Thus, even though there is no preferred *absolute* frame of
reference, observers in all frames of reference measure the
same *absolute* speed of light.

Einstein's theory predicts bizarre effects counter to
common sense if the encountered speeds become relativistic,
or close to the speed of light. For example, a clock moving
at this speed would appear to run slower to a fixed observer.
For light there is no time; what would be a mere second
for light, would be eternity for the rest of the universe.

Because of Einstein's work, the Newtonian belief in an absolute, universal time also had to be discarded. Nevertheless, relativity did not challenge such cherished classical ideas as the requirements of causality and the continuity of physical processes. Einstein treated time as a fourth dimension. Physicists can construct common space-time diagrams where one axis is time and the other axes are space. In practice we can draw at most only three dimensions. Einstein used geometrical models to describe physical effects. The geometry he used to describe relationships in his special theory of relativity is flat or Euclidean geometry, because light travels along a straight line. Since all relative velocities are constant, the paths of light particles are also straight lines.

However, it soon became clear that the requirement of the special theory of relativity that light velocities are constant is too restrictive. Suppose that the smooth train suddenly came to an abrupt stop. The passengers would be thrown forward, and they would have no doubt as to whether or not their train were moving. Einstein wondered how one would do physics if the frames of reference themselves were accelerating, as for example a frame in the gravitational field of the earth. His answer was quite ingenious. Imagine yourself inside a free-falling frame of reference, such as an elevator falling from the one hundredth floor of a skyscraper. Inside it, an object released appears stationary, since the object as well as the person who released it are falling at the same rate. Gravity appears to be transformed away, the inertial frames are free-falling and the laws of physics hold as usual.[3] This line of reasoning resulted in a more powerful relativity principle, known as the general theory of relativity, published in 1915—perhaps the most mathematically elegant theory that the human mind has produced. Simply put, the general theory of relativity holds that matter tells space-time how to warp, and warped space-time tells matter how to move.[4]

A profound consequence of the principle that gravity can be transformed away is that in the presence of gravitational fields, light appears to be "falling down."[5] Here on earth the effect is minute, but in the presence of strongly gravitating bodies, such as black holes, the effect becomes important. As in the special theory, one can construct space-time diagrams, but in this case gravity warps the flatness. Visualizing such four-dimensional space-time diagrams is a challenge to say the least, since our spatial universe is three-dimensional. Thus in Einstein's view, the presence of gravity distorts space-time from its flat, Euclidean form. Instead of forces which were mysterious, ill-defined concepts in Newtonian mechanics and which required instantaneous action at a distance, Einstein postulated curved space-time. Einstein's theory treats gravity in terms of geometrical curvatures in the space-time continuum. In his work, geometry again assumes the paramount importance it held in ancient Greek and Egyptian mathematics. But Einstein's geometrical picture is complex in its mathematics. Even a simple geometrical statement like Pythagoras' theorem—that the sum of the squares of the sides of a right triangle is equal to the square of the hypotenuse—assumes a non-trivial form in curved space-time.

Not only gravity but any other "force" manifests itself in the warping of space-time. We can visualize this warping by constructing a plastic rubber sheet which has a grid drawn on it representing space-time (Figure 3). When no

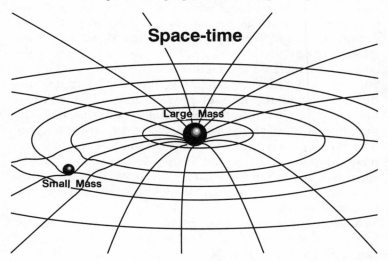

Figure 3. Warping of space-time caused by gravity

objects are placed on the rubber sheet, it is flat. A small object like a steel ball will travel in a straight line along the flat sheet, in accordance with the laws of Newtonian kinematics when no force applies. However, when a heavy object is placed at the center of the rubber sheet, a warping of the space-time grid results. The steel ball will now follow a curvilinear path around the heavy object and can even move along a closed orbit, in accordance with the laws of planetary motion. On warped surfaces, the shortest distances are no longer straight lines. In other words, warped space-time affects the motion of matter and even of light, and constrains them to move along paths which are not straight lines.

The ultimate warping of the space-time grid occurs around bizarre objects called black holes. The escape speed from the surface of a black hole is the speed of light, but in the interior the gravitational fields are so intense even light cannot escape.[6] Thus a black hole is perfectly black. A black hole is also a hole in space-time, and at its center exists the dreaded singularity—a region where all paths converge to a point, and everything collapses down to nothingness. We expect a black hole to form as a massive star collapses after it has exhausted all the nuclear fuel at its center. Supermassive black holes weighing millions or even billions of solar masses could also form at the centers of galaxies, as stars and interstellar gases collapse at the center of a star cluster.

The general theory of relativity is the only theory that we have to describe the universe as a whole. It states that the universe itself has a definite curvature. According to the theory, the universe can be open, like the surface of a saddle, or closed, like the surface of a sphere. The theory also permits dynamic, expanding models. Our universe seems to be in such an evolving and expanding state. Einstein's general theory of relativity implies an undivided wholeness. The presence of all the matter in the universe is responsible for the curvature of the universe—locally as well as globally. Local matter then moves in the grid of space-time established by the overall distribution of matter in the universe.

A profound difference between Einstein's relativistic

mechanics and Newtonian mechanics is that in Einstein's theory, measurable quantities like lengths, time and even masses acquire values as a result of the motion of the specific frame of reference in which these measurements are carried out. In this sense we have what physicist John A. Wheeler terms "observer participancy." In other words, what values we measure depend on the relative motion between frames of reference. Despite this difference, the theories of relativity are basically classical. Space-time is continuous—the theory allows no quantum jumps; causality still holds—the motion of matter is caused by the warping of space-time; and relativity is exact in its predictions—it contains no worrisome quantum probabilities. As in classical physics, the future is exactly determinable from what has already happened. Finally, no issue of realism enters here. Whether or not an observer measures time or any other quantity, the value of that quantity definitely exists as a real entity.

Einstein believed that any fundamental physical theory has to be elegant and simple. He was so convinced of this that time and again he was guided by his intuition to formulate theories that would later be confirmed by experimental evidence. It is said that Einstein would get absorbed in a particular problem, and after prolonged periods of silence, would provide the solution to his colleagues. They would then struggle to verify that his solution was correct. Einstein's sense of simplicity and elegance was intuitive and innate. Intuition is beyond mathematical formalism. Yet, in all creative processes—artistic, scientific or literary—intuition guides the artist, the scientist or the writer towards the completion of the work.

Einstein's theory of gravity is a perfect example of intuitive elegance and simplicity. His belief in the ultimate rationality and simplicity of the universe has all the characteristics of a religious feeling. In fact, Einstein believed in an impersonal God that manifests through the rationality of the universe. However, even the most elegant and rational theory must eventually break down. Einstein's theory breaks down at the center of the black hole where, presumably, quantum effects have to be considered. Physicists now anticipate that a more general quantum theory of gravity will eventually replace Einstein's general theory of relativity.

Summary

It seems reasonable to assume that our everyday experiences of the world are merely one aspect of the universe, perceived either directly by our sense organs or indirectly with the help of instruments. Yet, we know that often what we experience is not exactly what exists in reality. For example, we perceive the earth as flat, but we know that the earth is a vast sphere. What we observe is not an illusion. It is instead a very small part of a greater whole. By the fact that we are part of the universe, we cannot have a bird's-eye view of the entirety of our universe. In other words, we cannot perceive simultaneously all three aspects of our universe—the microcosm, the macrocosm and the world of our everyday experience. Moreover, our everyday experiences of the world are limited. We are like blind men touching different parts of an elephant. The one touching the leg thinks that an elephant is like the trunk of a big tree. The one touching the elephant's trunk thinks that an elephant is like a fat hose. Both are right based on their limited experiences. Neither however, perceives the entire elephant. Consequently, both are wrong in their generalizations of their perceptions. An elephant is not like a tree and not like a hose. Classical Newtonian physics describes everyday experiences accurately but does not describe accurately the entire physical reality. Assuming that classical physics is a complete description of the world is like insisting that the earth is flat, because that is what we perceive.

Since the Renaissance, classical physics has helped us expand our understanding of the universe. Classical physics was used in the invention of the steam engine, the airplane, the automobile and many other everyday objects, not to mention electricity, the telephone and radio. Here is our universe, a closed box according to classical physics, and we, the observers, puzzled, wondering, enchanted, outside the box, trying to understand and to discover the marvels inside. To this end, physicists began with hypotheses, developed theories on how things might work and then subjected these theories to laboratory tests. If the outcome of the experiments agreed with what was occurring in reality, they concluded that they had found a piece of the puzzle. They called their finding a "law" of physics and named it after the person who did the work. But if the results of laboratory experiments did not match what was going on in the universe, physicists modified their hypothesis and their experiments. They kept doing this until they developed another "law." This constitutes the scientific method.

The paradigm of classical physics was built on a number of assumptions about the nature of the universe and our relationship with it, which were never challenged because they were considered too obvious. First, classical physics assumed that there is an independently existing physical reality. Second, it assumed that physical processes are continuous, that there are no abrupt jumps or changes in the state of the system. Third, for this reason, it assumed that a classical system is determinate and subject to causality, that its future state can be determined from its present state if all interactions with the external world are taken into account. Fourth, it assumed that the act of observation is not necessary to take into account and that a system is unaffected by what we do to find out about its state. In other words, the observer-participant of the quantum vision simply does not exist in the classical view of the universe. Fifth, it assumed a one-to-one correspondence between the parts of a theory and physical reality—that mathematically theory exactly mirrors physical reality and that both are in some sense equally "real." This conception of a dualistic reality consisting of a world of abstract ideas existing independently of the physical world can be traced to ancient Greek beliefs, but it was reinforced and strengthened during the seventeenth century Age of Reason. It has survived as an integral part of the classical scientific paradigm to the present time. Finally, the paradigm of classical physics assumed that the classical system could be divided into independent constituent parts, which could be studied separately since the parts did not affect each other—the assumption of locality.

The philosophical vision of classical physics is that we live not only in a mechanistic universe but also in a completely deterministic one. Although profoundly different from the Newtonian universe, the Einsteinian universe presumed determinism at least in principle. Upon reflection, this vision is rather oppressive, since it provides no room for free will. The rational God of Laplace and Einstein, who does not play dice, leaves no room for chance or for human initiative. Despite the great conceptual changes brought about by the rise of quantum theory, modern science still has not broken away from this classical vision.

2

The Case for Wholeness: Modern Quantum Physics

Science thus brings us to the threshold of the ego and there leaves us to ourselves.

Max Planck

In contrast to relativity which is essentially the product of one man's work, quantum theory is the product of many minds. Interestingly enough, light is involved in the birth of both theories. At the beginning of the twentieth century, German physicist Max Planck found an explanation for the second cloud of Lord Kelvin—the mystery of black body radiation. Quantum theory did not arise because physicists faced deep, unanswered philosophical questions posed by classical physics. It arose because laboratory observations of how a black body or ideal radiator behaves did not agree with classical electromagnetic theory.

The Birth of Quantum Physics

Planck's work involved an empirical formula that he derived to explain the radiation emitted by a black body. Planck's theoretical radiator absorbs in a perfect manner all radiation that falls on it. This is the reason for its name— it is perfectly black at low temperatures. It also emits in the most efficient way, and its emitted energy depends only on its temperature, not its shape, texture or chemical composition. Many objects in nature approximate black bodies, such as stars and furnaces.[1] When radiation is emitted by a black body, its intensity can be measured.[2] Such measurements show that the overall shape and maximum point of emission are solely a function of temperature. Physicists attempted to reconstruct the observed intensity of a black body by assuming that it is made of a multitude of microscopic electromagnetic oscillators. As they vibrate, the oscillators emit electromagnetic waves or light in accordance with classical electromagnetic theory. However, when the emissions from the oscillators were added up to find the overall black body emission, the classical formula failed to account for the observed spectra. The second cloud of Kelvin had become a threatening hurricane.

Planck found an empirical mathematical formula that could accurately fit the observed black body spectra. More importantly, within two months of his discovery, he was also able to provide the underlying physical explanation. The results were so amazing that Planck—a rather brilliant but nevertheless conservative physicist—accepted them himself only because there was no alternative. To explain the observed data, Planck had to assume that a microscopic oscillator does not, as physicists had believed up to that point, send out a minute part of its total energy in a continuous way. On the contrary, Planck found that the emission was discrete, or "quantized." In total opposition to classical concepts, *the energy content of the oscillator is an integral multiple of the frequency of its vibration.*

The proportionality constant that enters this simple relationship between energy and frequency is named Planck's constant, in honor of the conservative physicist who never dreamed he was causing a revolution. It is one of the fundamental constants of nature, as important as Newton's gravitational constant or the speed of light. Also known as the quantum of action, h, Planck's constant has the incredibly small—but not zero—value of 6×10^{-27} ergs times seconds.[3] The non-zero value of Planck's constant is responsible for the strange world of the quantum. Without it the universe would be completely different: there would be no uncertainty principle, no wave-particle duality, no atomic or quantum phenomena. The announcement by Planck on December 14, 1900, of his solution to the black body problem marked the effective birthday of modern physics, the birth of quantum theory. Five years later Einstein published his theory of relativity and two other seminal papers. One was a paper on the photoelectric effect—for which he received the Nobel prize in 1921—and the other was on the Brownian movement. Each of the three papers advanced physics in a different way, but it was Einstein's paper on the photoelectric effect which expanded the quantum revolution that Planck's work had started five years before.

In simple terms, the photoelectric effect can be witnessed when light of sufficiently high frequency—usually ultraviolet—falls on a photosensitive metal surface and ejects tiny charged particles, or electrons, from the metal. Trying to draw a classical picture of this phenomenon leads to strange results. Let us assume that ocean waves are analogous to light waves, and electrons are analogous to beach pebbles. Experience teaches us that the higher the ocean wave, the more energy it contains. However, this conclusion, reinforced by everyday experience, is simply wrong when applied to light. If a monochromatic light source has a frequency below a certain limit, then, no matter how strong the light source, no electrons are ejected. For example, an ultraviolet source will eject photoelectrons, whereas low frequency red light will not. This result occurs even if the red light source is very bright, and the ultraviolet source very weak.

Classical physics simply cannot explain these results. The energy carried by a wave is related to its height squared. This height is called the amplitude by physicists. Tall and long waves—like tidal waves—carry a lot of energy and can seemingly move a great number of pebbles and other particle-like debris. The brightness of a light source is proportional to the amplitude of the electromagnetic field squared. Thus a bright red light source is analogous to tall and long tidal waves. A weak ultraviolet source is analogous to small, short-wavelength waves, such as the choppy waves one encounters when there is a strong breeze. This analogy seems to imply that choppy waves—even if they are very small—can move beach pebbles, whereas long-wavelength waves—even big tidal waves—cannot!

Einstein's genius consisted in his ability to question established ideas and to reject them if they did not work. His explanation for these bizarre results is very simple and at the same time very bold. He argued that the *energy of light is not distributed evenly over the wave, as classical electromagnetic theory demanded, but rather is concentrated in small, discrete bundles.*[4] Forget the wave picture, Einstein said. Instead, think of light as quantized, or composed of energy bundles or packets of energy. Think of light as having *particle properties.* These particles or quanta of light energy are called "photons," from the Greek word *phos,* which means light.

The photoelectric effect, Einstein argued, occurs because the energy of light quanta is proportional to the frequency of monochromatic light. Einstein's explanation agreed with Planck but was applied to a totally different physical phenomenon. In Einstein's photon picture, the brightness of the red light source does not really matter, since individual red photons do not have enough energy to knock out an electron from the metal. Einstein computed the constant

The Photoelectric Effect

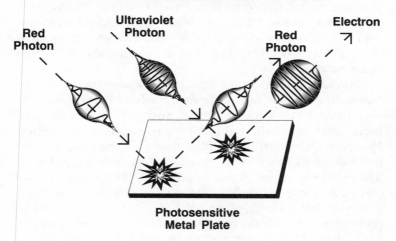

Figure 4. The photoelectric effect. Light of a sufficiently high frequency falling on a photosensitive metal plate can eject electrons.

of proportionality between energy and frequency of photons, and to his amazement he found that it was equal to Planck's constant. Not only did Einstein's idea of energy packets of light parallel Planck's idea of quantum oscillators, but the constant that appears in both ideas is the same. This certainly could not be a coincidence.

Even though photons have particle-like properties, one should not carry the analogy too far. Trying to use everyday experience to visualize photons as, say, tiny steel balls leads to problems. A more energetic ball moves faster than a less energetic ball; its ability to knock out another ball is in its motion. But all photons move with exactly the same speed. Their different energies have nothing to do with the kinetic energies of ordinary objects such as steel balls. The energy of a photon is an intrinsic energy, not a property that it acquires by external means. Quanta, though analogous to particles, cannot be accurately visualized.

By showing that the energy of light is quantized, Einstein contributed directly to the eventual acceptance of Planck's quantum hypothesis. Ironically, Planck himself was not happy with these developments. He feared that the entire classical electromagnetic theory would be undermined and, in his own words, "the state of physics thrown into confusion." Physicists in general do not like to throw away their theories unless they are left with absolutely no other choice.

Planck was also afraid that the old argument between Newton and Huygens on the nature of light would rear its ugly head. Planck and Einstein proved that Newton had been right after all: light does have particle properties. However, physicists knew that Huygens had been right too: light also has wave properties. How right Planck was! The dilemma threw classical physics into a state of confusion, but not by choice. The evidence was provided by nature in the laboratory, and the evidence was irrefutable. As hard as it was for the human mind to resolve the dilemma, both views of light seemed to be right. The microscopic world—the world of quanta—is a very strange world indeed.

Atomic Structure

The young Danish physicist Niels Bohr was responsible for the next important step in the development of quantum theory—the first successful theory of the structure of the atom. The multitudes of particles in aggregates of gases that James C. Maxwell and Ludwig Boltzmann had successfully described were believed to be small, hard spheres which collide with each other and with the walls of containers to give rise to such macroscopic effects as the pressure of the gas. Each particle obeys Newton's laws of motion, though this individual motion is inaccessible to the physicist. What is accessible is the average properties obtained by observing a large number of particles. Only then can the microscopic world be described by statistical theories, a situation which makes the assertions of Laplace about absolute mechanical predictability nothing more than wishful thinking.

The work of Maxwell and Boltzmann—though still classical—showed that the assumptions of Newtonian mechanics for predicting the future state of an individual atom were totally inadequate. Whereas the predictions of Newtonian mechanics worked for the macroscopic realm, a theory of statistical mechanics was needed to describe the state of the many microscopic particles. Moreover, as late as 1890 the existence of atoms was still doubted by many physicists, an uncertainty which existed until the early years of the twentieth century. Though Maxwell's and Boltzmann's statistical theory was eventually accepted, theirs was basically a classical probability theory. And classical probabilities are not like quantum probabilities. Classical physicists suppose that the individual properties of a particle, such as its velocity and location in space, exist and are real, *even if physicists cannot measure them.*

Einstein's work on the Brownian motion—the second paper he published in 1905—established beyond any doubt the existence of atoms. The British botanist Thomas Brown had discovered in 1827 that when a pollen grain floating in a drop of water is examined under a microscope, it appears to be moving randomly. Einstein demonstrated that this motion obeys a definite statistical law and that the path of a pollen grain is random as expected, if the pollen is being kicked around continuously by microscopic particles invisible under the microscope. By this reasoning, Einstein showed that atoms exist. But what was the structure of these atoms?

The ancient idea of Democritus that matter is composed of indivisible atoms remained just that, an idea, until it could be tested in the laboratory. When physicists studied the electrical properties of matter, they found two kinds of electrical charges in nature, positive and negative. They also knew that, overall, matter is neutral. Thus the two types of charges had to coexist in the tiny constituent particles of matter, the atoms. By the end of the nineteenth century the even tinier particles carrying negative charges had been isolated in the laboratory. Electrons, as these particles are presently known, were found to be very light. Next experimenters searched for the internal structure of atoms—how the electrons are distributed in the atom.

The actual structure of atoms became known as result of experiments involving radioactive nuclei. Ernest Rutherford, a New Zealand physicist, settled at the University of Manchester in 1907. In 1909 experiments were carried out in his laboratory involving the passage of alpha particles through a thin gold foil. Alpha particles—the nuclei of helium atoms—are a by-product of the decay of radioactive atoms. Experimenters observed that most alpha particles went straight through the foil, some were scattered at an angle to the original beam and a few bounced almost straight back.[5] Rutherford explained the observed phenomena in the following way: An alpha particle is much heavier than an electron—7000 times as heavy. If an alpha particle collides with an electron, the alpha particle continues on its course unaffected. The deflection of an alpha particle must, therefore, be caused when it collides with a positive charge in the atom.

Rutherford's work led him to develop a "planetary" model of the atom. However, this model has practically no similarity to the solar system. To begin with, the nucleus of an atom is extremely small, about 10^{-13} cm, or one ten trillionth of a centimeter across. It is embedded in an electron cloud, typically 10^{-8} cm, or one hundred millionth of a centimeter across. The sun is both the most massive and also the largest body in the solar system, but in the atom, the proton is tiny as compared to the electron cloud which occupies the outer region of the atom.

Neils Bohr, a young scientist who worked with Rutherford's team in Manchester, also studied the structure of the atom. He published a simple model of the atom in 1913. Up to that time, no one understood how spectral lines are formed in atoms. Bohr's model combined a number of ideas, some of them from classical physics, like the mechanical laws which govern orbiting masses. To explain the spectral lines of a hydrogen atom, Bohr assumed that the electron is found at specific distances from the nucleus, occupying distinct "energy shells" or orbits, and can never be found between these orbits. This theory explained quite nicely why every atom has a specific pattern of spectral lines, its own calling card. The pattern occurs because an electron always jumps between orbits in a given set of quantized orbits and in doing so absorbs or emits energy in the form of light. Thus

The Bohr Atom
Energy Levels Represented as Steps

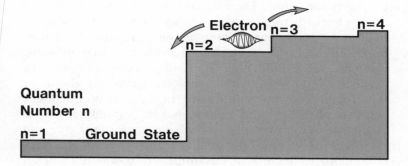

Figure 5. The Bohr model of the atom can be understood by the analogy of a set of steps of different heights. The electron is always constrained to one of these energy steps.

each atom has a particular pattern of lines. The structure of Bohr's atom is determined by Planck's constant. A jumping electron can absorb or emit an energy hν (in which h stands for Planck's constant, ν for frequency) in accordance with Einstein's photoelectric formula. The frequency ν characterizes the specific spectral line of the element. This simple picture of the atom seemed to explain beautifully the observations of atomic spectra.

And yet, Bohr's simple and beautiful picture of the atom runs counter to common sense. How can a jumping electron "know" exactly where to land—landing always at a quantized orbit and never between these orbits? Trying to visualize what is going on in the atom by using the classical analogy of planetary orbits leads only to counter-intuitive conclusions. If we use the planetary analogy—the electron being analogous to a planet—it would be as if the Earth could jump from its orbit to the orbit of, say, Mars by using or absorbing energy to make the jump, which would happen instantaneously. The next instant, the Earth could stay where it was, jump back to its original orbit or jump to the orbit of Mercury or Venus by getting rid of or emitting energy. Or it could jump to the orbit of Jupiter or Saturn by using or absorbing energy.

Bohr realized that the strange world of the quantum violates all common sense. However, "common sense" is derived from the observable macroscopic phenomena of our everyday world. There is no a priori reason to believe that what holds true in our everyday world of sensory input holds true everywhere. Common sense is fine in its own realm. If the mind is unsuccessful when it tries to apply common sense (which is after all nothing but its own product) everywhere, there is something limiting about the thinking process, not with nature. In the quantum dialogue between physicists and nature, nature replied that what holds true in our everyday world is not universally true and may even be wrong. Bohr realized and accepted this fact. His quantized picture of electronic orbits was not altered by future developments in quantum theory, though this picture was so disturbingly counter to classical notions that Erwin Schrödinger, one of the main architects of quantum theory, would eventually comment: "Had I known that we were not going to get rid of this damned quantum jumping, I never would have involved myself in this business" (Gribbin, 1984).

The next step in building an understanding of the structure of atoms had to await new theoretical developments. The Bohr model predicted the energy levels of hydrogen atoms rather well but failed for more complicated atoms. Wolfgang Pauli, a young quantum physicist who combined an unusual mathematical capacity with deep physical insight, provided the next development. Chemists already knew that each element has a specific number of electrons. In 1925 Pauli proposed that a maximum number of electrons can fit into any orbital shell. He assigned a quantum number, called the "spin," to each electron in a given shell.

A quantum number is one of a particle's various possible calling cards. The spin of an electron is analogous to the spin of a ball and can be thought of as pointing either up or down along a given axis of measurement. This distinction results in a double-valued quantum number. The value given to the spin of an electron is extremely small, equal to half a unit involving Planck's quantum of action. Pauli realized that with the addition of spin to the properties of each electron, the number of electrons in each shell had to be less than or equal to a maximum number. He determined that no two electrons in a shell can have identical quantum numbers. This idea is known as the Pauli exclusion principle. In a strange way it implies that even though all electrons in the universe are the *same*, they are not *identical*! Two electrons that have identical properties still differ in their spins, which are opposite to each other. Particles like the electron and the proton, which have half-integer spins, are called "fermions"—after the famous physicist Enrico Fermi. These particles, which also obey the exclusion principle, follow a new, strange kind of quantum statistics. Thus quantum particles are not identical, as were Maxwell's and Boltzmann's classical ball-like particles.

If electrons did not obey the exclusion property, our physical world would be much simpler but also terribly dull. All elements would have their electrons in one state, the lowest, and they would not differ from each other chemically. All elements would be similar to the hydrogen atom. Structure in our universe would be nonexistent—no crystals, no DNA double helix, no structure but spheres, only a boring sea of absolute uniformity. The exclusion principle, a quantum law which appears to run counter to common sense, is essential to the variety of structure in our universe (Heisenberg, 1971).

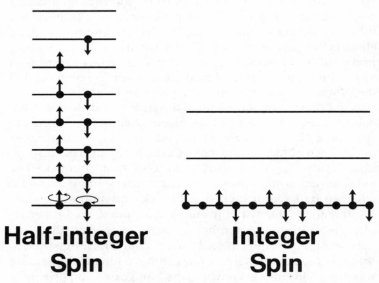

Half-integer Spin   Integer Spin

Figure 6. The particles at left, such as electrons, have half-integer spin. For energy states with all quantum numbers identical, only two electrons can be placed in each state, one with spin up, the other with spin down. The particles at the right, such as photons, have integer spin, and can all be crowded together in one energy state.

However, not all quanta are fermions. Photons and other particles with integer spins obey a different kind of quantum statistics. Einstein and the Indian physicist Satyendra Bose showed that these quanta, termed "bosons," can be crowded together in the same energy state. Planck's explanation of black body behavior follows from the properties of integer-spin particles.

Waves and Particles

The next step in the development of quantum theory resulted from the work of Arthur Compton in 1923. Einstein had found that the photoelectric effect requires that photons possess a momentum, p, related to the wavelength of light, λ, by the simple relationship $p = h/\lambda$, in which h is Planck's constant. Momentum is a particle-like property equal to the product of the mass and velocity of the particle. Compton had worked with X rays for a number of years. In a collision of a photon with an electron, Compton found, the photon behaved like a particle. If light, clearly a wave, could have particle properties, then perhaps the electron, clearly a particle, might also have wave properties. This was exactly the line of reasoning followed by French aristocrat Louis Victor Duc de Broglie.

In his thesis, published in 1925, de Broglie suggested that Einstein's and Compton's ideas regarding photons applied to particles as well. He reasoned that an electron should possess a wavelength, related to its momentum p by the same formula, $p = h/\lambda$. The wavelength of a particle is now called its de Broglie wavelength. De Broglie's idea implied the existence of "matter waves," subsequently found in experiments involving the scattering of electrons off crystals. Electrons were found to interfere with themselves as only waves are capable of doing. De Broglie's work demonstrated a new and unexpected kind of unification. Particles have wave-like properties, just as waves have particle-like properties.

De Broglie's work was seen by Albert Einstein, who published a paper in February, 1925, supporting de Broglie's ideas. Erwin Schrödinger, a professor at the University of Zurich, read Einstein's paper and went on to develop a theory of wave mechanics. Schrödinger, Einstein and de Broglie were crucial to the development of quantum theory, yet in the final analysis they turned against it because they were not willing to give up classical ideas, particularly the ideas of causality, predictability and, most importantly, realism.

In his version of quantum theory, Schrödinger tried to

restore easily understood physical concepts borrowed from classical physics. One such concept was the idea of wave motion. Schrödinger developed a famous equation describing the motion of quanta in terms of wave mechanics. He assumed the literal reality of electron waves. The community of physicists enthusiastically adopted Schrödinger's picture because it was old and familiar, similar to the view of nineteenth-century physicist William Hamilton. But the success of Schrödinger's version of quantum theory may have held back fundamental understanding of the strange world of quanta for many years (Gribbin, 1984). To begin with, and despite Schrödinger's own hopes, the discrete quality of quantum did not disappear. Also, Schrödinger's waves did not turn out to be as real as pond waves. The appealing picture of de Broglie's waves circling the nucleus of an atom was simply wrong.

The famous wave function ψ which appears in Schrödinger's equation is, according to some physicists, a superfluous auxiliary construct (Gribbin, 1984). Another theory published by Werner Heisenberg and his coworkers is equally descriptive without reference to wave functions, wave mechanics or matter waves. Max Born provided the proper way to understand the wave function. He argued that ψ itself can never be observed but that the square of the amplitude of ψ, namely $|\psi|^2$, provides a *measure of the probability of finding the particle at a particular point in space*. In other words, the possibility[6] contained in the wave function relates to probability through the simple relationship, probability = (possibility)^2. The amplitude of a quantum wave is its possibility. The square of a possibility is a probability. The quantum wave, unlike other waves in nature, carries no energy; it is an empty field, a field of possibilities. Einstein would call it a *Gespensterfeld*, a ghost field.

An alternate theory to Schrödinger's wave mechanics was developed by three young physicists, Werner Heisenberg, Max Born and Pascual Jordan. In contrast to Schrödinger's approach that electrons were real waves, Heisenberg's theory, known as matrix mechanics, deals only with quantities that could be measured by experiment. Central to this alternative point of view is the idea that electrons are particles. Max Jammer (1966) in his work on the conceptual development of quantum theory put it aptly:

It is hard to find in the history of physics two theories designed to cover the same range of experience which differ more radically than these two.

Schrödinger's wave mechanics emphasize the continuity of physical processes and the wave properties of electrons. Born, Jordan and Heisenberg's matrix mechanics emphasize instead the discontinuity of atomic processes. Since 1926, the two theories have been considered as two alternative— or as Bohr would put it complementary—foundations of the single quantum vision of the universe.

Nothing better illustrates the apparently strange complementarity of waves and particles than the double-slit experiment. In 1801, Thomas Young performed an experiment which provided the first solid evidence for the wave theory of light. Young created a narrow beam by letting a light source, O, shine through a slit, S_1 (see Plate I). The beam fell on a screen with two slits, S_2 and S_3 and shone on a screen, S. As Richard Feynman has emphasized, this classic experiment demonstrates all the fundamental concepts of quantum theory. Since quantum particles behave like waves, this experiment can be performed with either a light beam or a beam of electrons.

A similar experiment can be performed with pellets. Imagine a pellet gun shooting tiny pellets. We can graph the number of pellets falling on the screen directly across from the openings of slits S_1 and S_2. At first the pellets are allowed to go through slit S_1, slit S_2 being closed. Then the situation is reversed. Finally both slits are open. In this third case, the resulting graph of pellets hitting the screen is simply the sum of the two graphs produced when only one of the slits is open (Plate I, Panel A). However, when the same experiment is performed with light or electrons, the graph which results when both slits are open is not simply the sum of the graphs when each slit is open. When both slits are open the resulting pattern formed by electrons or photons is a wave interference pattern (Panel B). Imagine now that we allow electrons to leave the source one at a time. Obviously, the electrons are then acting as single particles. Common sense would say that after a sufficiently long time, the pattern on the screen would be like that obtained from the pellet experiment. Common sense, however, is wrong. As more individual electrons are allowed to fall on S, an interference pattern emerges again (Panel C)!

How can a single electron interfere with itself? Do electrons "know" in advance to guide themselves to fall on just the right spot on S so that an interference pattern will eventually form? Or does a single electron go through both slits as a wave interfering with itself and then somehow become a particle again upon impact? Or could it be that each electron splits into two parts, one part going through S_1 and the other through S_2, the two parts interfering with each other? Each possibility is rather unsatisfying. Trying to describe quantum phenomena in these terms sounds more like a Zen Buddhist *koan*, which is designed to stretch the mind to its limits, than a rational statement of an exact physical science.

Suppose we try to find out which slit each electron goes through. We place an electron detector D, at each slit. When an electron passes through S_1 detector D_1 goes "click." The same is true for S_2 and D_2 (Plate I, Panel D). Now we know for sure which slit each electron passes through. But when we place detectors at the slits, the interference pattern disappears! This can only mean that *the wave/particle aspects of electrons, photons and other quanta manifest themselves in response to the experimental situation which we set up to discover whether quanta are wave-like or particle-like.* In other words, when an experiment is set up for the wave aspect to manifest, the quanta exhibit only their wave aspect. When an experiment is set up for the particle aspect to manifest, the quanta exhibit only their particle aspect.

Measurement and Uncertainty in Quantum Theory

The double-slit experiment demonstrates dramatically that the nature of a physical object like a quantum of light or an electron is not independent of the experiments used to uncover that nature. This conclusion is certainly a drastic departure from the principles of classical physics. Quantum theory demonstrates that physical systems do not evolve independent of the act of observation. The discovery of the complementary nature of quanta gave birth to a new kind of realism—a realism which necessitates taking the measuring apparatus into account in any complete description of a system. The classical glass wall separating the observer from an observed system is shattered beyond repair.

Thus in a way quantum theory implies a holistic view of the universe. Classical physics constructs such as the "path" followed by a particle in space-time are meaningless in quantum physics. It makes no sense to ask what path the electron follows when it goes through the slits. We can only talk about a path when we know which slit the electron went through. But when we use detectors, we alter the experimental situation and the interference pattern disappears. When interference is observed the idea of a path makes no sense. We cannot have it both ways. Moreover, we cannot resolve this dilemma by saying that the electron has a path even though we cannot observe it. In essence, *a quantum has no properties when not observed.* Or better still, *we cannot say anything about such properties when the quantum is not under observation.*

These conclusions form the core of the Copenhagen Interpretation, named in honor of the home city of Neils Bohr. This interpretation of quantum theory was developed primarily by Bohr, Heisenberg, Pauli and Born. It revived the old question of whether physical objects have existence and properties independent of the act of observation. Contrary to what some people believe, quantum theory does preserve the observer-observed relationship. In fact, it clarifies that relationship in a way that classical theory never did. Measurement theory is a well-defined branch of quantum theory, which accepts the centrality of the observing process. Classical theory—like an ostrich hiding its head in the sand—addressed the role of the observer by completely ignoring the observational process. Quantum theory, on the other hand, necessitates a split between the observer and the observed to preserve scientific objectivity.

It opened the door to the view that perceived reality is a function of perception. However, quantum theory does not settle the question of what is real. If by "what is real" we mean *what exists*, scientific inquiry cannot provide the answer, because existence is forever beyond the object/subject duality of the scientific process.

Today most physicists follow Max Born's ideas about wave functions. Born's version of quantum probability is not like probability in classical physics. Classical statistical theory assumed that the properties of each tiny molecule are exactly determinable. Not so in the quantum world in which the positions and velocities of electrons are random. *Electrons cannot be said to have definite values, even in principle.* A scientist can know in advance only the probability—expressed by the square of the amplitude of the wave function—that the position and the velocity will exhibit particular values. When an electron or any other quantum is observed, its wave function gives a range of possibility, out of which one probable value of the physical quantity is actualized. The quantum jargon used to refer to this collapse of possibilities is called "the collapse of the wave function."

Because quantum processes are intrinsically random, two basic premises of classical physics do not hold in quantum situations: 1) that a physical system exists in a well-defined state in which changes to the system occur continuously; and 2) that the future state of the system can be predicted based on complete knowledge of the initial conditions, by using the correct laws of physics. In Born's and Bohr's view, quantum processes are inherently random and unpredictable, not just in practice but also in principle.

Another consequence of quantum theory which fundamentally changes our concept of reality is Heisenberg's indeterminacy principle, also known as the uncertainty principle. In 1927, German physicist Werner Karl Heisenberg proposed that certain pairs of physical quantities, such as position and momentum or energy and time, cannot be measured simultaneously with a high degree of accuracy. The more accurately we try to measure one quantity, the less accurately we can measure the other. The essence of

Heisenberg's principle is that nature herself imposes fundamental and unchangeable limits to our measurements. No matter how advanced our technology, we cannot go beyond what nature allows. This is again a radical departure from the notions of classical physics, which implied that one could predict with absolute certainty what is going to happen. The uncertainty relation, like all quantum phenomena, features Planck's constant, h. The uncertainty principle holds at all levels of reality. However, at the everyday level, the limiting uncertainty of measuring position and momentum is so small (because h is so small) that for all practical purposes, the uncertainty principle can be assumed to be nonexistent.

The uncertainty principle troubled Einstein; he considered it a flaw of quantum theory rather than an absolute limit imposed by nature. Starting in the middle 1920s, and continuing for about thirty years until his death, Einstein tried unsuccessfully to show that quantum theory is not a complete theory, because it implies unpredictability and, more importantly, because it denies classical realism. Other physicists, like Planck, Schrödinger, de Broglie and more recently David Bohm, also disliked the consequences of quantum theory. However, Einstein himself most eloquently and consistently argued against the theory that, ironically, he and Planck had first established.

On the other hand, the new quantum theory, in its Copenhagen Interpretation, was defended by the young physicists Dirac, Pauli, Jordan, Born, Heisenberg and, most vigorously, by Niels Bohr. The battle lines were drawn along age differences. The Copenhagen Interpretation physicists generally belonged to a younger generation, more willing to give up the classical worldview.

A debate ensued between the two world systems, or paradigms. The main actors were Bohr and Einstein, both great physicists, who were also close friends who admired and respected each other. The Bohr-Einstein debates are well documented. They provide a wealth of information for those interested in the history of quantum theory (Bohr, 1949). Ultimately, the debate was settled in the arena where all physical theories must be tested—the laboratory—

although this took place after both men were dead, when Bell's theorem was finally tested. Before this theorem is considered, let us examine the principle of complementarity.

The Principle of Complementarity

For all its successes, quantum theory has not been able to provide metaphysical or ontological principles, or to settle conclusively the issue of reality. Bohr's principle of complementarity shows us how to view the world, although it is anchored in the way a physicist studies quantum phenomena rather than in metaphysical principles; in other words, quantum theory is based more on epistemology than on ontology. The system of metaphysics implied by classical physics was overturned by the existence of a fundamental constant of nature, Planck's constant. Thus classical metaphysics was not really an ultimate, self-evident truth. The quantum view showed that ultimate truths are hard to come by in the world of science. Yet despite this loss of certainty, the principle of complementarity provides a general view of the cosmos, more exciting than the assumptions of classical metaphysics.

Bohr first developed the principle of complementarity in 1927 (Bohr, 1928). In doing so, Bohr considered seriously the constituents of the classical framework. The ideal goal of observation in classical mechanics is to provide a space-time description of the motions of various bodies in a "closed" system—a system isolated from the observer and from the rest of the universe (Folse, 1985). In other words, since the total momentum and energy of a closed system is conserved, one can discover the state of the components of a system after a specific interaction by knowing the state of any one component. This is accomplished by applying the principles of conservation of physical variables, such as momentum, angular momentum or energy.

This procedure has one catch—one needs to know the initial conditions of the system (Folse, 1985; Kafatos and Nadeau, 1990). In order to determine the initial conditions, a scientist needs to perform an observation. However, the observation itself constitutes a physical interaction between the measuring apparatus and the observed system. Thus, the system cannot henceforth be considered closed. In classical systems, the interactions caused by measurement usually have a negligible effect. Because the states of classical systems change continuously, it is possible for the scientist to distinguish between the system being observed and the physical apparatus through which the observations are carried out. This makes the idealization of a closed classical system possible. However, the uncertainty principle and the discontinuous changes of state in a quantum system prevent scientists from attaining this ideal in the microcosm, both in principle and in practice.

By the mid-1920s, wave-particle dualism had been fully established. In classical physics, waves in a field structure and localizable particles are antithetical and preclude each other in specific applications. How could something continuous and seemingly unbound, such as an ocean wave, be one aspect of something completely localizable, such as a pebble? But Bohr argued that the two constructs are complementary, and that both manifest themselves in the double-slit experiment. Complementarity is not then an empty principle. Rather, it is the core of all strange quantum behaviors. To the classically trained mind which requires absolutes, complementarity is an anathema. James R. Newman summarizes the agony of the classically trained mind, which demands absolute truths (Cline, 1987):

> In this century the professional philosophers have let the physicists get away with murder. It is a safe bet that no other group of scientists could have passed off and gained acceptance for such an extraordinary principle as complementarity, nor succeeded in elevating indeterminacy to a universal law.

It is important to emphasize that quantum effects apply even when they are not recognized as such. For example, macroscopic structure as we know it is really attributable to quantum effects which our instruments cannot perceive. As physicist Victor F. Weisskopf notes, "the uncertainty principle has made our understanding richer, not poorer." When we gave up the idea of absolute knowledge of the physical universe, we discovered a wealth of phenomena unimaginable before, all based on complementarity. To make matters even more uncomfortable for the mind that requires absolutes, Bohr did not intend to limit complementarity to the quantum domain. He argued that complementarity was already evident in Einstein's theory of relativity; space and time, he said, are complementary constructs that can be distinguished sharply in the classical domain only because of the smallness of the speeds encountered when compared with the speed of light (Bohr, 1949).

In general, two complementary physical variables are always linked so that the more we know about one, the less we can know about the other. Because of this relation between variables like momentum and position, the principle of complementarity becomes essential. We cannot experience the "wave-like" and "particle-like" properties of quanta under the same conditions. Nevertheless, neither the wave nor the particle picture, with their associated mathematical formalism, can be said to be more actual or real. Rather they are two phenomena which should be considered together in a complementary fashion to provide a complete description of what we call light. The same holds true for all complementary variables in the quantum domain: a description of their state splits into two mutually exclusive classes, both of which are needed to describe the state of the system completely.

In Bohr's view, physical constructs or theories can be said to be complementary if they fulfill four conditions: 1) the constructs are individually complete; 2) the constructs are premised on antithetical assumptions; 3) the constructs preclude one another in a description of the physical situation to which both apply; and 4) taken together, the constructs constitute a complete description of a physical situation. This points up an important difference between complementarity and dialectics. In complementarity, opposites represent a more complete picture of the whole. In dialectics, opposites always stand in seemingly irreconcilable juxtaposition to each other.

During and after World War II, work on the philosophical problems in quantum theory more or less ceased. Bohr continued to campaign for complementarity, but the new generation of quantum physicists was more interested in the many impressive applications of quantum theory (Bohr, 1958; Folse, 1985; Kafatos and Nadeau, 1990) than in philosophy. Only recently have we witnessed a resurgence of interest in the philosophical implications of quantum theory, as result of the experiments designed to test Bell's theorem and to settle the issue of what is real.

Bell's Theorem and Quantum Non-Locality

In May, 1935, Einstein, Boris Podolsky and Nathan Rosen published a paper known by the initials of its authors. The EPR paper became famous for the turmoil it caused in the world of physicists (Einstein, Podolsky and Rosen, 1935). It is often stated that Einstein's central criticism of quantum theory was directed at its probabilistic view of the universe. This objection is summarized in Einstein's famous statement, "God does not play dice." In a recent article N. David Mermin (1985) argues that Einstein's main criticism of quantum theory is contained instead in the EPR paper and is focused on the question of realism—the belief that in the quantum world, physical properties have no objective reality independent of the act of observation. To Einstein the central problem of quantum theory was "that the description of quantum mechanics has to be regarded as an incomplete and indirect description of reality" (Mermin, 1985). It is important to remember that Planck's constant, or quantum of action, is responsible for both the probabilistic view of the world and the peculiar quantum effects that make up Bell's theorem—the so-called "superposition" effects. Thus the statement "God does not play dice" is intimately related to the question of what is real. To turn Einstein's statement around, quantum theory says that *independent reality does not exist for the same reason that God likes to play dice.* In other words, uncertainty and the lack of absolute knowledge or independent reality are integrally interwoven.

In the EPR paper, Einstein and his collaborators were trying to show that quantum theory asserts that properties in region B are the result of an act of measurement performed in another region, A, which is so far from B that there is no possibility that what happened in A could possibly influence region B. Einstein maintained that the properties in B must have existed all along. Therefore, he said, quantum theory is not a complete theory, since it allows for "spooky actions at a distance" (Mermin, 1985). What Einstein meant by "spooky actions at a distance" is a definite value for a physical quantity at B resulting from a measurement carried out at position A (Figure 7). The EPR paper is another ingenious thought experiment of the kind that Einstein was so good at. However, this thought experiment eventually was tested in the laboratory as a real experiment, in a version proposed by J. S. Bell as easier to test than Einstein's original version (Bell, 1964).

In a 1964 paper, Bell proved his now famous theorem that if the statistical predictions of quantum theory are correct, our "commonsense" view of the universe cannot be right (Zukav, 1979). It is interesting that Bell's theorem postulates a situation opposite to what Einstein was trying to show in the EPR paper. According to Bell, not only is the quantum view of the world right, but quantum phenomena spill over to our everyday world or macroscopic experiences. In other words, the concept of the independent reality of physical objects, seemingly reinforced by everyday experience, is limited in a fundamental way. In the words of physicist Henry Stapp (1975):

> The important thing about Bell's theorem is that it puts the dilemma posed by quantum phenomena clearly into the realm of macroscopic phenomena . . . it shows that our ordinary ideas about the world are somehow profoundly deficient even on the macroscopic level.

Bell's theorem is based upon correlations between paired particles, either pairs of photons or pairs of electrons. Alain Aspect and his coworkers at the University of Paris in Orsay have recently carried out experiments to test Bell's theorem involving pairs of photons (Aspect, Dalibard and Gerard, 1982).[7] The investigators measured correlations between the linear polarizations (or direction in space of the electrical fields) of two photons emitted when a calcium atom decays from an initial state to a final state. The paired photons move away from the calcium atom in opposite directions. Quantum theory requires that the linear polarizations of the two photons be parallel. Quantum theory also insists that it makes no sense to talk about the polarization of either photon until a measurement is carried out on one of them.

Testing Bell's Inequality with a Polarization-Type EPR Experiment

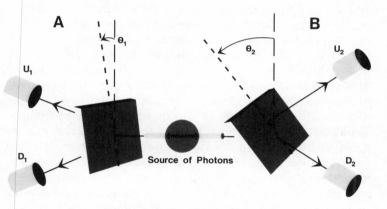

Figure 7. A simplified version of the experiment designed to test Bell's theorem

As shown in Figure 7, a source of photons containing calcium atoms is placed at the center of the apparatus. Pairs of photons are emitted in opposite directions, passing through two polarizers. Behind the polarizers are photomultiplier tubes, which detect the passage of a photon by making a "click" sound. You can think of the polarization of a photon as an arrow in space. Photons can show a preferred direction in space, analogous, say, to soldiers marching one at a time all carrying their spears pointing upward. The spears are polarized in the vertical direction (the "up," U, direction measured by detectors U_1 in region A and U_2 in region B, as shown in Figure 7). If the soldiers (the photons) pass a gate (the polarizer) which is very tall, their spears will fit and they can go through. But suppose that the soldiers are carrying their spears horizontally (the "down," D, direction measured by detectors D_1 in region A and D_2 in region B, as shown in Figure 7). If the gate is tall but not wide, the soldiers and their spears (photons) will not fit, and the marching will stop.

If both polarizers are aligned in the same direction (the angles of both polarizers with the vertical direction are the same (or $\theta_1 = \theta_2$ —see Figure 7), then whenever the photomultiplier at A goes "click," the photomultiplier at B also goes "click." If, however, the situation is reversed, and the two polarizers are aligned at 90 degrees with respect to each other (when the angles shown in Figure 7 differ by 90 degrees), then whenever the photomultiplier at A goes "click" the photomultiplier at B does not respond. Bell proved—and Aspect and his collaborators showed he was right—that no matter what the angles or alignments of the polarizers, the clicks in area A correlate too strongly with the clicks in area B to be explained purely by chance. The two regions are connected somehow. The actual experiment is a bit more complicated than what has been presented here. It allows the physicist to choose what polarization to measure *after* the two photons have left their source, and they are so far away from each other that *no possible signal can get from one photon to the other to "tell" it what direction was picked.* Still somehow one photon "knows" what happened to the other. The worst fear of Einstein— "spooky actions at a distance"—is very much a part of quantum reality, now documented in the Aspect experiments.

Most scientists would hold true a worldview which consists of three premises: First is realism—the doctrine that physical reality exists independent of human observers. Second is that scientists can use logic, algebra and the other wonderful weapons of the mathematical arsenal to derive theories. Third is that no influence can propagate faster than light. This premise is called Einstein separability. Theories that follow these three premises are called "local realistic theories." However, Bell's theorem states that if the statistical predictions of quantum theory are valid (and they are observed to be very valid indeed), then whether quantum theory is "right" in an ultimate sense is immaterial. Its predictions are totally different from those of local realistic theories, but its predictions can be tested in the laboratory. Bell derived an inequality, which is violated by quantum mechanics but which is obeyed by local realistic theories. Bell's inequality shows that two particles that have ever been connected remain connected in a mysterious way, even if they are light years apart. This inequality applies to experiments with particles that have three stable properties, for example, three axes of spin, each of which has the value plus or minus. An excellent account of Bell's inequality and of the experiments designed to test it is given in *Scientific American* articles by Bernard d'Espagnat (1979) and Abner Shimony (1988) and in the book *Quantum Reality* by Nick Herbert (1987).

The overwhelming experimental evidence collected from many experiments testing Bell's inequality shows not only that local realistic theories are invalid but that Bell's inequality is violated precisely as quantum mechanics predicts. Global realistic theories—theories that allow interconnection in the universe over vast distances—may still be valid. David Bohm (1952) and his coworkers Basil Hiley and David Peat proposed a pioneer view[8] of the cosmos, which allows for interconnectedness at a deep level which they call the "implicate order" (Bohm, 1981). Our own universe is the "explicate order," made explicit from the deep level which implies it. Bohm's theory is holistic. It has the added beauty that at a deep level it is fully de-terministic. Nevertheless, the theory allows instantaneous actions at a distance, and as such it is as non-classical as orthodox quantum theory. Eventually Bohm's implicate order may be testable in the laboratory, but even without experimental verification, it postulates a remarkable wholeness to the cosmos unachieved by any other theory.

Physicists are still debating what the violation of Bell's inequality implies for the universe. Most physicists still cling to the premise of realism, because the alternative is too difficult to work with (d'Espagnat 1979; Kafatos and Nadeau, 1990). Most physicists have adopted Bohr's attitude toward realism. He rejected classical realism but followed

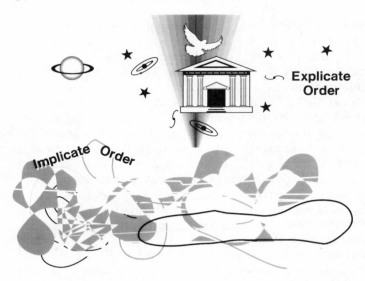

Figure 8. Bohm's implicate and explicate orders

a kind of critical realism; he accepted that nature exists independent of human acts but realized that complementarity should nevertheless be taken into account. This view of realism in turn implies limits to what we can know about nature. These limits make any experiment designed to discover the ultimate Reality of things through scientific means likely to be an empty exercise. It may well be that God does not play dice, but in the physical realm, it appears that this happens! Thus physical reality is contingent on what we do to find out about it, or, in other words, on consciousness itself. It is not yet clear which of the three premises of local classical realism a modern physicist should reject. Perhaps the easiest premise to give up is Einstein separability—the notion that physical influences are limited by the speed of light. However, the quantum correlations evident in Bell's theorem cannot be used to send a signal, thus they do not violate relativity. Only when the observers at A and B compare notes do the correlations between events at A and at B become apparent. Nature has shown us that our *concept of reality, consisting of units that can be considered as separate from each other, is fundamentally wrong.* For this reason, Bell's theorem may be the most profound discovery of science (Stapp, 1975).

Of Cats and Other Paradoxes of Reality

The issue of ultimate Reality bothered Einstein. He believed that mathematical reasoning should ultimately be able to unravel the mysteries of the universe. Implicit in this assumption is the old belief that a one-to-one correspondence exists between elements in a physical theory and objects in the universe. However, mathematical formalism belongs to the mental realm, while the universe we study with science is physical. Why should the two realms correspond exactly? This old belief can be traced to ancient philosophers, particularly Pythagoras and Plato. In believing this, Einstein was more a classical physicist.

The split between the universe and our mathematical description of it—the latter somehow thought of as superior to the former—did not occur in antiquity but fairly recently in the Age of Reason. Quantum theory shows that such a split—philosophers of science often refer to it as ontological dualism—is not justified. *Quantum theory implies a holistic view of the universe, although quantum theory cannot say anything about how one would arrive at such a view.*

Einstein even went as far as stating that accepting quantum mechanics as a complete description of microscopic phenomena would somehow undermine our common belief in the independent existence of objects in the universe. One night his friend and collaborator A. Pais (1981) recollects:

> We often discussed his notions on objective reality. I recall that during one walk Einstein suddenly stopped, turned to me and asked whether I really believed that the moon exists only when I look at it.

Einstein, of course, was correct on this point. It is likely that the moon exists whether or not human observers are looking at it. However, quantum mechanics, and for that matter all scientific fields, which are *based on the object/*

subject duality, cannot answer or even ask questions on matters of existence. Existence cannot be proven externally. Sensory input can tell us only facts about an object, while its existence itself is beyond object/subject dualism. Later chapters show that this is what mystical traditions have held all along. Modern physics has reached the limit of what science can know, but by its very nature science is not allowed to go beyond.

Quantum mechanics asserts that the perception of existing physical objects depends critically on the experiment we set up to find out about them. However, the problem lies in confusing *existence* with *properties of existing objects*. It is reasonable to assume that physical objects exist whether or not we are looking at them, or whether or not we are interacting with them. But the nature of objects when we are not looking at them, when all sensory input has been cut off, cannot be known within the context of scientific inquiry. This book argues that existence can be experienced only directly. In other words, existence is a totally subjective experience. Perceptions of existing objects, on the other hand, constitute objective activity, or scientific inquiry.

As humans, we commonly share similar perceptions and commonly share such validating perceptions with each other. But this is as far as we can go. Even if all the organisms on the entire earth and ourselves were removed, how could we be sure that no being somewhere else was looking at the moon or feeling its presence? Quantum mechanics asserts only that perceptions of objects are contingent upon the act of observation. In this way, quantum mechanics has opened the door to a new perception of reality. It may well be that objects exist only when someone is conscious of their existence. But even if we eliminate the entire universe and all its observers, how can we know for sure that the moon itself is not conscious of its own existence? *Proving existence objectively then becomes identical to proving the consciousness of existence.* If we can prove the first, we can prove the second proposition as well. However, proving objectively the existence of consciousness seems an impossible task. In the words of Schrödinger, "consciousness is never experienced in the plural, only in the singular." We know that we exist and that we are conscious. It is also reasonable to assume that other humans exist and are conscious as we are. But that's as far as it goes. Extending human consciousness to objects like the moon eventually leads to absurdities.

One such absurdity is the famous paradox of Schrödinger's cat (cf. Gribbin, 1984). Imagine that a cat is put into a box with a mechanism that has a 50 percent probability of killing the cat in any interval of time. (No one has said whether Schrödinger's cat is curious!) If observation confers reality upon an object, then by opening the box we somehow either "cause" the cat to be killed, or we "cause" the cat to be alive. The paradox, according to Schrödinger, is that the cat is neither dead nor alive until someone decides to open the box! To complicate the issue further, a macroscopic system with a large number of degrees of freedom, such as a cat, does not exhibit the binary choices exhibited by simple quantum systems. Some macroscopic systems, such as superconducting rings, do exhibit simple binary choices, and experiments are currently underway to determine whether or not they "choose" a particular state until a measurement is made (as exhibited by the pairs of particles in Bell-type experiments) (see Kafatos and Nadeau, 1990). The cat paradox, which Schrödinger rejected, becomes a problem if we assume that human observation is the only kind of observation implied by quantum theory. Perhaps the cat is conscious too! In that case the cat knows before we open the box if it is alive and can feel the death experience if the mechanism kills it. Where is then the paradox? It seems to be only in our minds!

Further Unification

As we have seen, the early 1920s and 1930s were times of extraordinary change in the history of science and philosophy. Quantum theory was developed, and with it came a new view of physical reality. The next step was unavoidably a step towards unification. The impressive success of quantum theory meant that it had to be combined with the other successful scientific theory of the twentieth century—relativity. In the early 1940s the two were blended together into a relativistic quantum field theory, dubbed quantum electrodynamics, or QED. To this day, this theory remains the most successful and accurate product of the scientific mind.

QED combines two complementary constructs, the field and the quantum. Since a field is a continuum, it is antithetical to a distinct, particle-like quantum. In QED electrons, protons and other charged particles interact with each other electromagnetically by exchanging quanta of energy, in what appears macroscopically to be a field interaction. In QED the quanta that mediate the electromagnetic interactions are photons.

A series of diagrams developed by Nobel laureate Richard P. Feynman (1988) describe visually what is going on. Imagine an electron moving through space-time following a "world line," a continuous path of connected points in space and time. In a typical Feynman diagram such as Figure 9, the horizontal axis depicts a dimension of space, and the vertical axis depicts the passage of time. A second electron interacting with the first scatters off it, and the two exchange what is called a "virtual" photon. Macroscopically we can think that each electron sets up an invisible electromagnetic field around itself, which the other electron somehow "feels," because according to classical physics, the two fields interact. But just as Einstein did away with the concept of force in the realm of macrophysics, when he described gravity as the warping of the space-time continuum, in the realm of microscopic physics, QED physicists also did away with the concept of force. What appears to be an invisible force acting instantaneously at a distance between electrons is nothing more than an exchange of quanta, which travel at the speed of light. When the two electrons exchange a virtual photon, each is thrown out of its uniform motion as if each felt the other's "force."

The exchange of the virtual photon can be understood more easily if one brings Heisenberg's uncertainty principle into the picture. During the minute interval of time during which the electrons cannot be observed, they can exchange

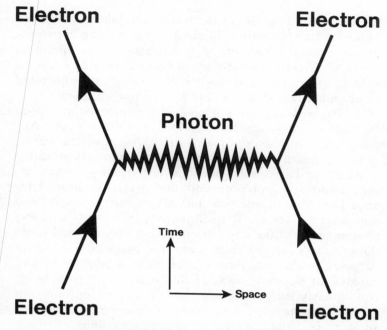

Figure 9. Feynman diagram of an electron-electron scattering

an amount of energy carried by a photon. Heisenberg's uncertainty principle relates the interval of time to the energy exchanged. An electron does not live in isolation, since it can borrow energy from the vacuum, as long as this takes place in an extremely short time. Thus in the strange quantum view of the universe, a vacuum is not empty. On the contrary, it is full of energy which is unmanifest. If the time interval is short enough, a large amount of energy can be borrowed through the mediation of a virtual particle, a particle which goes unnoticed by the rest of the world.

An analogy to this occurrence would be somebody walking into a bank after hours, borrowing a large sum of money, keeping it overnight and returning it in the morning before any clerk finds out. The problem with the bank analogy is that there is not an infinite pool of money. Also, if the borrower uses the money in any way, the bank could eventually find out about the illicit overnight use of funds. However, there is nothing illicit about an electron borrowing energy from the vacuum of space, because the energy of the vacuum is virtually infinitely abundant. A correspondingly infinite amount of money—if such a thing existed—would be abundantly easy to find but also totally worthless.

Not so with the infinite pool of energy existing within the vacuum of space. Here perfect democracy exists. Any particle can and does borrow as much energy as it wishes, in fact as much energy as is required by all particles in the universe to carry out their dance. Virtual particles are the abundantly available currency of the cosmos. They arise from the infinite pool of vacuum energy and to that they return. They are not counterfeit, only totally invisible or unmanifest. Like any currency, they can be used to do things; they can be exchanged in interactions between particles, just as real money is exchanged between human beings. An electron—and for that matter any particle—is continuously surrounded by a "cloud" of currency of virtual photons, virtual electrons, their oppositely charged antiparticles, the positrons, and many other currency particles.

All this may sound strangely familiar to anyone knowledgeable in Indian philosophical systems. The ancient Indian sages talked about universal Consciousness as continually creating an infinity of universes without the mediation of material substance. These universes arise out of the fullness of material emptiness and eventually return to the same emptiness.

Even though invisible, virtual particles can be felt indirectly. Their presence has also been confirmed in the laboratory.[9] QED predicts that empty space itself is full of such virtual particles. At the ultimate level where QED is unified with gravity, one can imagine that space-time itself is broken up into an infinite sea of seething activity. At the unimaginably small dimensions of 10^{-33} centimeters, the so-called Planck length, space-time becomes foamy.[10] There, virtual tiny black holes appear and disappear in continuously violent activity. This sea of virtual particles and virtual black holes is responsible for a vast reservoir of energy. The energy density of empty space is unimaginably large. One cubic centimeter of empty space contains 10^{90} kilograms of mass-energy, or 10^{37} times more mass-energy than the entire observable universe! In other words, a volume of empty space not bigger than the tip of your finger contains as much energy as ten billion, billion, billion, billion universes put together!

The unification of QED with gravity at the Planck length implies that there are real limits to physics. What we study in physics, namely the physical universe, is but a tiny drop in the great ocean of energy contained in "empty" space. It goes without saying that perhaps physicists are missing the whole point. What we study, the "observable" universe, is nothing compared to what is beneath it, huge energies which are unobservable and yet nonetheless real.[11] Foamy space-time is literally under our very eyes and yet unobservable directly, because at the unimaginably small dimensions of 10^{-33} cm, everything, including the very fabric of space-time, breaks down. This makes the task of unifying quantum theory with gravity very difficult. Einstein equated gravity to curved space-time. Quantum theory also requires the presence of space-time, but the seething activity of particle interactions can be assumed to take place against an impassive backdrop. In other words, quantum field interactions occur over a flat, imperturbable sheet of space-time. How can the imperturbable space-time sheet of quantum theory also be the macroscopic, rubbery, warped space-time hypothesized in Einstein's gravity theory? Physicists have no answer. But one thing is sure— at the Planck length, both flat and warped space-time get torn up and turn into totally chaotic foam.

Recently an idea has been advanced that the Planck-length particles are one-dimensional "strings." An alternate modern view holds that at the Planck level space-time is made of quantum "loops." Other physicists hope that a supersymmetric theory called "supergravity" will succeed in unifying gravity with the other three interactions explained below.[12] Recently, physicists have pinned their hopes on the "superstring" theory,[13] which may be a good candidate for the "Theory of Everything" (TOE). It is presumptious, to say the least, to assume that the human mind can reduce all the complexities of the cosmos to a single mathematical theory, produced by the mind itself. In any case, the ultimate unification of Einstein's gravity with quantum field theory will not be easy to accomplish.

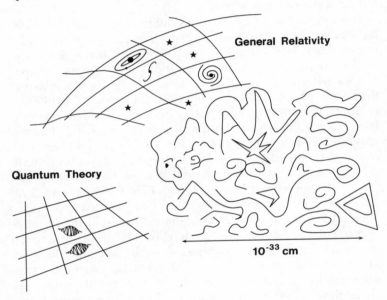

Figure 10. At the Planck level, the flat imperturbable space-time sheet of quantum theory and the curved, rubber-like space-time sheet of gravitational theory both end up as chaotic foam.

Despite the ultimate chaos of the vacuum, our universe is also magnificently predictable. At the macroscopic level, God does not play dice. Einstein stated that "the most incomprehensible thing about the universe is that it can be comprehended." The hope of a mathematical understanding of the universe is what seduces the scientist. We would really like to know everything there is to know about the universe, and the many successes of science seem to promise reaching that goal. However, quantum theory clearly shows that at the micro level where everything starts, the universe is *unpredictable in principle*. Even worse, Bell's theorem shows that even the concept of an independently existing reality has to be called into question. How can anything be comprehended if we don't even know what is real? Deep inside we want to agree with Einstein that God does not play dice, and that ultimately the universe will be comprehended in its entirety, but the successes of quantum theory point to a nature that stubbornly behaves in an unpredictable way. *However, our inability to know everything makes this universe what it is.* We cannot have both the marvelously intricate universe we live in and love and perfect, complete knowledge of that universe. Perhaps the issue is like the old wave/particle dilemma. Absolute predictability and total randomness are two sides of the same coin—two complementary constructs—both needed to make sense out of our universe.

Besides gravity and electromagnetism, two other interactions are known in nature, the strong or nuclear, and the weak. The properties of all four interactions are summarized in Table 1 (see Gaillard, 1982; Kafatos and Nadeau, 1990). The strong interaction is responsible for holding particles such as neutrons and protons together in the nuclei of atoms. The weak interaction manifests when, for example,

TABLE 1

FOUR ELEMENTARY INTERACTIONS FOUND IN NATURE

INTERACTION	PHYSICAL PHENOMENA	RANGE[#]	RELATIVE STRENGTH	RADIATION[¢] QUANTA	MATTER[*] QUANTA
STRONG	nuclear forces	10^{-13} cm	1	gluons	quarks[&]
ELECTROMAGNETIC	atomic forces, optics, electricity	∞	10^{-2}	photon	quarks, leptons (i.e. electrons, muons)
WEAK	radioactivity, nuclear reactions in stars	10^{-16} cm	10^{-10}	$W^{\pm}$, Z	quarks, leptons, neutrinos
GRAVITATIONAL	planetary orbits, binary stars, galaxies, clusters of galaxies, black holes, etc.	∞	10^{-38}	graviton	everything

Notes: [#] 10^{-13} cm is about the size of a nucleus
[¢] These are the quanta which are responsible for the transfer of the interaction
[*] These are the particles which interact with each other under the particular interaction
[&] Quarks are the constituent particles of neutrons and protons and other heavy particles

a free neutron decays into other particles. The elusive neutrino particle partakes in weak reactions. Weak and strong interactions occur in the multimillion degree furnaces in the central regions of stars. Because of them, stars shine, planets can sustain life and human beings can live and think. The fourth interaction, gravity, is what holds the universe together. Gravity is the weakest of all the interactions, but it reigns supreme over the large scale of the universe. As can be seen in Table 1, the range over which the electromagnetic and gravitational interactions are felt is infinite. The carriers of these interactions—the photon and the hypothetical graviton—have zero rest mass and travel with the speed of light, 300,000 kilometers per second. On the other hand, the range of the strong and weak interactions is extremely small. These two interactions drop to zero beyond a distance about equal to the size of a nucleus or one trillionth of the tip of a human finger.

Physicists are pursuing Einstein's dream of bringing together all four interactions in a single, elegant unifying field theory. Any attempt at unification involves symmetry principles (Zee, 1986). All conservation laws arise because of adherence to symmetry, as the German physicist Amalie Emmy Noether proved in a beautiful and powerful argument. For example, conservation of energy occurs because physical laws are equally valid if time is reversed. Today physicists build quantum theories for the strong interaction and other interactions by adhering to symmetry principles. In some ways, the search for unification is the search for beauty in physics. QED, a theory which is accurate to the fifteenth decimal place (Polkinghorne, 1984) is a good example to follow in this search for beauty.

An elegant quantum theory of strong interactions, called quantum chromodynamics, or QCD, has recently been developed. According to this theory, the fundamental building blocks of particles like the proton and the neutron are quarks. Theoreticians distinguish the properties of these strange particles by giving them the names of colors. A proton, for example, consists of three quarks, each with a different color. These colors have been called red, blue, and green, although one should not think of them as colors in the ordinary sense. Quarks also have a property that quantum theorists dub their "flavor," namely up, down, charm, strange, bottom and top. Unlike any other particle seen in nature, quarks have a fractional charge. The down, strange and bottom flavored quarks have a charge of $-\frac{1}{3}$ of the charge of the electron; the up, charm and top flavored quarks have a charge of $+\frac{2}{3}$ of the charge of the electron. Quarks are very elusive, and physicists believe they will never be found alone as free particles. Quarks appear to be glued together by quanta called "gluons." It now appears that light particles like the electron are truly elementary and point-like; in other words, light particles have no size whatsoever! Similarly, quarks also seem to be point-like. One wonders if the ultimate building blocks of all matter will ever be found. Although physicists do not presently believe that quarks are composite particles, it probably would not surprise them if at some future date physicists conclude that they need to look still deeper to find "the ultimate fundamental structure" of matter.

As far as our present knowledge of micro interactions goes, quantum theory has allowed progressive unification to take place. The weak and electromagnetic interactions have been unified into an electroweak quantum theory by physicists Sheldon Glashow, Abdus Salam and Steven Weinberg. This partial unification has raised hopes that at some future time, quantum theory will explain all interactions. Thus Einstein's dream of a unified field theory may one day be fulfilled. It is now certain that such a theory—probably to the dismay of Einstein if he were around to witness it—will be a quantum-type theory. The experimental evidence in favor of quantum theory is so strong that no physicist could take seriously a nonquantum unifield field theory.

A candidate for the next level of unification, uniting the strong, electromagnetic and weak interactions, is the so-called "grand unified theory," or GUT. Experimentalists are looking for clues to the validity of GUT (Davies, 1984) in ultrahigh energy particle accelerators. However, it appears that the only place where it may be realistic to search for evidence of this theory is in the very energetic processes which took place in the early universe, near the beginning of time, when the big bang occurred.

Questions about the ultimate "stuff" of the universe and its basic structure go back to ancient times. The philosophers of the Ionian school, Thales, Anaximenes, Anaximander, Parmenides and others, thought that the fundamental philosophical question ought to be "what is the ultimate substance—stuff—of the universe?" Plato, Pythagoras and to a certain extent Aristotle, on the other hand, believed that the critical philosophical issue was the world's form, the order and structure we see in the universe. Ironically, despite the great successes of quantum theory, the answers to these questions still elude us. If we are tempted to say that the ultimate stuff is quanta, in elementary or composite form, we must remember that these strange particle-like, wave-like things are neither permanent nor immutable. Under our eyes quanta transform into other quanta all the time. How can something be the ultimate stuff if it is never the same? Strange indeed is our universe!

However, many physicists today still cling to the idea that the ultimate substance of the universe is the elementary particles, a belief that can be traced to Democritus. We presently know a number of the elementary particles, but even if we forgot for a second that a particle is not an indivisible, immutable something, as Democritus' particles were, where would our list end? How do we know that future experiments will not reveal more and more particles, which we do not presently even suspect to exist?

This brings back the old question of reality. A quantum continuously changes into other quanta, forming loops of virtual quanta that dance in and out of existence in an eternal flow. If we are still seduced by Democritus' dream of finding an elementary particle, we quickly reach an impasse. How can something be the ultimately "real" stuff if that something perpetually changes? However, if we prefer Pythagoras' and Plato's view, the problem dissolves. What remains is the flow—the "dance" and not the substance. In fact, in modern quantum theory *substance is flow*. Consider a proton. Flow creates a proton, and yet a proton is not just a proton. It is also an infinity of other particles appearing and disappearing into nothingness. Yet somehow, a proton still retains its identity.

What modern quantum theory says about the primacy of flow can be found elsewhere, in traditions of the past. In fact, the perennial philosophy says that everything in the universe, from Universal Consciousness down to a simple blade of grass, undergoes the same ever-flowing changes—the three fundamental processes of creation, maintenance, and reabsorption or disappearance. Thus modern quantum field theory is distinctly Platonic and Pythagorean in its basic outlook.

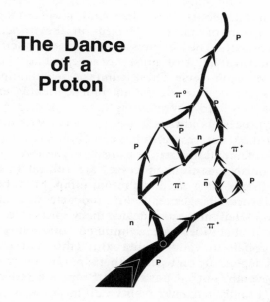

The Dance of a Proton

Figure 11. The dance of a particle. A proton continuously undergoes creation, sustenance, and dissolution.

Summary

The theories of relativity and quantum theory both lead to an increasing level of wholeness. Specifically, according to these theories, the act of observation is central to the way physical phenomena appear. Einstein's relativity treats time as simply another dimension. In fact, time and space together form a more general unified substratum than any implied by Newton's physics—a four-dimensional space-time continuum. However, Einstein's theories are classical in the sense that space-time is continuous, that cause and effect relationships are strictly obeyed and, of course, that space-time, gravity and mass are all real. Einstein's vision does differ profoundly from classical physics in one way: What one observes depends on one's own state of motion.

A pivotal issue in quantum theory is the dual nature of light. How can light and matter exhibit opposite tendencies and be simultaneously wave-like and particle-like? The quantum vision of nature is based on the principle of complementarity. The features of this view often seem counter-intuitive but still must be accepted as objective properties of the universe. These features can be summarized as follows: First, if there is an independently existing reality, physics can say nothing about it. Second, the observing process is always present in what we are trying to find out about nature; reality has to include us as observers. Third, complementarity manifests itself in the wave-particle duality. Fourth, quantum processes are subject to abrupt changes of state, such as the quantum jump. Fifth, because of these abrupt changes, causality and determinism must conform to Heisenberg's indeterminacy principle. Sixth, quantum probabilities are computed differently from classical probabilities, and quanta exhibit different statistical properties depending on whether their spin is integer or half integer. Seventh, not all parts of a theory are reflected in the world. Finally, whatever reality is, it has to be non-local. In essence, quantum theory implies that atomic processes are discontinuous and can only be predicted probabilistically. In other words, the observing process has an inherent limitation. Quantum phenomena should be understood in terms of the principle of complementarity developed by Bohr, which asserts that a complete, objective description of a phenomenon, such as light, requires the use of the complementary constructs of wave and particle.

Since everything in the universe is made of quanta, the

macrocosm arises from the microcosm. It does not seem realistic that there would be two domains with conflicting physical laws. It would be like insisting that a house and its foundations follow different laws. Quantum physics seems to provide a general framework based on what we now know, and it wisely insists that we do not and cannot know everything. Recent experiments designed to test Bell's theorem have shown that realism remains an unanswered problem. Quantum physics does not answer the question of what is real. Perhaps the problem lies in confusing the reality of existence with the properties of existence. But quantum theory has opened the scientific door to the nature of consciousness. It has brought us, as Planck stated "to the threshold of the ego." Though it does not provide an answer, quantum physics' newly opened door on the boxed walls of the Newtonian universe has revealed a remarkable wholeness behind physical phenomena. In other words, the completely deterministic Newtonian universe has become a non-local, indeterminate quantum universe, manifested through complementary relationships.

Finally, quantum theory has allowed for an increased level of unification. Unification features profound symmetries. Physicists even hope that the strong interaction will be unified with the electroweak in a more general theory. Though gravity stubbornly resists attempts to be quantized, there is optimism that we are close to the goal of a unified field theory. Yet, despite all the successes, it is not clear that even if we eventually understand what happens at the elementary particle level, even if we quantize gravity, that these accomplishments will enable us to understand more about the universe, including our own place in it. Recent developments in physical theory are bringing us closer to unification but also leading us more and more toward what cannot be visualized. Will current theoretical developments survive the test of time? Actually, this matters little, for it is the unification, the wholeness, and the implication that reality cannot be visualized that must be the prescription of the new glasses with which we will view our wonderfully intricate and knowable universe.

3

A New Vision of
the Universe: Seeing Out

We agree much more than you think.
Niels Bohr

The vast expanse of the universe reaches to a distance at least ten billion light years from the solar system. It contains more than a billion galaxies, each containing hundreds of billions of stars and planets, some likely to support life. All matter is made of tiny atoms, which in turn are made of elementary particles such as protons, neutrons and electrons. Protons and neutrons are composed of even more elementary particles called quarks. The total number of elementary particles in the observable radius of the universe is in excess of 10^{78}, or one million trillion trillion trillion trillion trillion trillion protons and electrons! An even vaster number of photons or quanta of light exist in the universe, since the universe is filled primarily with light. For each particle of matter there are some ten billion particles of light. Thus the number of photons in the universe is estimated to be about 10^{88}, or ten thousand trillion trillion trillion trillion trillion trillion trillion! At the other end of the scale of size, each atom measures about one hundred millionth of the tip of a human finger across, and most of the mass of an atom, the nucleus, is concentrated in a region not more than one ten trillionth of a fingertip. The tiny nucleus of a simple hydrogen atom is vastly greater than the Planck length, one hundred million trillion times bigger, at which point our knowledge of the universe reaches a horizon.

How can the human mind comprehend these scales, these quantities, this vastness? Mathematical language is the only language useful in discussing such concepts. And yet as physics developed in the last three hundred years, it became clear that mathematics by itself was not sufficient, that physical insight was necessary as well. Newtonian mechanics dealt with objects that could be visualized, like pulleys and colliding spheres. As physics progressed to the description of electromagnetic phenomena, the common objects used to study these phenomena—batteries, magnets, wires and the rest—still remained within the realm of what can be visualized. To be sure, no physicist had a clear idea of what a force is, and Newton himself declared that natural science could not answer such questions. No physicist could comprehend or visualize the constituency of a force field. However, since the effects of forces and fields were easy to observe, physicists retained a false sense that forces and fields could be visualized. But twentieth-century physics' movement toward unification has led it first to the paradoxical and then to the realm of relativistic quantum interactions, which can never be visualized.

What Is Real and What Can Be Known?

As modern physics has progressed to its limits, qualitative and quantitative descriptions of reality have tended to approach each other. Quantum field theory is complex mathematically. To grasp its statements truly one needs to be an initiate in the abstract mathematics of group theory. The problem is that at both the very large and the very small ends of the scale of lengths, common experience fails us. How can the human mind comprehend a black hole, a place where space and time come to an end by the infinite curvature of nothingness? How can the human mind understand the stuff that makes up quarks and colored gluons? These strange names describe something that is totally alien to anything we can perceive.

Despite its paradoxes and its inability to be visualized,

relativistic quantum field theory is very successful in describing nature. Scientists hope that if we put together a unified view of the cosmos, we may even understand its origin. If there is any fundamental simplicity to the physical universe it is that all fundamental particle interactions obey the universal principle of adherence to symmetries. Some particle physicists, drunk with the wine of success of field theory, declare that we are, at last, close to understanding everything. Impressive names have been devised for the theories that may fulfill the dream of unification—grand unification theory, theories of multidimensional reality or superstring theories and, ultimately the theory of "everything" or TOE (Zee, 1986).

Of course everything to a particle physicist is not everything to anybody else. To the particle physicist, everything refers to fundamental particle interactions. It certainly does not include the vast complexity of life, thinking and conscious processes. And even in the realm of pure physics, gravity has stubbornly refused to marry its quantum suitor. One is reminded of the boastful statements of Lord Kelvin during another time when physicists thought they were close to understanding everything. As a result, many theoretical physicists remain skeptical. Past experience teaches that the universe is much more complex than whatever theories are in vogue. It is not at all clear that the human mind can achieve closure—that it can comprehend what may turn out to be an incomprehensible universe. As Herman Weyl (1949) put it:

> The example of quantum mechanics has once more demonstrated how the possibilities with which our imagination plays before a problem is ripe for solution are always far surpassed by reality.

The fundamental problem which remains is that no one has shown convincingly that the reductionist approach of science guarantees an ultimately successful theory of everything—a theory which, in addition to particle interactions, accounts for all the observed phenomena in the universe. It is certainly not clear why mathematical physics has been so successful in accounting for physical phenomena at the micro and macro levels. Physical scientists somehow assume that they alone can unravel the mysteries of the universe, since only science possesses the element of objectivity. Whether ultimate knowledge has to be rational and objective or not is a metaphysical question (Weyl, 1949); science itself cannot determine it. Think, for example, about music, which has its own rules of composition and standards of how it should be performed. Is music less objective than science? If so, it is only in the sense that the object music concerns itself with is closer to the human psyche than the external objects of scientific study. If, instead of knowledge of external objects, one searches for ultimate meaning and for union with the core of all else in the universe, science, as it is practiced today, is clearly limited.

Scientific inquiry requires consensus, even the obvious consensus that we will accept as objective truth only what can be tested in the laboratory. If, for example, the community of scientists suddenly decides that repeated verification of laboratory results is not necessary, science as we know it would certainly change. Science, then, is another field of human activity with its own rules, its own truths, its own definition of objectivity. To call science more objective because it deals with the physical universe and not with the human psyche, human feelings or human existence is rather arbitrary.

Within science as well different scientists use different kinds of expressions. The way Einstein understood and expressed quantum theory was different from the way Bohr understood and expressed the same theory. Ultimately, these various personal belief systems clouded scientific objectivity. To his death Einstein remained unconvinced of the completeness of quantum theory. Science may be an objective system of knowledge; yet its objectivity is inexorably connected to human scientists and their instruments. In other words, we can no longer talk about absolute objectivity, a reality divorced totally from the methods designed to reveal it. Nature does not allow us to forget the game of dice that so disturbed Einstein, the game of trying to unravel what is "real." Sir Arthur Eddington (1929) put it as follows:

It is time we came to grips with the loose terms Reality and Existence, which we have been using without any inquiry into what they are meant to convey.

Furthermore, if, as quantum field theory implies, the emphasis of scientific work should be on process rather than on substance, we must ask, "Can a process be scientifically objective?" Western philosophy and science implicitly assumes that what is real has a certain sense of permanency and that scientific truths should thus be self-evident, universal and everlasting. Even today scientists take for granted Einstein's view of an unchanging reality. This belief certainly fits well with the philosophical beliefs of Renaissance natural philosophy, traceable to Plato and Pythagoras. If, however, the emphasis of modern physics is on process, on change and flow, wouldn't the philosophy of the Greek Heraclitus be more appropriate? If time and space are not fixed, if particles continuously engage in a dance of change, reality must have a new meaning.

Scientific "truths" emerge as the community of scientists practice according to the current rules of science. However, these rules are not self-evident and eternal. Ever-changing, they are a product of Western human history, hardly more than four hundred years old. If the rules of science were self-evident, science would have been around for as long as human history. An objectivity that needs to be defined and agreed upon by definition cannot be absolute or universal. By its very nature science does not accept dogmas or self-evident truths. And yet paradoxically, scientific inquiry would be meaningless if science *as a matter of principle* could never reach an ultimate understanding of the universe.

What would in fact happen if the rules of science were changed or not accepted by everybody? Would science cease to be a successful system of knowledge? Science cannot answer these questions, because they belong to metaphysics, the foundation of scientific knowledge. In the West objectified rationality has been elevated to a supreme belief system despite the fact that human beings often operate irrationally, as witnessed in the dream and deep sleep states and in other processes of the subconscious. Although we have extended scientific knowledge to the inner and outer reaches of the universe, humans don't seem to have progressed very far in understanding themselves.

How can we be so sure that we are close to comprehending the incomprehensible universe if we don't even know ourselves? It may not work to examine the complex processes of life, such as thinking and consciousness itself, using the methods by which we study the comparatively simple processes between particles. No one has developed a successful mathematical theory of the origin of life, nor has anyone shown convincingly that biology and psychology can emulate the successful example of physics. Biology and physics may actually be fundamentally different.[1] Even though biological processes involve countless particle interactions, the evolution of life on earth must be studied from the historical record. In contrast to physics, in which researchers can run the same experiment over and over, changing the initial conditions until they achieve agreement with the theory, there is only one Earth with a unique history and complexity of life. Had astronomers found many living planets in the universe, they would at least be sure that life on Earth is not an aberration. Perhaps they could then develop a "rational" field to describe how life begins under different conditions. However, we are not sure if we are alone in the universe, or if there are trillions of planets which support life.

Biology does have some universal principles, such as the right-left symmetry prevalent in living species and the universality of the genetic code. Some biologists even believe that the entire Earth should be viewed as a living entity—the so-called Gaia hypothesis (Lovelock, 1979). However, these principles cannot be placed in a neat mathematical framework as can, for example, the simplicity of symmetries in fundamental physics. The statement that before we can understand individual species, we must understand the ecology of the whole Earth has a certain ring of truth to it, but it is not a mathematical formula. Moreover, it is not clear that such statements get us nearer to posing the right questions about life and consciousness. Even in principle, we may not be able to come up with quantitative mathematical means to approach the disciplines of biology, psychology and the other sciences that study animate matter.

One of the fundamental challenges facing quantum theory—and for that matter all physical science—is that it cannot account for individual events, things that happen only once. Quantum theory makes statistical predictions and is, therefore, based on repeatable experience. Here one encounters what Pauli called the *irrationality of reality*, the inability of quantum theory to describe individual events unambiguously (Wilber, 1984). In biology, individual events are the norm. For example, a critical component of evolution is the many unpredictable events that cause mutations in the cells. Although quantum in nature, these events cannot be predicted statistically. In some ways, life appears to be the product of random events, which if different, would have resulted in an entirely different biosphere.

In contrast to the unpredictable events of biology in the macro world, nature at the micro level can be described statistically. Of course a statistical universe is precisely opposite to Einstein's conviction that "God does not play dice." At the microscopic level at least, it appears as if God were throwing dice. In other words, a particle exhibits properties of waves and vice versa, and this behavior introduces an inherent uncertainty into the observed phenomena. It follows that the only way to reconcile what appear to be irreconcilable opposites is to apply a fundamentally statistical description of nature. Thus one might come up with a different version of Einstein's famous statement: "God *appears* to play dice *precisely* in order to reconcile the irreconcilable dual nature of quantum phenomena." Note the word "appears." What Einstein referred to as "God" was, of course, his sense of the ultimate mathematical simplicity of the universe. In Einstein's view, quantum theory is not complete because it does not allow a *precise* knowledge of the properties of a quantum system. He thought that things which are obviously real should be knowable. In this line of thinking, *reality is subtly equated with the ability to know that reality.* Einstein's bias is very similar to Descartes' statement, "I think therefore I exist," in the sense that rational thinking and understanding are presumed to be as primary as existence.

To presume that scientific knowledge can *in principle* access ultimate reality is an incredibly self-centered view of the universe, to say the least. Yet most scientists implicitly assume this in their everyday endeavors. Moreover, the notion that ultimate reality has to be expressed in scientific terms goes against what Pauli termed the irrationality of reality. Such a belief denies the possibility that there are other realities, where rationality and objectivity in the narrow scientific sense do not operate.

Bohr and the Copenhagen Interpretation physicists preferred a more pragmatic and humble view. To them, the universe is real, but scientific descriptions of physical phenomena cannot describe their real essence. They establish only a framework to describe our own interactions with nature. As laboratory confirmations of quantum paradoxes indicate quantum theory *can say nothing about the fundamental nature of external objects, not just in practice but, more importantly, in principle.* For example, the "real" properties of an electron are unknowable except through its interaction with laboratory instruments. Thus the Copenhagen Interpretation of quantum theory points to the limitations of science. We don't know how things really are, only how they appear as we carry out our dialogue with nature.

In our search for ultimate answers we need to examine the philosophical foundations of quantum theory. The cornerstone of the Copenhagen Interpretation is complementarity. This principle hints at a way to view our universe which allows the integration of opposite human endeavors, such as science and art, the rational and the irrational. It also allows human horizons to expand beyond the presently narrow boundaries of scientific practice. This view makes the inherent flexibility of science a practical reality. Because science in principle accepts no preconceived ideas, its nature can be changed. Future science may retain little resemblance to present-day science. This evolution will not be painless, because science is a human product; and scientists—like all human beings—resist change.

These issues are in essence philosophical (see Stapp, 1989). Upon reflection it is easy to believe that metaphysics is primary, prior to physical science. All great scientists, including Einstein and Bohr, struggled with metaphysical issues (Wilber, 1984). Both were painfully aware that the answers cannot be found simply in physics. If, however, there are unifying principles to the universe, they must be evident in physics. Our experience with quantum theory shows that metaphysical principles must be connected to scientific reality. Since science searches for the unifying principles of external reality, and since metaphysics searches for the truth about inner and outer realities, the two disciplines are ultimately searching for the same thing.

What Is Time?

In Newtonian physics, everything perceived by the senses, either directly through observation or indirectly through its effects, is real. Newtonian reality is objective, local and eternally the same. However, local realistic theories were dealt a serious blow by the evidence of the violation of Bell's inequality. Thus the worldview of quantum theory strongly disagrees with common sense. Since this is so, why does classical physics do so well in the world of macroscopic observations and experiments? This dilemma has not been completely resolved. Central to its resolution is the concept of time (see Griffin, 1986). We know that classical physics, which describes the world of everyday experience, is more limited than quantum physics; nevertheless, when the differences in energy between neighboring states is very small, quantum physics reduces to classical physics. In the jargon of quantum theory, this idea is called the "limit of large quantum numbers."

In classical physics time was presumed to be universal, the same everywhere. Einstein's theory of relativity showed the falsity of this assumption. However, when we think

about the "arrow of time"—the notion that at least macroscopically time has a preferred direction—we cannot see
how quantum physics reduces to classical physics. In the
world of the quanta, time has no preferred direction. If we
reverse the arrow of time, new particle interactions emerge.
These time-reversed quantum interactions are as real as
the non-reversed interactions. This is certainly not the case
in the world of everyday experience. Imagine the bizarre
sequence of events if we reverse what happens when a
swimmer jumps from a diving board into the water.

In working with time, physicists usually bring entropy
into the picture. Entropy is a measure of the disorder of
a system. The second law of thermodynamics states that
in a physical process, entropy has to increase, thus providing
an arrow of time.[2] The direction of the arrow emerges as
the combined statistical   tendency of many microscopic
events to go in a certain direction, which eventually becomes
"irreversible." Thus, the arrow of time is nothing more
than a macroscopic illusion of the probabilistic tendency
of events to proceed in a certain order. This explanation
is not entirely satisfactory. No human being asked about
the passage of time would term it an illusion of probabilistic
tendencies. As humans, we know for sure that time passes
inexorably, and that, in the words of the Pythagoreans,
"time demands the end of things."

Many physicists now believe that we will not understand
the arrow of time until consciousness is brought into the
picture. However, orthodox quantum theory itself has
something profound to say about time. A wave function
changes in two ways. As a result of the passage of time, a
wave function changes continuously according to the
Schrödinger equation. A wave function also changes
discontinuously, according to probability laws, if a measurement is performed on the system. Physicist Eugene P.
Wigner believes that these two changes constitute the
most fundamental dualism of quantum theory (Wigner, 1983).
If a system is left alone, the uncertainty in the behavior of
a wave function does not increase over time. If, however,
the system is subjected to measurement—if we try to check

whether its properties did change over time—uncertainty enters the picture.

This dualism is reminiscent of the two types of time proposed by physicist Henry P. Stapp. It is also in accordance with Alfred N. Whitehead's philosophical system (Whitehead, 1929). According to Stapp (1988), the first type is time in the Einsteinian sense—as a fourth dimension. The second type is "process" time, which is the time associated with cumulative processes. Einsteinian time enters physics only through the content of observations, which by themselves cannot say anything about the order of things in a process. Thus quantum theory has not resolved the problem of time, though it has introduced the observational process itself as intricately interwoven with the nature of objective reality.

Since time is closely related to consciousness, it is important to examine what philosophies which concentrate on consciousness say about time. Time seems to be central to any physical process, and scientists can only speak of a universe in time. In Eastern metaphysics, however, time is not the first step in the unfoldment of essential reality. In these philosophies, consciousness is a priori to both space and time. The creative process of unfoldment is examined in the next chapter. For now it suffices to point out that time is of fundamental importance to sentient and thinking beings, but this in no way makes time a predicate of reality.

The Evolving Universe

Time is also of paramount importance in cosmological theory, which views the universe as a system beginning from origins and evolving over time. A simplified version of the evolution of the universe is illustrated in Figure 12.

At the instant of the big bang, the universe emerged from the initial singularity in conditions of unimaginable high density and temperature. Present-day physics breaks down completely in any attempt to describe the big bang itself. Gravitational theory will have to be unified with quantum theory to provide a complete picture of the origin of the cosmos. Conditions during the big bang were the same as conditions at the Planck level at every point of dimension smaller than 10^{-33} centimeters. If we could figure out how to view the Planck level and understand vacuum physics, we would understand the big bang singularity. The reverse is also true.

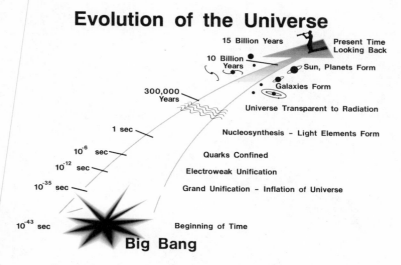

Evolution of the Universe

Figure 12. Evolutionary view of the universe from its origins to the present era. Some milestones in the presently accepted history of the universe are shown.

Einstein's general theory of relativity is a powerful tool for understanding the large-scale structure of the universe. In the 1920s and 30s, American astronomer Edwin Hubble[3] discovered that the more distant a galaxy, the faster it appears to be moving away from us (Trefil, 1983). However, Hubble realized that this effect is simply an illusion, arising from our vantage point. Observers in a distant galaxy would see an identical effect. Actually, the entire fabric of space-time is expanding, carrying with it all galaxies, just as dots drawn on a rubber balloon recede from each other as the balloon expands.

Following the expansion backward in time, Hubble was able to estimate when matter started its expansion. His estimate has been revised many times, and today most cosmologists believe that the universal expansion started between ten and twenty billion years ago. Implicit in this, of course, is the assumption that the universe is expanding today as it has always expanded since it emerged from the big bang (see Gibbons, Hawking and Siklos, 1983).

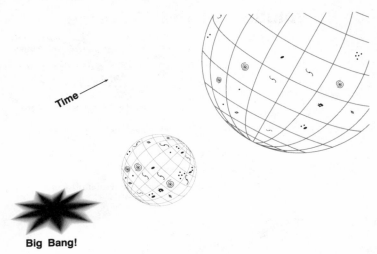

Big Bang!

Figure 13. An analogy for the expansion of the universe. Dots drawn on the surface of a balloon recede from each other as the balloon expands just as galaxies recede from each other as the fabric of space-time expands.

Cosmologists also believe that the universe is isotropic. This means that no matter what direction one looks, the universe appears the same. Moreover, the density of matter is the same in all regions of the universe. In other words, the universe is also homogeneous[4] (Harrison, 1981).

Despite what appeared to be early observational confirmation, big bang cosmology faced a troublesome theoretical challenge—the initial singularity. To avoid this problem and construct an esthetically pleasing model of the universe, Bondi, Hoyle and Gold proposed the steady-state theory in 1948. In their view the universe obeys a perfect cosmological principle: Not only is the universe homogenous and isotropic, but *it looks the same to all observers at all times*. However, since the universe also appears to be expanding, one has to conclude that new matter is being created continuously[5] out of the vacuum of space to fill the voids left behind by the expansion of the universe (Harrison, 1981). Steady-state proponents claim that the universe had no beginning—it has always been expanding.

Despite its philosophical simplicity, the steady-state theory has not survived the test of time. Two observations are hard to reconcile with the theory. The first is the discovery by Arno Penzias and Robert Wilson of microwave background radiation. This radiation, a relic of the initial big bang flash, was first predicted by George Gamow in the 1950s. However, it is hard to reconcile with the steady-state worldview. Today the radiation that fills space has cooled down to 3 degrees above absolute zero. But since in the steady-state view there was no initial flash, the source of this radiation is unclear. The second observation that challenges the steady-state model of the universe is the discovery of quasars. First detected in the early 1960s by astronomer Maarten Schmidt and others, these extraordinary objects are so distant that they are literally at the edge of the observable universe. Thus they would have to be extremely bright for us to be able to detect them at all. Astronomers presently believe that quasars are very ancient, bright active galaxies, the brightest members in a scale of ascending galactic activity, perhaps containing supermassive black holes at their centers. The existence of an evolutionary sequence clearly argues against the principle of a universe that looks the same to all observers at all times, since an evolving universe must have appeared different billions of years ago.

The big bang itself is not without problems. Two particularly difficult challenges are the *horizon problem* and the *flatness problem*. Concerning the first, observations, particularly those made from the recently launched NASA satellite *Cosmic Background Explorer* (Kafatos and Nadeau, 1990), indicate that every condition in the early universe, including background radiation, was extremely smooth. Nevertheless, theory requires that the big bang itself was totally chaotic. Radiation we observe today from opposite directions in the sky was emitted about 10^5 years after the big bang. But at the time the radiation was emitted, these opposite directions were separated by 10^7 light-years. If we insist that there is a causal connection between the opposite sides of the universe, as classical physics demands, then in order for the temperatures of the background radiation observed today from opposite directions to be so similar, we have to assume that at emission the temperatures were equal. The dilemma then is that big bang theory implies chaos at the origin of the universe, but observations indicate that initial conditions were perfectly smooth.

The second problem with the big bang is the flatness problem. The universe appears to be remarkably flat to distances of billions of light years. Thus the geometry appropriate to describe warped space-time is Euclid's flat geometry. If the universe is exactly flat, it started from the big bang some ten to twenty billion years ago and will expand forever. Cosmological theory tells us that an exactly flat universe will come to rest in the infinitely distant future (Harrison, 1981), while an open universe will never come to rest, even in the infinitely distant future.

However, to know for sure the future of the universe, one has to know how much material it contains. If it contains sufficient matter—measured by a critical value of the density of matter—the universe will eventually collapse back on itself and end in a "big crunch." Perhaps this collapsed universe will re-emerge in another big bang and begin another cycle of expansion. In this case, the geometry of the universe would be closed, like the surface of a sphere. Many twentieth-century cosmologists, including Einstein, like the idea of an oscillating closed universe because of its philosophical appeal. Human beings like to feel that something is permanent, that something is not as ephemeral as their mortal lives.

The idea of an oscillating universe is a recent product of Western science. However, the ancient sages of the East came to a similar conclusion. In the *Puranas*, ancient Indian books of epic myths, is the following passage (Wilkins, 1990):

Who will count the universes that have passed away, Or the
creations that have risen, Afresh, Again and again, from
the formless abyss of the vast waters? Who will number the
passing ages of the world, As they follow each other endlessly?

In fact, the Puranas make specific predictions. Book III
of the *Shrimad Bhagavatam* states that one day of Brahma,
the Creator, is 4,320,000,000 human years. A day of Brahma
is followed by a night of Brahma, also lasting 4,320,000,000
years. Four billion years is not quite ten billion years, the
estimated cosmological age of the universe, but it is very
close. In fact four billion years is nearly the presently
accepted age of the Earth. Could this be a coincidence?
How could the sages who wrote the Puranas, who possessed
no telescopes, no calculus and no general relativity theory,
have derived the right order of magnitude for the age of
the universe? If one is quick to dismiss the calculation as
pure coincidence, the Puranas also say that the Creator
will last one hundred Brahma years, in which each day
counts as 4,320,000,000 human years. In other words, the
universe will exist for a total of 311 trillion or 311,040,000,000,000
human years! Then everything will dissolve back into
formless Consciousness and stay that way for another
311,040,000,000,000 human years, until the cycle begins
again. In Hindu cosmology, there was no beginning, and
there will be no end, only an infinity of cycles. Present-day
cosmology does not make a specific prediction of 311 trillion-
year-cycles. Should one then dismiss these ancient statements as pure myths?[6] One could take that point of view,
or one could see whether these ancient predictions can be
proven by scientific inquiry.

Returning to modern cosmology, if the universe contains
little matter—below the critical value of density—it will
expand forever. This type of universe is open, and its geometry
is similar to the surface of a saddle—an unbound surface
that extends to infinity.

When cosmologists try to add together all luminous
and non-luminous matter to estimate the average density of
the universe, they find that the observed average density of
matter in the universe is close to the critical value. This means

that the universe may indeed turn out to be exactly flat or Euclidean. To visualize how small the critical density is compared to the density of matter we are accustomed to in everyday life, imagine a cube one meter to the side. Within this volume, in the darkness of intergalactic space, there is hardly one atom. Compared to the almost perfect vacuum of space between galaxies, the tip of your finger contains almost 10^{24} atoms, or one trillion trillion atoms! The universe is indeed vast, cold and almost completely empty. In order for the value of the density of observed matter in the form of stars and galaxies to be close to the critical density today, one must conclude that the initial density was equal to the critical value to an exactness of one part in 10^{50} or one followed by 50 zeros! How could the initial conditions have been so finely tuned as to be exact to one part in 10^{50}? Standard big bang theory cannot explain this.

To retain an evolutionary picture of the universe, one needs to assume that very special conditions existed at the beginning. Partly to get around these problems, a revised evolutionary model called the inflationary model has been proposed by Alan Guth and others (Guth, 1982; Linde, 1982). According to this model, the universe underwent an extraordinary inflationary expansion at an exponential rate shortly after the big bang, or at about 10^{-35} seconds. After this point the universe evolved as the standard big bang scenario says, but in the crucial period between 10^{-43} and 10^{-35} seconds after the beginning, the future of the universe was determined. During this period of rapid expansion, every tiny part of space could inflate to the size of the present-day universe, or become a space-time "bubble." And since each part of space was causally connected before inflation began, this model implies precisely equal temperatures of the background radiation observed from opposite directions in the sky.

The currently accepted evolutionary history of the universe can be summarized as follows (Schramm, 1983): First came the big bang, where the space-time description breaks down completely. Then followed the inflationary era some 10^{-35} seconds later. Next, in the time between 10^{-3} seconds and 10^{-6} seconds, quarks and electrons formed a primordial soup. Then, at 10^{-6} seconds neutrinos decoupled from matter and quarks combined to form heavy particles, such as neutrons and protons. Between 10^{-6} and 1 second after the beginning, electrons, protons and neutrons formed a primordial soup of higher complexity. Between 1 second and 3 minutes, protons and neutrons underwent nuclear reactions forming the nuclei of heavy hydrogen—deuterium and tritium—and the nuclei of helium and other light elements and their isotopes. Most heavy elements were formed millions of years later, when massive stars first began to evolve and explode into supernovas. Up to about 100,000 years after the big bang, photons and matter were coupled together, and the universe was opaque to radiation. The 3 degrees Kelvin black body microwave photons that we presently observe were emitted after this time. The soup of microwave photons fills the entire universe and is the remnant of the initial big bang which formed the universe.

Some 100,000 years after the beginning, light quanta decoupled from matter, and it was possible for atoms to form. The formation of neutral atoms allowed huge clouds of gas to undergo gravitational collapse and to form giant clusters of galaxies, individual galaxies and clusters of stars. It then became possible for ancient galaxies such as quasars to form and shine, and we today observe their light from billions of light-years away. Some five to fifteen billion years after the beginning, an insignificant star that we call the Sun formed from a protostellar cloud some 30,000 light-years away from the center of an average spiral galaxy we call the Milky Way. And some five billion years later—ten to twenty billion years after the beginning—on one of the nine planets of this star, human beings looking at a night sky adorned with an infinity of stars, try to figure out how it all began (Figure 12).

It is a great irony that one of the most important clues to the big bang universe—background radiation—cannot itself be used to probe the big bang or the early times when important physical processes were taking place. The opaqueness of the early universe to its own radiation prevents us from studying such data. The presently observed expansion of the universe thus must be extrapolated, perhaps arbitrarily, to very early times. However, this extrapolation cannot be verified by means of light. Light is in fact the main tool of observational cosmology. Thus to prove the inflation theory of the universe, one must derive the early conditions of the universe—about which experiments reveal little and theoretical ideas are incomplete—from current observations (Kafatos, 1989). Thus the origin of the universe is forever beyond our reach. Could the beginning then be nothing more than a product of the human mind?

The fact that we are looking at the starry sky may be so significant, some physicists claim, that the very origin of the cosmos hinges on it. This theory, called the anthropic principle, was developed by Robert Dicke, Brandon Carter, John A. Wheeler and others (Barrow and Tipler, 1986; Harris, 1991). It holds that the initial conditions of the universe were not randomly chosen. The values of the fundamental constants of physics, such as the speed of light, the gravitational constant and others, are such because the universe contains conscious beings. Take, for example, the so-called "fine structure" constant which determines the size of an atom. This value is so finely tuned that a one percent difference up or down would have resulted in a universe with either massive stars, which would have died billions of years ago, or faint red stars incapable of supporting life. In either case, we would not be here.

The proponents of the anthropic principle state that the universe is what it is because it contains life. Unfortunately, if one really thinks about this statement, one realizes that it may be a tautology: The universe is what it is because we are here, and we are here because the universe is what it is. Nevertheless, the anthropic principle is profound in its simple recognition that we will never understand the physical universe unless we bring into our theories the existence of conscious beings and consciousness itself.

The big bang picture rests on one assumption—that the shifts of the spectral lines of galaxies arise because of motion away from us. But suppose that one could find evidence challenging the usual cosmological interpretation of the shifts of lines (LaViolette, 1986). Such evidence might cause theorists to question the evolutionary picture of the universe, and some sort of steady-state theory may again be plausible. Astronomer Halton Arp and others (Arp, 1980a, 1980b; Sulentic, 1983) have found evidence that some quasars are located near galaxies, even though the spectral shifts of these quasars are vastly different from the spectral shifts of the associated galaxies. This finding has been very controversial, because it challenges the commonly held view that the universe is expanding. If nearby objects have vastly different velocities of recession, how could they be close in space and, at the same time, be so far away from each other, as implied by their different velocities? Others have proposed that a new physical mechanism can explain the redshifts of quasars (Cocke and Tifft, 1983).

The Universe: A Quantum System?

The universe, unlike anything else in experimental physics, is a vast system which contains the observers who are trying to study it. An astronomer observes distant objects with no interaction with them other than passively recording their photons on a photographic plate or other apparatus. The stars, galaxies and distant clusters shine in the emptiness of space, impervious to whether we observe them or not. On the other hand, it is clear that in any evolutionary model of the universe, quantum effects were important. At the big bang itself, total chaos reigned and black holes appeared from and disappeared into quantum nothingness (Hawking, 1976; Hawking, 1989).

At the time of the big bang, and for a time afterward not exactly determined by cosmological theory, ours was a quantum universe. The theory of general relativity cannot determine when the universe began to obey the laws of classical physics, because Einstein's theory is not quantized. However, it is clear that the universe was not always a classical system. Thus cosmologists cannot extend the laws of classical macrophysics back into the early time, because at origin, such a description breaks down completely. Moreover, no matter whether we use classical or quantum physics, we cannot actually observe anything from the very early universe. For this reason a basic requirement of all science—the test of empirical confirmation —also breaks down, and our theories about the big bang can never really be confirmed directly.

Moreover, there is an important difference between the universe and classical systems. The systems that one usually examines in the laboratory can be considered to be isolated or closed. In such macroscopic systems interactions usually have a negligible effect upon the observed system. In observing the universe, this idealized situation is impossible. Even though astronomers' observations have a negligible effect on the overall state of the universe, *the universe cannot be considered to be a closed system*, separate from the observing apparatus. After all the universe contains everything, including all observers and their apparatuses.

Can the universe, on the other hand, be considered a quantum system? Yes, because quantum theory and specifically Bell's theorem show that once quantum effects are present, they will, under appropriate conditions, manifest macroscopically. However, the presence of observers and observing apparatuses[7] presents a conceptual problem in a quantum view of the universe. In quantum theory the division between the observed object and the observing apparatus is primary, but no one has as yet developed a quantum theory in which the observer and the observed are part of the same system (Kafatos and Nadeau, 1990). Despite this basic problem, quantum theory provides a more appropriate framework for understanding the universe than does classical theory, which does not take into consideration the intricacies of interaction between the observer and the observed system.

Quantum theory leads us to the realization that what we consider to be the objective universe can never be fully objectified. This realization cannot be proven in the usual scientific way; it is rather a working hypothesis, which may appear more reasonable when we present our argument about the mystical view of reality. In this context, the correlations evidenced in Bell's theorem, which tie together the observer and the observed system and which seem to be outside space and time, may be relevant. These may be the same correlations that manifest in the wholeness of the universe. Since the universe is more a quantum than a classical system, correlations between different parts of the system may forever remain apparent. In this case, understanding, for example, the smoothness of the microwave background, would be identical to understanding the implications of Bell's theorem. In other words, cosmological correlations may be nothing more than quantum correlations.

As we extend quantum mechanics into cosmology, the only conceptual tool that remains at our disposal is the principle of complementarity. Contemporary cosmology has ignored the simple and obvious fact that the astronomical observations that validate our theories about the early universe are a function of light, the main tool of observational cosmology. And since the wave-particle nature of light only makes sense when complementarity is the starting point, it follows that complementarity should be brought into cosmology as well.

Cosmological Observations and Complementarity

In astronomy one relies on one of two general categories of tools and techniques—either the spectra of light sources or pictures of these sources. Individual photons are always recorded in the observing process (kafatos and Nadeau, 1990; Fang, et al., 1982). But certain observations can only be understood properly if one considers that light exhibits wave properties before the photons are recorded as the spectrum of a light source. The first category of techniques can, therefore, be best understood in terms of the wave nature of light, and the second in terms of the particle nature of light.

The spatial non-locality of quantum phenomena is manifested in the Bell correlations. Another non-local peculiarity connecting the "past" with the present has been pointed out by Wheeler (1981, 1983). Central to Wheeler's argument are the "delayed-choice experiments"[8] designed to illustrate that "past events" are influenced by observations made in the "present." The simplest version of this experiment is a modification of the double-slit experiment. The temporal correlations in the delayed-choice experiments take place over vast distances in the universe, linking the most distant quasars seen as they were in the past to the present. The spatial correlations in Bell's theorem can also take place over vast distances. Thus Wheeler's delayed-choice experiments are closely related to Bell's theorem, and both are manifestations of the non-classical correlations brought about by quantum theory. Light from a distant quasar travels to us, but the choice of which path the light followed is made now. A question about which path the light "really" followed is meaningless. The question only becomes meaningful when the observer chooses one of the complementary aspects of light present. Kafatos and Nadeau (1990) propose that all observations of cosmological import allow us this type of choice—whether to utilize the wave properties or the particle properties of light.

Wheeler (1981, 1983) puts it aptly when he states, "No elementary phenomenon, whether now or in the earliest days of the universe, is a phenomenon until it is an observed phenomenon." "Observed" in this context means registered by some physical measuring instrument, as for example when a photon darkens a silver compound crystal on a photographic plate. Wheeler even goes as far as asserting that the act of observation confers reality on what is observed. However, objects exist whether we choose to perform specific observations of them or not. Rather our various observations confer a specific view of the universe. Confusing "existence" with "views of that existence" is an unnecessary confusion not warranted by quantum theory. To put it another way, the universe exists, but views of that reality are conditioned by the specifics of acts of observation.

There are three kinds of non-localities (Kafatos and Nadeau, 1990). The first is a spatial, Bell-type non-locality.

It connects distant regions, too far from each other to be connected by light signals, but events at the two regions are, as Henry Stapp puts it, "influenced" by each other. This is called a *Type I non-locality*. The second is a temporal, Wheeler-type non-locality. It connects the "past" with the "present" and is called a *Type II non-locality*. In other words, the past and present are connected together by an act of observation which happens in one region of space. By choosing now one of the two aspects of light, we allow the past to happen in two different ways. Thus, the past did not happen in the past, it happens now! The third type, called a *Type III non-locality*, is the most general case. It connects distant space-time regions.

The universal correlations evidenced by the smoothness of the background radiation may be an example of a Type III non-locality. Since the early universe exhibited quantum correlations, when we carry out observations and find these correlations, we are finding the deep interconnectedness of the universe that quantum theory implies. As such Bell's theorem has profound implications for any philosophical view of the universe. A non-locality is a non-locality whether it is centered in the relatively small dimensions of a laboratory or across billions of light-years. When we understand one, we understand the other. Understanding, though, cannot be taken to mean describing a non-locality within space and time, since a non-locality transcends the boundaries of space and time. Thus it implies an individual wholeness which ceases to be whole if subjected to spatio-temporal description.

The statement that the past exists only in the context of the specific observations made by conscious beings sounds strange to the Western mind. But the perennial philosophy hammers the same point over and over: Past and future are illusions; only the eternal Present exists. Western science now seems to be making a similar statement. Are the conclusions arising out of modern quantum theory identical to ancient philosophical statements? Not quite, because physical science is not the same as the perennial philosophy. Yet, the similarities are striking, showing us once again that humans totally outside the scientific tradition using only intuition reached insights which seem to be supported by modern science. The illusion of the past, the non-locality of the universe, the cyclic universe and similar ideas must be profound truths, transcending culture, language or tradition, if humans keep discovering them over and over at different times and by different methods.

Returning to the question of whether the universe is open, closed or exactly flat, present-day observations give conflicting results. Observations which reflect the particle aspect of light tend to indicate an open universe, while observations which reflect the wave aspect of light tend to favor a closed universe (Kafatos and Nadeau, 1990). The apparent correlation suggests that something more fundamental than a limit to observation is revealed by cosmological investigations. If the universe is a quantum system, then complementarity must be a dynamic of our understanding it. The open and closed models of the universe could then be viewed as another complementary relationship. A logical conclusion of this line of thinking might be that a workable model of the universe is something between open and closed—namely a flat universe. Observations indicate that this conclusion is valid. This argument says nothing about whether the universe experienced inflation; its sole purpose is to bring complementarity into the cosmological realm.

Another complementary relationship has cosmological import. Advocates of both the steady state and the big bang models agree that universal constants, such as the speed of light, Planck's quantum of action, Newton's gravitational constant and others, do not change, except possibly in the event that a new universe emerges from another big bang. Yet the findings of Dirac (1937) and others, that certain large numbers such as 1 followed by 40 zeros keep appearing in seemingly unrelated ratios of physical quantities,[9] has led to the speculation that these constants may not be constant at all, but rather change with time. There is no other reason for totally unrelated ratios to be so close to each other in numerical value. Dirac concluded that these ratios take on their specific values as a result of the present age of the universe. However, how in this case could anyone keep track of time, since we would have no standards by which to measure its passage? Proponents of the anthropic principle try to provide an alternative explanation for the similar ratios of unrelated physical quantities. Maybe the coincidence of these large numbers points to the fact that our universe contains us. Exactly how and why remains a mystery.

When we extend complementarity into the cosmological realm, we can explain the coincidence more easily. If as one theory holds, the universe is evolving, perhaps the constants are truly constant in time. However, the universe also has a complementary aspect—the view that the constants themselves are changing, and that it is this change that creates the illusion of an evolving universe. We may never be able to exclude one or the other point of view.

As discussed, cosmological shifts (or the shift of lines seen in the spectra of distant galaxies due to the expansion of the universe) and noncosmological shifts (or shifts which are not due to a universal expansion) may be another example of complementary constructs. Neither construct can account by itself for all the observed facts. Unfortunately, the assumption that spectral shifts are cosmological is so well ingrained in the minds of most astronomers that alternate views are dismissed or, even worse, not tolerated. This is nothing new. Human beings dislike questioning established points of view. In the old debate between Newton and Huygens, Huygens' point of view was accepted by most physicists until Einstein explained the photoelectric effect. It finally turned out that both Newton *and* Huygens were right.

Since complementarity appears to be at the foundation of any way of viewing the universe, the usual assumption that science will eventually reach complete understanding of the cosmos may turn out to be wishful thinking. For example, in cosmology the evolutionary effects in distant galaxies cannot be exactly known. Therefore, the behavior of the expanding universe at large distances is in principle indeterminate. For this reason, building larger and larger telescopes may never give a definitive answer about the origin of the cosmos.

A Generalized Principle of Complementarity

The principle of complementarity was formulated because of the contradictions encountered when a researcher tries to apply antithetical classical constructs to the quantum domain.[10] However, the principle of complementarity may turn out to be a much more general principle. Such a principle, applicable to both the macroscopic level and beyond, may help solve many puzzles in physics as well as in other scientific fields. It may even tell us something profound about the human mind, or about consciousness itself. The dilemmas created by Bell's theorem require that complementarity be viewed as a powerful means to comprehend the universe. Perhaps, the way consciousness unfolds and works can be viewed as the unfolding of a Reality which always takes the form of complementary constructs—analysis/synthesis, object/subject, wave/particle, transcendence/immanence. These and countless other complementary pairs may be clues to the unfolding of the universe itself. The unsolved but tantalizing cosmological coincidences examined above may therefore provide clues about our own nature.

The discussion so far has suggested why complementarity should be viewed as a powerful general statement about our universe, one that goes beyond microscopic and macroscopic physics. In fact, complementarity can be extended to mathematics, biology and psychology, just to mention a few fields outside physics. When we extend complementarity to other disciplines, we should be guided by the experience gained from physics. First, we must remember that each member of a complementary pair is an individually complete theoretical construct. Second, each member should be premised on antithetical assumptions. Third, each construct should preclude the other in specific applications. And fourth, both constructs taken together should constitute a complete description of the particular situation under consideration.

The examples of complementary constructs which we present below meet the first three requirements. The fourth requirement provides evidence for the "unity of knowledge" that Bohr himself considered essential to any description of nature (Folse, 1985). Bohr stated many times that we should never forget "that we ourselves are both actors and spectators in the drama of existence" (Kafatos and Nadeau, 1990). Following Bohr's thinking, we should expect that the extension of complementarity should take place in cases in which we cannot control the effects of observation on the system being studied. In other words, the resultant description of the system under question cannot be assumed to be independent of these observations. What follows examines complementarities similar to those found in physics, drawn from mathematics, biology and psychology.

One complementary pair is ordinary language and mathematical language. Ordinary language developed as a result of the interactions of humans with other humans and with the surrounding world. Sense organs play a vital role in this interaction because they mediate experiences which are then recorded in either the subconscious or the conscious mind. In order for us to communicate our experiences to others—and incidentally to ourselves by the process of feedback—we use language as the tool. Thus ordinary language developed from the concrete experiences of our ancestors.

Mathematical language is also closely related to human experience. In ancient times, it developed in Egypt, Babylon, Greece, India, and in the Middle Ages, in the Arab world. For example, the ancient Egyptians were very skilled at geometry and in architecture; they used their mathematical knowledge to build magnificent temples and pyramids. In ancient Greece, however, mathematical language underwent a qualitative change. The Pythagoreans believed that numbers were perfect, transcendent quantities that represented concrete, creative principles manifested in the physical world. Later, the Copernican revolution utilized the language of mathematics as a tool to study the universe.

In modern times, scientific theories have become so

abstract that the boundaries between pure mathematics and physics have become fuzzy. Many theoretical physicists implicitly hold the Pythagorean view that the universe is essentially mathematical. Yet, the mathematical description of a quantum cannot be visualized. No one can say or even imagine what an electron looks like. What is real is then an infinitely complex web of interactions between physical entities that are accessible to us not through our sense organs, but through the abstract language of mathematics. Thus the modern physicist faces a curious dilemma: the world of the quantum is beyond the reach of sensory input and can be described only in a language which is abstract and unrelated to everyday experience. Nevertheless, quanta make up the universe, including ourselves, and therefore must be responsible for our everyday experiences as well. Bell's theorem and the other quantum phenomena which spill over to the macroscopic domain have only made this dilemma more obvious in the sense that quantum phenomena cannot be delegated to an unobservable, out-of-reach realm of physical reality.

The only way we can resolve this seeming contradiction is to consider mathematical language and ordinary language as complementary aspects, which coordinate the experiences of the self in the universe. Seen in this light, ordinary language is not completely divorced from mathematical language, and vice versa. Each has something important to say about our role in the universe.

Mathematics also has several obvious complementary relationships, such as: 1) the analytic and synthetic modes of description—analysis entailing the breakup of a whole set into distinct mathematical units, and synthesis, the combination of many units to form a mathematical whole; 2) the relationship between zero and infinity—zero signifying complete absence, and infinity, complete fullness; 3) the relationship between order and chaos—order implying the mathematical predictability of the future evolution of a physical system, chaos signifying the inherent or intrinsically unpredictable behavior of a dynamic system (see also Prigogine and Stengers, 1984). Mathematical theory has progressed to the point where it is now possible to see the onset of chaos develop in solutions of classical nonlinear dynamical equations, which are the most general equations describing the evolution of dynamic systems (Ott, 1981; Gleick, 1988). In fact, the laws of classical physics imply nondeterminism of the future evolution of a system as the rule rather than the exception. Ironically, quantum theory and classical physics have recently converged via entirely different routes, in the sense that both imply an *inherent* unpredictability of the behavior of physical systems under certain conditions.

Complementarity can also be witnessed in the field of biology. This may not be as surprising as it first appears, because quantum effects are responsible for many biological processes. For example, were it not for the existence of the Pauli exclusion principle, the structure of matter, including, of course, animals and plants, would be different.[11] Bohr realized that mechanistic biology was limited in trying to explain biological phenomena.[12] He believed that life as a concept should be accepted in biology the same way that the quantum of action is accepted in modern physics. Both preclude a purely mechanistic description of the systems under question. Even today, despite our understanding of biochemistry, biomedical engineering and similar developments, we do not really understand the phenomenon of life.

Central to biological complementarities is the relationship between nonconscious and conscious entities. An animal is clearly aware of its environment and is, thus, a conscious entity. However, an animal's consciousness is limited. Consciousness obviously involves much more than simply an awareness of the environment. An organism cannot be considered simply the sum total of its constituent parts—ultimately the atoms that make it up—unless we assign consciousness to its atoms as well. To study consciousness scientifically, we must reduce an organism to its constituent parts and isolate it from its environment. When we do this, the organism no longer possesses awareness of its environment.

Since Darwin's time, biologists have accepted the evolution of species as a matter of faith. The evidence in favor of the evolutionary picture is impressive indeed. The biochemistry of DNA, genes, and other aspects of the process by which genetic information is passed on from organism to organism has provided a convincing framework to support the hypothesis of evolution. Nevertheless, some nagging problems remain. For example, if complex biological molecules were formed from an inanimate, primordial soup by a purely random process, it would require much longer than the three to four billion year timescale available in earth history. Moreover, researchers cannot repeat nature's successful experiment in the laboratory. Such an experiment would require billions of years and conditions of the early earth that cannot be duplicated today. Thus life is a unique experiment which, like the universe, cannot be repeated in the laboratory.

Finally, the recent hypothesis of Louis Alvarez and others about massive extinctions that occurred in the past has shown that Darwin's ideas give an inadequate account of the evolutionary process. If massive extinctions occur periodically, the Darwinian assumption of a slow evolutionary process cannot be reconciled with sudden, massive changes in the species. The biologist is then faced with the situation that experiments carried out in the laboratory to test evolution cannot recreate evolution as it occurred billions of years ago.

Perhaps evolution should be viewed as one construct in a complementary relationship with the idea of immanence, or existence a priori. Species do evolve, but the ecosystem on earth also evolves as a unit. The anthropic principle is relevant to this thesis. The tendency of matter to evolve biologically fits into the picture of the evolving inanimate universe as a given, not as an afterthought that occurred after billions of years. This view explains the symbiosis and cooperation abundantly evident in the ecosphere of the earth. Without cooperation in the biosphere, no life would be found today; competition between species would result in the extinction of all species. Something holds this competition in check, allowing life as a whole to survive, even though parts—the various species—are in continuous competition. Harmony is a part of the process that we call life, as competition is. Immanence should not be viewed as an agency of causation; rather it is the complementary construct of the tendency of individual species to compete and survive. Until biologists give up the idea that strict causality should always be a part of any attempt to account for life, a number of puzzles will remain.

A closely related issue is how the shapes and instincts of organisms are determined. Biologist Rupert Sheldrake (1981) points out several unresolved problems in biology and the inadequacy of genetic information to explain them.[13] He proposes that the form, development and behavior of organisms are shaped and maintained by what he calls "morphogenetic fields," which carry information about the structure of biological organisms beyond the information contained in the genetic code. These fields, which operate outside of space and time, are molded by the forms and behaviors of other organisms of the same species. The hypothesis of morphogenetic fields may be viewed as a complementary construct to the usual mechanistic view of genetic processes by which information is passed to the cells of a new organism. Both the traditional view and the idea of morphogenetic fields may be needed to explain the evolution of species.

Bohr also extended complementarity to the field of psychology by examining constructs like free will and determinism. Central to all complementarities—not just those in psychology—is the complementarity between object and subject. Bohr used Immanual Kant's ideas of the "transcendent ego" as the background of consciousness on which all sensory input is recorded. This background of consciousness can never be known as an external object. Sensory input in turn shapes the "personal ego," which—in contrast to the immutable transcendent ego—is continually changing. The two are always present, locked together. The analogy from quantum theory is apt here: the observed object cannot be independent of the observations which bring out its properties.

In any formulation of how human consciousness,

thinking and other psychological processes operate, one cannot ignore the structure of the human brain. The complementary relationship between the left brain and the right brain colors the way we perceive the universe. The hardware of the human mind operates in two, totally different ways. The right brain synthesizes; the left brain analyzes.

A final example of a complementary relationship in psychology is found in Jung's work—the "animus/anima" relationship. These terms refer to the male and female aspects of human beings. Every man has feminine archetypal aspects—the anima; and every woman has male archetypal aspects—the animus. One aspect is clearly dominant, yet both are important.

The Unfoldment of the Universe

Complementarity seems to be at the center of not just physical phenomena but everything that constitutes consciousness. Usually the evolving or unfolding universe is thought of as occurring objectively, independent of human perceptions. However, our discussion so far suggests an alternative view. Perhaps *unfoldment is central to the way consciousness perceives objective experience.* An example of the unfoldment of emerging complementary relationships can be seen in Figure 14 (see Kafatos and Nadeau, 1990). This figure is what one may call a "Universal Diagram" (Kafatos, 1985, 1986). More such diagrams appear in Chapter 7 (Figures 24-26). In general, they are plots of the relationships between objects in the universe. Figure 14 shows physical size on the horizontal scale, from the Planck length to the observable universe, a scale that spans about 61 orders of magnitude. The vertical scale does not represent a physical quantity, but rather various complementary relationships in a tabular format.

The space-time complementarity spans all scales, since space-time is the foundation of all physical descriptions. All scales are also contained in the range of the Type III non-locality which connects regions of the universe. The Type I (spatial) non-locality exists at the laboratory scale. The Type II (temporal) non-locality ranges from the

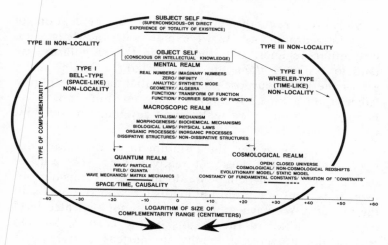

Figure 14. Universal Diagram relating the scale of objects (horizontal scale) to the type of complementarity encountered (vertical scale). Shown are complementarities which have a physical scale, because they belong to the physical universe, and complementarities in the purely mental realm.

laboratory level to the "past" universe—in other words, to the most distant regions of the universe.

Quantum complementary relationships span scales from the tiniest elementary particle (10^{-13} centimeters) to the size of an atom (10^{-8} centimeters). Biological complementarities span the range from the tiniest virus, about 10^{-5} centimeters across, to the size of the biosphere itself, a few thousand kilometers across.

At the top of the diagram, under the heading "mental realm," we find mathematical complementarities and the complementary relationships from psychology. The arrows connecting the two parts of the diagram are meant to indicate fluidity—complementarity connects the two realms; thus their separation is not a hard boundary.

The unfoldment apparent in this figure is relational over physical scales, from the smallest distance—the Planck length—to the largest—the observable universe. The expanding or evolving universe may be better comprehended if we realize that the terms "evolution" or "expansion" actually represent the evolution of our perception of everything around us. As we expand our knowledge into unfamiliar regimes, like those near the singularity, we tend to assign to them the term "origin." "Origin" really serves the same purpose as the familiar fairy tale phrase "once upon a time." It implies that something must have happened; although we really can't say much about how, when or why.

One may notice that the unfoldment of the knowledge about the universe does not really address the issue of the end. As human beings, we do not like to consider our own ends, and we project that dislike into our views of the universe. We have achieved a rather sophisticated level of understanding of the origins of the cosmos, but the end of the universe is totally uncharted territory. The universe may expand into the infinite future, eventually suffering a distant cold death, or it may expand, collapse and, perhaps, re-emerge. In other words, anything is possible. Ironically, the statements about infinite cycles found in the *Puranas* are of a degree of sophistication totally unknown to modern cosmological theory.

The Wholeness Vision

A generalized principle of complementarity allows us to conceive a holistic view of the universe. However, the wholeness vision emerging from physical theories cannot be expressed in strict scientific formalism (Capra, 1975). In that case wholeness would be subjected to analysis, to division into parts, and would cease to be wholeness. We thus have an apparent paradox: physical science hints at an underlying wholeness; yet physical science is unable—by its very nature—to describe that wholeness. Wholeness should be viewed as complementary to the singular aspect of entities. Physical science, which always studies units, is unable to account properly for wholeness; yet, physical science has uncovered the wholeness of the cosmos (Briggs and Peat, 1984).

What is fundamentally whole? What is always experienced in its fullness? Our thesis is that Consciousness is fundamentally whole. This thesis cannot be proven in the usual scientific way, because our consciousness and that of other individuals cannot be examined as an object of perception. Consciousness is rather the constant background, the source of all sensory processes and mental perceptions. If Consciousness is whole, it must be the core of our being. It has to be there always, outside of space, time, the physical body or even the mind. If Consciousness is the background of all perceptions, it follows that it *cannot be comprehended as an object of perception; it can only be experienced.* In fact, Eastern sages declared that Consciousness *is* experience. When we search within us, we find that what is always there no matter who we are, or who we think we are, is the constant sense of I-awareness. It is this background which gives rise to all complementary relationships—from which they all arise, and to which they all return.

It may indeed turn out that the origin of the universe will remain a mystery forever if we attempt to comprehend it with the mind alone. In the context of the generalized principle of complementarity, we can see why this is the case. There may never be one final answer, because as our horizons of knowledge and experience expand, we will asymptotically reach more refined truths—like a straight line that approaches a curve but never meets it. These truths will consist of what at first appear to be contradictory statements. One answer may contradict another; yet both will reveal different aspects of what is being examined. Since all complementary relationships arise from the constant background of I-awareness, we can never know the object of perception *in itself,* apart from the perceiving agency. This perceiving agency is sometimes referred to as the Self, and sometimes as the Witness—the observer that can never itself be perceived as an external object. Kant called it the "transcendent ego," and Bohr, the "background of consciousness." Whatever term one uses, it is the foundation of being, and includes the body and mind even though it is not limited to the body and mind.

To emphasize that there is a part of ourselves greater than the conscious, thinking mind, we suggest a new term, the *metamind*, which refers to everything that is beyond or below the conscious mind. The metamind bears the same relationship to the mind as metaphysics bears to physics. It is the foundation of the mind, that from which the mind springs and on which the mind is based. The innermost core of that metamind is the Self. By definition, the metamind and its central core can never be understood by the mind, since the metamind is the mind's foundation. The Self is what is left when there is no more mind—conscious, unconscious or subconscious—in fact, no objects of perception whatsoever. The core of the metamind is the ultimate witnessing agent, the irreducible background of ourselves. Even though unknowable as an object of perception, the ultimate Witness—the Self—can be experienced. This concept is the subject of our subsequent discussion.

Accepting underlying wholeness means that we have to realize that by definition, the Universe is whole. The capital *U* in the term "Universe" indicates that it includes both the physical universe and everything else there is. Every human is aware that what is whole, what cannot be divided by time, space or external circumstances, is the constant background of I-awareness in each of us. This background is always there, no matter how old or young our physical body may be. Behind the diversity of individuals, an undivided wholeness of Consciousness, *identical in all individuals*, remains. Without it we could not share similar views or sense perceptions, and we could not communicate with each other. Each one of us would constitute a universe totally separate from every other. We would not even be aware of anything else.

Moreover, if the Universe is whole, and the background of Consciousness of each individual is also whole, it follows that the two have to be identical. The reason for this is quite simple. Any single wholeness has to be identical to every other wholeness, because if they were different, they wouldn't be whole. Since the background of an individual's Consciousness is the same as everybody else's, individual consciousness must be universal. We then conclude that if the Universe, individual consciousness and universal Consciousness are whole, these three are also identical. Otherwise, they would not be whole. In other words, since the observer is always involved with the object of observation, and since no one can step outside the universe to describe it externally, the Universe must be the ultimate endosystem. This term implies that the Universe has no outside, only an inside, which is what the prefix "endo" means. Also part of the endosystem is the innermost part of every one of us. As a working hypothesis, let us assume that the Universe and the Self are identical, and that these two make up the ultimate endosystem. The Self is the endosystem of our innermost being. The Universe is the endosystem of everything we experience outside. We use the word "hypothesis" rather than "proof," because the existence of an ultimate endosystem cannot be proven externally.

If we are to progress beyond these points, we have to turn to systems which study the inner core of human beings—consciousness and the mind. These systems, found in all cultures, constitute the perennial philosophy of inner knowledge. The philosophic systems of the East provide precise and detailed knowledge of the intricacies of consciousness. The seers and sages of ancient India and Kashmir held that when studying one's inner reality, one finds universal principles at work. In the process of going within, the ancient sages discovered profound truths about the Universe. Rather than studying the external, physical universe in the hopes of discovering the secrets of human nature, they studied the inner secrets of human nature and, in the process, found principles that apply to the external universe. This study of inner realities was extremely practical. Its concern was the betterment of humankind. The ancient sages were psychologists of a rare kind. In turning within to study themselves, they discovered in their own depths the creative unfoldment of universal Consciousness.

This discovery cannot, of course, be proven using the usual methodology of dividing the object from the subject. It is better to look within and check to see if one's own experiences confirm what the sages have said. Sages from all cultures felt unshakable faith in the truth of their own experience. Despite differences of culture and language, the similarity in their statements bears witness to the validity of the ancient philosophical statements. Moreover, the experiences of the sages can be repeated today. The wholeness they experienced implies that object and subject are not just related; they are identical. However, physical science cannot accomplish this merging of object and subject unless it transcends itself. In this case, the object will not be examined outside in some external laboratory, rather, the object and subject will be the laboratory.

If complementarity is accepted as the guiding principle of the way knowledge is obtained, science will expand in an unlimited way. Rather than trying to find the answers to everything, scientists will be aware that there are limits to any system of knowledge based on a division between objects and the perceivers of objects. Complementarity can then be utilized to unravel a universe more rich, more profound, more subtle than anything we can imagine now. The process of knowing will become far richer than the compartmentalized knowledge of present-day science. In this process the perceiving subject will be given the central role it deserves. Scientists will continue to study parts as they presently do, but at the same time, they will accept the underlying wholeness.

To proceed, we turn to what the ancient sages experienced, taught and wrote down about the creative process. The starting point is that undivided wholeness is the central principle in the Universe, the concept that holds everything together. If this is the case, the perennial philosophy, to use the term of Huxley and others, will reveal something identical in all individuals. It will turn out to be more profoundly scientific than physical science. The term "science" refers to a systematic body of knowledge. The justification in turning to the East is that Western science says little about Consciousness. Even Western psychology devotes a lot of effort to understanding the mind, yet treats the mind as an object. If the mind is an object, then what is the subject? Psychology does not ask about the source of the mind, or the subjective background of awareness —what we have termed the metamind. It is that core which is identical in all individuals and, the sages insisted, in everything else as well.

In the perennial philosophy the object, the subject and the process of knowing are connected; the Universe, Consciousness and the process of knowing form an undivided whole. *The creative process is nothing other than the unfoldment of the relationship between object and subject.* Eastern philosophies shed light on the inner center of the metamind or the Self and the process of unfoldment which gives rise to the objective Universe of countless objects. A most profound view of the unfoldment of Consciousness can be found in Shaivism, the most ancient faith of the Indian people. Kashmir Shaivism is a philosophical system developed by sages in ancient Kashmir. It was basically pre-Aryan and pre-Vedic in its origin, but it found its way into the Aryan Vedic religion. Although it has unique features—primarily its monism—it is in harmony with the broad principles of other major Eastern systems. We chose it to represent the Eastern view of Reality because of its insight into the nature of Consciousness.

Kashmir Shaivism is a monistic philosophical school of thought (Pandit, 1977). It accepts that ultimately there is only one Reality. It differs from some other monistic schools in that it accepts that everything in the universe is Universal Consciousness. *Paramashiva* or Ultimate Reality comes from *Para*, which means supreme, and *Shiva*, which means Consciousness. Kashmir Shaivism not only states that everything was and is continuously created by Shiva but that the entire universe is the body of Paramashiva: *Everything is Consciousness.*

This simple statement and its profound ramifications are not merely intellectual. They arose from the countless experiences of the sages in Kashmir, experiences which revealed to them the presence of the Universal within themselves. Sages in all countries from all traditions at all historical times have stressed the same point over and over again: individual consciousness is identical with

Universal Consciousness, and everything in the Universe is interconnected in the ever-changing "dance" or unfoldment of Consciousness. In Kashmir that experience was developed into a magnificent philosophical system which is remarkably rational and objective in its lucid description of the process of unfoldment. It is particularly appealing to Westerners.

In this book we attempt to give credence to this profound view, but it really cannot be understood by intellect alone. For intellect itself is illuminated by *Atman*, the Self within, the central core of the metamind, which is identical to Paramashiva. How can the illuminated understand what illuminates it?

A popular image of Shiva in Indian culture is the dancing Shiva or *Nataraj*. One can find this form in statues in most Indian stores throughout the world. The dancing Shiva continually performs five actions or functions: emanation, existence or sustenance, dissolution, concealment and bestowal of grace (Figure 15).

Emanation. Sound, the vibration of Consciousness, gives forth creation, and this is symbolized by the playing of the small drum. The creative process of sound unfolding is examined in detail in the next chapter. Also, as the creative process is examined, it becomes apparent that *Consciousness unfolds through the appearance of complementary pairs at each level of creation.*

Sustenance. Paramashiva sustains everything, and this is symbolized by the *mudra* or gesture of the raised palm facing outward. This gesture signifies fearlessness: recognizing that Consciousness sustains everything removes all one's fears.

Dissolution. Sometimes the term "destruction" is used for this function, although this term does not really convey the right understanding. Dissolution signifies the merging of everything back into Consciousness. Nothing is destroyed; it only changes form: the form changes; the substance remains the same.

Since in the Shaivite view everything is Consciousness, the first three actions can also be viewed as steps in an ever-changing universal dance. Dances in all cultures

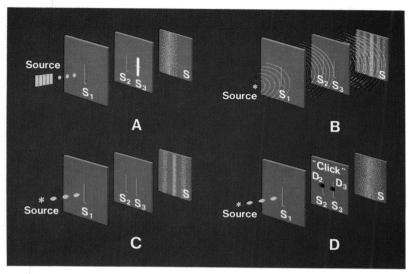

Color Plate I. The double slit experiment

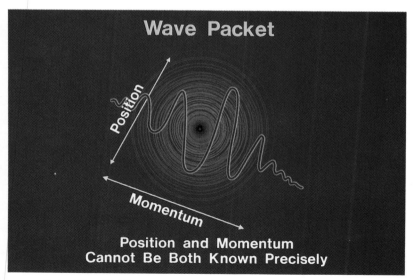

Wave Packet

Position

Momentum

Position and Momentum Cannot Be Both Known Precisely

Color Plate II. The uncertainty relation showed that it is impossible to determine exactly both terms of certain pairs of physical quantities, such as position and momentum.

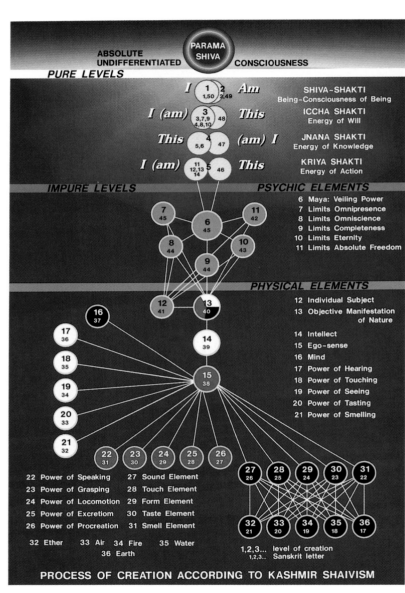

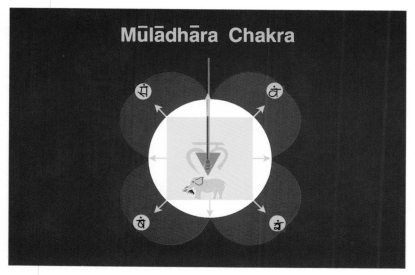

Color Plate IV.

Color Plate V.

Color Plates IV, V, VI are three important milestones of the inner journey: the muladhara, anahata and sahasrara subtle centers depicted in their symbolic representations.

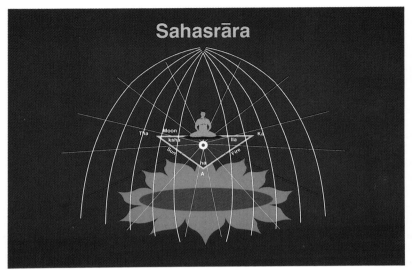

Color Plate VI.

Color Plate VII. Consciousness should be included in any modern view of the universe.

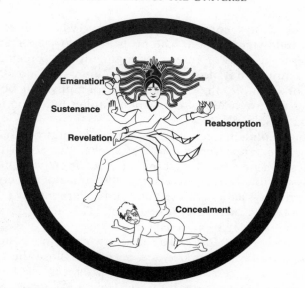

5 Cosmic Functions of Paramashiva

Figure 15. Supreme Consciousness performs the five actions eternally.

signify a ritual. Dances are not random steps; they follow a prescribed sequence which repeats itself. The sound or music, the steps and postures, the feeling all have a part in creating harmony. The feeling of the dance expresses itself in the specific steps and sounds necessary to the dance. For example, the dancing Shiva is always depicted with a serene look and a slight smile. This represents the inner posture of contentment. Without it there would be no dance of Shiva. Later we will see that contentment—along with Beingness—is of the fundamental nature of Consciousness. If there is any primal cause of the universe it is this aspect of bliss, *ananda*. As such, contentment is viewed as the female aspect of Consciousness, the Universal Mother, who gives birth to everything.

The first three actions are allegorically represented in the form of the dance of Shiva. However, they do not follow a strict sequence in the temporal sense: dissolution does not always come after sustenance, which does not always follow emanation. The proper way to view them is as different aspects of an ever-changing drama. Emanation of something may follow the dissolution of something else. For example, the sustenance of our physical bodies requires that we take in food, which implies that food itself must be dissolved.

In the second chapter we saw that quantum processes involving the appearance and disappearance of virtual particles can be viewed in terms of emanation, sustenance and dissolution. In fact, *everything* in the universe undergoes these primary actions. It is not only Paramashiva that plays out those acts; everything does. This must be so if everything is indeed Paramashiva.

Concealment and Grace. The other two actions, concealment and bestowal of grace, are needed to close the loop. Concealment represents the ego. Shiva dances on the ego and tramples it beneath his feet. He points down to it, making a gesture revealing grace. Grace should not be taken to mean something that comes to us from the outside. An equivalent term is revelation. Our real nature is not necessarily revealed to us by an external agency; it is simply revealed. Concealment and revelation or grace are not easy to visualize in physical processes, but they are nevertheless there. In the example of the ever-changing quantum, say a proton, the virtual particles appear to be something else—concealment of their nature as protons. Eventually they are revealed as having been protons all along but in the form of different particles—revelation or grace.

If we ponder all five actions we see that they are related; they all change into one another. Emanation, sustenance and dissolution give rise to what appears to be different from Universal Consciousness, the variety of infinite forms contained in the Universe. When they appear as different from Paramashiva, their true nature is concealed. When they dissolve back into Paramashiva, their true nature is revealed. Emanation and sustenance serve to conceal, whereas dissolution may actually be an act of grace. It is said that if one truly understood the essence of the five-fold act, there would be nothing more to look for in this world.

The one who understood would be liberated from worldly existence.

If we view these acts as pairs, each pair reveals complementarity. Each function in the pair needs the other and could not exist without it. For example, emanation could not exist without dissolution; sustenance could not exist without emanation; grace could not exist without concealment. Also, each function can turn into its opposite. For instance the emanation of something may be the dissolution of something else. What remains in the end is the dissolution of the pairs of opposites into the eternal process of transformation. *Only transformation itself is permanent*, the eternal dance of Universal Consciousness. Here all complementarities are finally consumed, so that what remains is the process and not specific acts, properties, attributes, concepts or opposites.

The profound understanding of the five-fold act does not provide a sequential view of the unfoldment of the Universe in a historical sense. Rather, it shows us how everything now, in the past and in the future unfolds and is enfolded within the all-supporting, ever-present Universal Consciousness. This view is very practical, very "scientific" in the sense that it applies in all aspects of one's life. If we ponder it, the mystery of the objective universe begins to unravel before our eyes.

Summary

What we describe as the objective evolutionary reality of the universe is nothing other than an unfolding process of complementary views, which is happening in our minds. Our theories of the universe reflect the unfoldment of our understanding, our presuppositions and the way we set up our observations. In this sense the observer is always a part of the system. Physical theory says nothing about the nature of consciousness, nor does quantum theory resolve the problem of observation and reality. It only points to the existence of the problem. Nevertheless, for this reason we consider quantum theory superior to classical theories about the universe. Western science does not address the issue of consciousness. But consciousness is a factor in our existence, and therefore we cannot ignore it or bypass it without a penalty. We assert that this penalty might be the conflict between reality and our attempts to describe reality that we have been discussing so far. Bohr's attempt to resolve the conflict resulted in the introduction of the object/subject complementary relationship, which he felt was at the core of all complementarities.

Experience from quantum theory teaches us the following clear lessons: 1) Common experience is plainly wrong when it comes to microscopic phenomena. 2) Any view of the universe has to take into account the process of observation. 3) In order to understand the role of time, we have to somehow include consciousness as an inseparable part of what we call "objective" reality. 4) Whatever theory one uses to describe the fundamental processes in the universe, wholeness is a fundamental, probably the most fundamental, property of the universe.

Where does all this leave us? Henry Stapp—who along with Bell has probably best understood the implications of Bell's theorem and the experiments verifying the violation of classical locality—has concluded that faster-than-light influences are entailed in the framework of standard quantum theory. This is in agreement with experiments validating Bell's predictions (Kafatos and Nadeau, 1990) that show reality is non-local. Complementarity should then be seen as a powerful principle for revealing the properties of the universe. Emergent complementarities give the universe its appearance. If complementarity is extended to cosmology, it may help to solve certain puzzles in our understanding of the universe. A generalized principle of complementarity can be extended to other fields, such as mathematics, biology and psychology. Complementarity cannot be simply a principle with limited application to the hard sciences. It must ultimately reveal the process by which the universe is manifested, the fundamental way by which we interact and comprehend it.

In this light the five-fold act of universal Consciousness makes perfect sense. The acts cannot exist by themselves. But in pairs of what appear to be opposites they bring forth the Universe. Heraclitus' statement that the Universe would cease to exist if one of the opposites ceased to be is a profound truth.

We have to realize the subtle difference between complementarity and dialectics as understood today. To be sure, Zeno's dialectics is not quite the same as Plato's dialectics or Aristotle's, and they are all different from Hegel's or Marx's. Dialectics as it has come to be understood by most people today implies irreconcilable separation. The opposites stand firmly apart from each other; they can be reconciled only when in the final analysis one wins over the other. Viewing the five-fold act in the spirit of complementarity reveals something different: the opposites are not eternal in themselves, though they appear as opposites in relation to each other. In this way the eternal dance of Consciousness, the eternal process which manifests the Universe, reveals itself.

4

Sound, Letters
and the Power of Creation

Throughout the Universe, that divine sound has been vibrating from time immemorial.

Swami Muktananda

As we saw, the paradigm emerging from science provides a view of an undivided wholeness at the physical level. Quanta are not hard atoms, not individual particles; rather, they are vibrations of energy moving forward and backward in space and time. Space and time itself, or space-time which is the more modern term, can be described in a first approximation as a fixed background on which particles or quanta move. Physicists believe and hope that space-time itself will be shown not to be primary but to emerge out of the ultimate quantum chaos of the vacuum. Space-time, energy and the quanta would then be part of a seamless whole constituting the entire cosmos. If physics succeeds in this effort, Einstein's dream of the unified field would be realized.

The question remains: what is the seamless whole which in its vibration gives rise to everything? Calling it the "unified field" or anything else does not provide an answer to the fundamental paradox. Quantum theory cannot say whether particles and the fields from which they arise are real, whether they have an independent existence. Physical theory can describe quanta only in terms of probabilistically defined possibilities. The physical scientist insists on a "hard" reality, but quantum theory provides a ghost-like

126

reality of possibilities. Probabilities and possibilities do not exist by themselves but are intricately interwoven with the mind that perceives them. Therefore, quantum theory allows for the *possibility* (although it does not require it) that the reality of the physical world is inexorably interwoven with the mind that perceives that world.

The next step might seem to the reader as a leap of faith, and indeed *is* a leap because it requires leaving the world of physical theory. And yet, what we propose does not contradict physical theory. In a curious way, quantum theory implies that one must leave quantum theory if one is to ask questions about the nature of reality of the cosmos and the quanta which make it up.

If the description of cosmos is inexorably interwoven with the mind that provides descriptions of the cosmos, could it be that the cosmos and the mind are fundamentally one? If this seems hard to swallow, remember that quantum theory implicitly indicates that one cannot extract the "observer" from the "observed"; they are interwoven in a seamless process of observation, an undivided process of consciousness. Might it be simpler to assume as a starting point that the observer and the observed, the mind which creates theories about the cosmos and the cosmos itself, are common aspects of an undivided wholeness, the wholeness of Consciousness? Taking this a step further, it is reasonable to propose that the mind is a vibration of Consciousness. In fact this could be taken as a working definition of the mind. Since the mind cannot be extracted from the cosmos, could the cosmos itself be a vibration of Consciousness?

In proceeding in this direction, we need to keep in mind that quantum theory has squarely put in front of us not only its own limits but the limits of all physical theories, of all purely objective ways of viewing the cosmos. To find more integrated views, we cannot leave out the thinking agency which derives these views. Thus we are led to the core of ourselves. In this case the object is the subject itself. We leave external physical laboratories behind but not concrete experience, which includes physical experience. The laboratory is now ourselves; the emphasis changes

from seeing out to looking in. It is a leap, a flip from the
outer to the inner, as simple perhaps as closing one's eyelids.

What follows is an exposition of the creative process
found in ancient philosophical systems. It is closely tied to
the direct experiences of many sages and thus acquires an
objectivity that goes beyond a particular individual's
system of thought.
A vibrating medium causes sound and is caused by sound,
in fact it *is* sound. One could explore how the analogy
of sound applies to vibrations of Consciousness. In fact,
this is not a mere analogy. Ancient sages of the East insisted
that sound is fundamental to the process of Consciousness,
to the creative process itself. We needed a term which
indicates that ordinary sound and all vibrations of matter
and energy are special cases of a universal vibration; but
there is no such term in the English language. For lack of
it we will use the term "sound" to imply the *vibration* of
an underlying medium.
More formally, definitions of ordinary sound found in a
dictionary are: a. The sensation perceived by the sense of
hearing; and b. Mechanical radiant energy that is transmitted
by longitudinal pressure waves in a material medium (as
air) and is the objective cause of hearing.
The energy of sound causes the material medium in which
it occurs to change its initially uniform distribution of
molecules. In some locations the concentration of molecules,
say in the air, increases, and this causes the pressure there
to increase, too. The distance between two places of high
pressure represents the wavelength of the sound wave. In
all experiments that are conducted in acoustics laboratories,
results indicate that sound needs a material medium in
order to be propagated. In a vacuum, however loud one
screams, there is no sound because there is no matter to
carry the vibration. If sound is to be heard, the presence
of matter is absolutely necessary. Otherwise we hear nothing.
Does this mean that what we consider as "sound" is an
effect rather than a cause? And, if this is so, then what is
causing the experience we call "sound?"

Soundless Sound

In ancient Indian metaphysical systems, sound followed to its source was considered to be the cause and not the effect of vibration. The Hindu sages considered sound as primal potential energy. They termed it "potential sound" or "soundless sound." They considered sound capable of rearranging particles from their originally undisturbed patterns into other patterns.

The validity of this phenomenon has been shown in experiments conducted in the laboratory. The first scientist to show the correspondence between sound vibrations and visible forms was the German physicist Ernst Chladmi, who lived in the eighteenth century. He scattered particles of sand on steel disks and observed that various notes played on a violin produced different harmonic patterns or standing-wave patterns in the sand (Blair, 1976). The source of the same vibration, in this case the violin, causes two different effects: a. the sound that is heard as musical notes; and b. the harmonic patterns that are seen on the steel disk. What we call "sound" is the audible effect. The harmonic patterns were created at *the same time* by the same source of vibratory frequency. We do not call them "sound" and yet, they are the visible form of the same vibration.

The explanation for this effect is that the vibrations from the violin make the disk resonate in certain places. The sand moves to those areas that do not resonate. Thus, there are actually two patterns on the disk for each sound vibration: a. the pattern made as the sand accumulates on those parts of the disk that do not resonate; and b. the pattern created by those parts of the disk that do resonate.

These two patterns are interdependent. It is interesting to note that what is observed as the primary pattern on the disk is the pattern of sand accumulated on those parts of the disk that do not resonate. However, the cause of this pattern is the resonating areas of the disk: the accumulation of sand is secondary, at best. The visible expression of the sound energy is the inverse of the actual vibratory pattern, which is invisible. Both patterns are indispensable in the manifestation of the visible effect. The Taoists called this concept of complementary aspects *yin* and *yang*; the Hindus named it *Shiva-Shakti*. Complementary constructs are found at all levels, including the physical universe, as electrons and positrons, north and south poles, male and female.

Twentieth century physics reveals that light, matter and sound can all be thought of as energy vibrations, and far exceed the range of what we can see and feel, touch and hear. When a specific vibratory energy of oscillating matter of certain frequency tunes onto our ear-drum, we perceive it as audible sound. When a specific vibratory energy of oscillating electromagnetic fields, but of a higher vibratory frequency, tunes onto the retina of our eyes, we perceive it as light. Since all interactions at the physical level of our bodies involve, as quantum theory states, the exchange of photons between charged particles, the same must hold true for other senses like smell, taste and touch. We also know from physics that there are vibrations that are not perceived by our sensory organs such as ultrasonic sound, infrared and ultraviolet light. Vibratory energies of frequencies that cannot be detected by the most sophisticated current instruments cannot be ruled out either. As we go to more refined frequencies, we progressively approach the ancient concept of "soundless sound": sound that is not heard by human ears; sound that in its silence contains all possibilities.

The secret texts of India stated that sound holds the key to the mysteries of the Universe. Through sound, the world is created, sustained and dissolved, and human beings can evolve their consciousness beyond the limits of their ordinary experience of themselves as limited and imperfect beings. In this ancient tradition the physical world is considered as a reflection of an infinite number of sound patterns, an infinite number of combinations of these patterns, all arising from the underlying level of soundless sound. Great philosophers from ancient times and from many cultures have recognized in this process the underlying order of creation.

According to ancient traditions, soundless sound goes

through four levels of unfoldment to become audible sound. The scriptures state that, similarly, *the unfoldment of the world is indispensably linked with the unfoldment of sound.* In a series of unfoldments, sound springs out of the soundless level to become the manifest Universe of objects and phenomena.

Symbolically the unfoldment of sound begins with a circle, representing the Absolute. Undivided, undifferentiated, the circle represents the oneness of the Absolute before the formation of the world. Then, comes the point (Figure 16), which symbolizes the supreme sound, *para shabda,* (*para* meaning supreme, *shabda* meaning sound). It is the subtlest level of sound. At this point sound is unmanifest, the unstruck sound. It is the first vibration pulsating in the cosmic primordial sea of Consciousness. It is the germinal seed in the process of becoming the Universe. The supreme sound is sound with practically no vibration, with infinite wavelength; and at the same time, it is sound with zero wavelength, with infinite vibration. At this level zero and infinity are still undifferentiated. Para shabda is sound beyond silence, the silence of silence, *metasilence.* The Universe is not yet manifested, but it is all contained in the seed form of the sound, in the same way that a tree is contained in its seed. Everything is contained in the point (Singh, 1979a).

The Universe, which is becoming ready to manifest, is thus gathered up into a single point. Then as sound unfolds, a slightly denser level emerges, the seed form of sound, prior to any differentiation of word and object. In Indian metaphysics, the word for an object is its sound form, its audible but invisible record. The object is the final condensation of the pure energy in this process of creation. At this level the word and the object are still in their oneness, not yet differentiated. This is the second level (*pashyanti*) represented by two vertical lines.

A triangle represents the third level of sound unfoldment (*madhyama*). It is the first stage of differentiation of word and object. Here, subtle sound is just about to manifest itself on the gross level. The subtle letters begin to take form, creating thoughts and feelings. The fourth level (*vaikari*) is the final stage of the densification of the under-lying causal sound. It is the complete differentiation of word and object. It is speech, the words and letter sounds used daily, and also ordinary sound. An image of the process of unfoldment is found in the ancient Indian texts, the Upanishads (e.g. Bahadur, 1979; Gambhirananda, 1977): "The Vak, Word, which sprouts in para, gives leaves in pashyanti, buds in madhyama, and blossoms in vaikari."

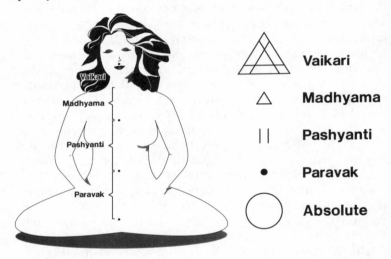

Figure 16. The four levels of sound which spring from the Absolute and are found in the subtle human body

This process of unfoldment is an active on-going process within all of creation, including ourselves as human beings. These same four levels of sound exist within each of us. The physical body is the final densification of the individual consciousness. When we dream, our awareness shifts to another level of consciousness that some call the subtle body, dream body or emotional body. The scriptures tell us that in this subtle body there are power centers or energy nodes of consciousness (chakras) which, even though not sensed or detected by medical instruments, nevertheless correspond to and control the ductless glands. Within these power centers sound manifests in four different levels (Figure 16).

Nothing remains still in our Universe; everything is throbbing. Ordinary sound is the audible vibration of matter. In subtler levels of sound, Consciousness is vibrating, and this vibration may be heard within that Consciousness. The same four levels of throbbing Consciousness are found in the individual human being. It is said that during deep meditation these levels of unmanifest sound can be experienced and actually "heard" as inner sounds. The sages, who experienced them in their meditation for thousands of years, state that ten different kinds of inner sounds can be heard in the inner space within the subtle heart (cf. Muktananda, 1978). They are:

1. the roaring of waterfall,
2. the buzzing or whistling of bees,
3. a bell,
4. a conch shell,
5. an Indian stringed instrument (*Veena*),
6. cymbals,
7. a flute,
8. a two-headed South Indian drum (*Mritang*),
9. a kettledrum, and
10. thunder.

Is it possible that these inner sounds are the musical tones of the planets described by Pythagoras? The Pythagorean theory concerning the harmonic sounds of the planets was based on the observation that every fast-moving object produces some sound. This phenomenon, they argued, should also be present in the motion of the stars and the planets. The frequencies of the sounds produced depend on the distance of the stars and planets, and they correspond to the frequencies of the musical notes. According to Pythagoras, humans are not aware of these sounds because they form the background of sound that we are accustomed to from birth (Graviger, 1982). It is likely that Pythagoras was referring to inner sounds and inner "planets," which are representations of cosmic forces or archetypal patterns within us.

The whole cosmos is resonating in sound. The world is a vast symphony of sounds we can hear and sounds we cannot hear, but which affect us nevertheless. The source of Sound is right inside the human body. The entire process of unfoldment from the soundless sound to the concrete sound of letters we produce with our tongues is under our control. Sound coagulates into what we experience whenever it comes out of its earlier stages (paravak, pashyanti, and madhyama), as blood coagulates when it comes to the surface of the body from a wound. The entire process of creation is within. Sound, letters, words, feelings are all vibrations which come from the ultimate level of soundless sound, the level beyond silence, the level of metasilence.

If this entire process is under our own control, then, perhaps, we ourselves might be the creators of the individual worlds we live in. The Hermetic statement "as above so below" may be seen as a profound truth.

The Creative Power of Letters

Letters compose words. Words are very powerful because they create pictures in our minds and feelings in our hearts. Our experience of the world around us is based on these images and feelings. They can color the way we see and relate to the world. A word or certain group of words can cause an intensely pleasurable inner experience or a violent reaction. For example, praise creates joy and satisfaction within us, while harsh words make us unhappy. It is important to know the right meaning of words. It is far more important to understand their power and where this power comes from. When we do not know the power of the words, they control us. The power of words dictates our beliefs, our feelings of what is right and wrong. It influences how we see ourselves and others. We experience the power of words when we speak them, as well as when other people use them. If someone grows up with continuous exposure to words such as "stupid," "bad," "ugly," after a while this person will become all of these.

This power of words is mysterious because we do not experience it at the gross level of our perception. However, it does affect us profoundly in more ways than we are aware of. The Hindu sages called this power *Matrika Shakti*, the power of letters. *Matrika* literally means the unknown or un-understood mother. Shakti is the female, active, creative, aspect of Universal Consciousness, termed God by many. According to ancient knowledge of the creative process, Matrika Shakti is the power of sound, and her manifested form is the letters of the alphabet. The letters are that group of powers from which evolve all the words and objects in this universe. Here the term "letter" indicates the sound or conscious vibration of the letter rather than the graphic symbol. The symbols by themselves, without the energy of the sound, are like clothes hung on a hanger, with no life within. Letters in the sense of Matrika Shakti are concrete sound vibrations capable of creating actual sensations, feelings, mental pictures and images in our mind. All these inner sensations, impressions, feelings, mental images together form our inner universe. We project this personal consciousness onto the outer universe.

The same outer universe is experienced differently by people, because every person has a different inner universe. People perceive the outer world through the organs of perception. However, the process of perception is occurring in the mind; it is an inner process. It is happening through the mirror of each individual's inner universe. "The world is as you see it" (Singh, 1979b).

Sound has supreme creative power when it operates at the deepest level (paravak). On the level of speech (vaikari) words have only limited power to create. Still, every word does convey some power. Even the most gross level of speech maintains a hint of its underlying divine origin. Letters of all languages ultimately come from the same source and embody the same power. However, we concentrate on sound vibration as understood in the ancient Sanskrit language, because in Sanskrit the science of sound was refined to a subtlety unknown to most other traditions.

It is hard for us to grasp the concept of the power of letters because, with the exception of the power of the meaning of the words, we do not experience any power coming from letters. Modern languages have evolved through the centuries in an arbitrary and haphazard way, reflecting social changes and political and economic turmoils. They are so far removed from their original sources that they have lost most of their original intention and structure. Nowadays, letters and words are mere tools for verbal communication. Arbitrary changes have been made in the structure of the languages and in the spelling of the words. This robs the language, any language, from its original power and effectiveness.

Some linguists believe that the structure of the most highly evolved ancient languages was actually designed to represent the structure of the cosmos, the way it was perceived and understood by the sages and seers of those traditions. For example, the 22 graphs or letters of the Hebrew alphabet were 22 proper names used to designate different states of structure of the one cosmic energy. In contrast to *A, B, C,* and so on, which are representations of vocal sounds, the names *Aleph, Bayt, Ghimmel,* etc., are living structured energies in unfolding stages of organization (Ponce, 1973).

According to this concept, the languages of the great ancient civilizations were expressions of the harmony and structure of the Universe. The seers and the sages of these ancient civilizations, including the Hebrews and the Hindus, reached the depths of their own being, their own consciousness. They uncovered a science of sound that does more than represent objects and ideas.

Perhaps the greatest of all fundamental languages is Sanskrit. Sanskrit is a member of the Indo-European family of languages to which most of the languages of Europe belong. Considering it outside the confines of linguistics, Sanskrit may be considered a sacred language because its alphabet was revealed to the ancient seers in deep meditative states. The letters of the Sanskrit alphabet are actual expressions of the subtlest energies of the creative process. They are the gross approximation of the subtle energies during the process of creation, just as audible words and music broadcast from a radio station are the gross manifestation of subtle electrical impulses.

The main point is that in this ancient cosmology the

creative process is indispensably linked with the creation of the letters of the Sanskrit alphabet. The process is not sequential or linear in time; we cannot argue which came first. The creative process of the manifestation of the physical universe brought the letters into being, and the vibrational subtle energies, which we relate to through the letters, began the entire process of creation. Which came first, the chicken or the egg?

The Sanskrit letters are the audible forms of the principles of creation. The sound *a*, the first letter of the Sanskrit alphabet, is very significant. It represents the first level of creation, *Shiva*, and all the other letters evolve from it. This sound exists in all the letters of the alphabet and supports their existence, just as Shiva, pure Consciousness, exists at all levels of creation and pervades them. There is more to the Sanskrit alphabet, though, since its very structure evolved from the structure of creation. The sequence of the letters represents the actual step-by-step unfoldment of the Universe, from the level of pure Consciousness to that of physical objects.

In Eastern cosmology sages of different traditions outlined and explained the process of creation in different ways. *Kashmir Shaivism* relates the letters of the Sanskrit language to the creative principles: the Supreme Absolute, *Paramashiva*, is the ultimate Reality (Muktananda, 1980). Paramashiva is supremely independent and complete in itself. (Emphasizing that the Absolute is beyond all dualities, one should properly use neuter terms—it, that, its.) The Supreme Reality is both transcendent and immanent. Its nature is to manifest, just as the bird's nature is to fly, the tiger's nature to hunt other animals, the scorpion's nature to sting. Although changeless, the Absolute is the underlying principle of all changes. Although formless, it pervades all forms. It becomes the entire Universe of forms, and yet never loses its unchanging state. It becomes all, though it is one. But Paramashiva has two aspects:

a. The power of manifestation, known in Shaivite philosophy as *vimarsha*. This the power of determinate knowledge and action and is characterized by content. It contains all that is to be. As the tree lies as potency in the seed, so the entire Universe, with all its beings and concepts and objects, lies as potency in the vimarsha aspect (Singh, 1979a).

b. The light of Consciousness, known as *prakasha*, by which everything is known. We do not see anything in a dark room full of objects, and when we turn on a flashlight, we can only see the objects upon which it shines. The flashlight (prakasha) did not create the objects; it only makes them known (Muktananda, 1980).

When there is no creation, the Absolute, Paramashiva, is in its transcendent nature. In our physical universe we experience its immanent nature. It manifests the world through its power or *Shakti* aspect. Shakti, which literally means "power," is therefore the active aspect of the Absolute, its power of manifestation. The Consciousness and power aspects are inseparable, like the light and the heat of the sun. They do not exist separately. Shiva-Shakti in Shaivism, as prakasha-vimarsha, is analogous to the concept of potential and kinetic energy in physics. Any object placed above the surface of the earth possesses potential and kinetic energy at the same time and in different degrees of manifestation. But in this example from physics potential and kinetic energies are finite, whereas Shiva and Shakti are limitless in any respect, such as time, space and quantity.

The Sanskrit alphabet has a unique characteristic that, as far as we know, is unparalleled in any other alphabet: it is the only alphabet where the letters have a one-to-one correspondence with their numerical values. This property might hold a fundamental secret for understanding the creation of the Universe. In Hindu thought the letters correspond to vibrational energy levels in the unfoldment of the creation. Numbers, according to the ancient Egyptians, on the other hand, represent the principles of creation (Khanna, 1979). It seems then that in the Sanskrit alphabet the universal principles of creation and the vibrational energies of creation unfold together. They are not the same, but they unfold in harmony with each other. For example, the 16 Sanskrit vowels represent the pure vibratory principles of creation which underlie the Universe as a whole.

The numerical value of the first letter, *A* is 1. The numerical value of the second letter, *AA* is 2, and the numerical value of the fiftieth letter, *KSHA* is 50. The first 16 letters are the vowels, which in Hindu thought represent the female aspect of Paramashiva. The Universe of names and forms is then nothing but the creative unfolding of the Absolute.

From the Supreme's first impulse to create down to the grossest matter, there are 36 levels of unfoldment. Of those, the first five are called "pure levels," because there is not yet any gross manifestation. It is the gestation period of creation, similar to the preparation inside a cell before the cell breaks into two. At the pure levels there is still unity: subject and object exist in a state of undivided equilibrium. Creation begins when this equilibrium is disturbed. The creative power, Shakti, causes a strain on the "surface" of Universal Consciousness. At this point the Absolute polarizes into positive and negative, subject and object, static and dynamic, passive and active, even though it is still one (Singh, 1979a; Rudrappa, 1969).

Levels of the Creative Process

The complete creative process represented by the various Sanskrit letters is a fascinating subject beyond the linguistic realm. The correspondence of the levels of creative process to the Sanskrit letters can be found in the Notes[1] (see Plate III and Figure 18). Here we provide only the main ideas (see also Singh, 1979a).

At the first level of creation, the level of pure Being (Shiva), the subtlest level of vibration is expressed by the first letter of the Sanskrit alphabet, *A*, अ. The second level, the level of power (Shakti), is expressed by the second vowel and second letter of the Sanskrit alphabet *AA*, आ . Each level of the creative process has a specific power or shakti associated with it, which brings that level into existence from the undivided state of the Absolute. The first level is predominated by the power of supreme existence, the second by the power of supreme completeness, contentment or bliss. The formation of these two levels takes place simultaneously. The union of the two primary principles, static and dynamic, creates a stress, a throb or vibration that moves out from the undifferentiated and undivided Paramashiva to give rise to the whole creative process represented by the entire alphabet. The third level is predominated by the power of supreme will or desire, the will to create the objective aspect of individual experience (*Iccha Shakti*). This level is the first stage of the motion in the unfoldment of Consciousness.

The fourth level is predominated by the power of perfect knowledge (*Jnana Shakti*), and the objective side of manifestation becomes more defined. At this stage the distinct blossoming of the creative plan for the Universe emerges, and awareness of the Universe becomes clearer. Then at the fifth and final level of pure creation the power of supreme action (*Kriya Shakti*) comes into being. At this level subjective

Process of Cell Division

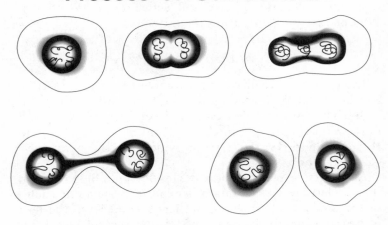

Figure 17. The division process in the cell

and objective sides are equal and balanced; there is no emphasis on either. Both remain unified, but clearly distinguished. In the pure levels, there is only the divine desire to manifest and the creation of the right conditions and tools as a plan, a Thought or the beginning vibratory process in the Universal Mind. Nothing is materialized yet, though the groundwork necessary for manifestation has been completed. Diversity in unity is at hand. Consciousness is ready to split into two. The cornerstone of our physical universe, the power of duality or *Maya*, is ready to manifest. Right after the pure levels the outer nature of Shiva, which manifests as the Universe, begins to materialize.

An analogy of the creative process at the pure levels can be found in the microcosm as a cell undergoes division (Figure 17). Each individual cell has a nucleus. When time for partition arrives, the nucleus prepares for complete bisection. From the original single nucleus a series of distinct stages leads to the formation of two nuclei. At the last stage, before the membrane of the cell is actually broken, there are two fully separate nuclei in the same cell. This is analogous to the stage of the last of the pure levels, where Shiva-Shakti has been polarized, but both aspects are still in oneness.

It is extremely interesting that the creative process, whether in the cosmic undivided state or in mundane human activities, manifests the same prerequisites for the creation of the Universe. All creative activities must satisfy the following requirements before the activities can manifest:

    a. one must first exist and be conscious (power of being and awareness); *sum ergo cogito*, I exist, therefore I think;
    b. one must have the desire to create (power of will);
    c. one needs to know what to do (power of knowledge);
    d. one needs to take action (power of action).

There is no human creation, from the most menial to the highest and noblest, that does not necessarily have all the elements above. If even one is missing, no creation can take place.

Following the pure levels, the process enters the impure levels. The term "impure" does not have moral value attached to it; it does not mean that the rest of creation is dirty. After the fifth level, Maya comes forth. Maya is the dualistic power, the power to veil, the power of illusion, where the sense of difference emerges. Through its power of Maya, the Absolute or Paramashiva conceals itself; Maya obscures the nature of ultimate Reality. The ephemeral seems real and permanent, the noneternal seems everlasting. The original unity of Shiva-Shakti begins to move towards differentiation.

From Maya emanate five qualifying limitations (*kanchukas*) (Muktananda, 1980; Rudrappa, 1969). Each of them limits one of the universal conditions of the Absolute. The *kala kanchuka* limits the omnipresence of Shiva-Shakti and gives rise to the notion of individuality. This is the experience of the individual soul being confined in a mere human body. Anything outside the human body gives rise to the experience of "not me." The *vidya kanchuka* limits the power of omniscience of Shiva-Shakti and gives rise to the experience of limited knowledge. It brings into focus our ignorance of Reality. We take the unreal as real, the part as whole. The *raga kanchuka* limits the wholeness of Shiva-Shakti. By limiting the power of completeness, it gives rise to desire for particulars and attachment to them, and leads us to discontentment. The *kaala kanchuka* limits the power of eternality of Shiva-Shakti. It gives rise to limitations of time, creates the sense of past, present and future and gives rise to mortality. The final limitation (*niyati kanchuka*), limits the omnipotence of Shiva-Shakti and gives rise to limitations of cause, space and form. It conditions us to fate, predestination and the round of life.

As a seed is covered by different layers of husk, so the Absolute is covered by these six layers of restrictions. The Supreme, through the limitations of Maya and the five limitations, becomes the individual self with all its powers veiled (Rudrappa, 1969). In this state, the Absolute is called *purusha*, which represents the Primordial Male Principle. Although purusha retains its absolute substance, it appears limited. At the same time the Absolute, through the same limiting process of Maya and the kanchukas, becomes the objective side of individual experience, the root cause of all the remaining levels of manifestation. The objective side is called *prakriti*. It is the Primordial Female Principle and is the embodiment of the active and creative qualities, constituting the objective manifestation of nature.

Prakriti consists of three qualities called *gunas: sattva*, the quality of radiance or intelligence; *rajas*, the active, kinetic quality; and *tamas*, the inertia quality (Muktananda, 1980; Dyczkowski, 1987). As the process of unfoldment continues, the intellect or higher insight (*buddhi*) comes into being; the ego (*ahamkara*) follows; the mind (*manas*) evolves next.

Then directly from the ego emerge the five organs of senses, colored by the sattva quality of prakriti; the five organs of actions, colored by the raja quality of prakriti; the five subtle elements, colored by the tamas quality of the prakriti. Finally, the last five gross elements evolve from the subtle elements. The entire creative process[1] is illustrated in Plate III and Figure 18.

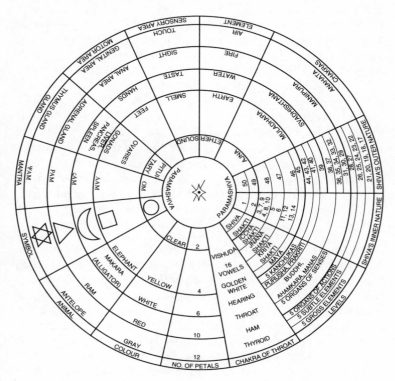

Figure 18. The various steps in the creative process and their associated properties shown in a circular diagram, all emanating from the central point of undifferentiated Consciousness.

All the material objects of the cosmos are comprised of the five principles of the gross elements—earth, water, fire, air and ether. In any object all the five gross elements must be present, with one predominating. All these coexist in any physical manifestation, even though this is not immediately obvious from our mundane experience. A rock, for example, obviously has the element of the earth, solidity, but we would have a hard time seeing fluidity or fire in it. However, rock heated to an appropriate temperature will manifest its water element: it will release the water that it holds inside. Two cold rocks struck together produce sparks, revealing the latent fire principle within them. The manifested world, however, is not composed of just the five levels of vibration constituting the five gross elements. Each level unfolds from the previous, carrying on energy qualities from the level above it. In that respect, even a rock is the representation of the entire creative process. The energy qualities of all the 36 levels of creation are present in the rock, including the five pure levels. The central essence of Kashmir Shaivism, as of many ancient philosophies, can be summarized as: *everything in the Universe is Universal Consciousness or God.* We are that Consciousness, and it is only because of the veiling power of Maya that we perceive ourselves as separate from each other and from the rock. In this context, the Shaivite statement that Chiti, the Supreme Universal Energy or Shakti, creates the Universe out of her own Being (Singh, 1980a) acquires a deep meaning.

It is equally important to understand the creative process in ourselves, as human beings. Since the 36 levels of creation represent universal principles in action, we can contemplate them in our own nature. In fact, the pure levels are beyond individual consciousness: they represent Pure Being, or in Christian terms, the Son of God (Yukteswar, 1984). Levels 6-11, Maya and the five limiting powers, represent the "causal body," the root cause of limited experience. Levels 12-31 represent the constituent elements of the subtle or astral body (Yukteswar, 1984), the sum total of all our subtle experiences. Finally, levels 32-36 are the constituent elements of the physical body: ether, air, fire, water and earth.

Mantra

Mantras are not mere words or combinations of words to be repeated in order to blank the mind and stop the ceaseless inner chatter. Mantras have a far more important role. The scope and usefulness of mantra science are enormous. By reproducing at the gross level of sound the fundamental subtle energy patterns of the entire Universe, the mantra provides a simple method for aligning and harmonizing ourselves with the Universe as a whole. Through a correct and fundamental understanding of the use of mantra we can transcend our limited experience of reality. We can experience and recognize the existence and the presence of Consciousness or God beyond the rational mind, in a mere rock, in an insignificant bug, in the most disagreeable neighbor, and finally in ourselves. At its deepest levels, the mantra can connect us to the source of the vibratory principles that underlie our very existence. In many traditions, the spiritual teacher gives his or her students personal mantras that suit the students' particular vibratory needs for spiritual unfoldment. The whole purpose of mantras is to assist us in our journey back Home: from the level of the five gross elements, through the reverse process of the unfoldment of the Universe, back to the state of the pure levels and union with our true nature, which is the transcendent nature of Paramashiva. Many people in various traditions throughout the ages have completed this journey through the practice of repeating a mantra, of gaining mantra awareness.

Mantras are composed of letters and syllables. Yet these vibrations relate to the creation of the entire Universe, from the supreme level of Paramashiva down to the smallest grain of sand. In a sense the human body contains the symphony of the creation of the entire Universe. The classic philosophical Shaivite text *Pratyabhijnahridayam* states (Singh, 1980a): "The individual experient, in whom consciousness is contracted, has the Universe [as his body] in a contracted form."

The science of mantra focuses on the aspect of consciousness as sound vibration that exists within everyone. The

mantra can align us with the sound form of the Supreme
Shakti and can reveal to us our true nature as pure Consciousness. *Matrika Shakti*, the "Un-understood Mother,"
is the subtle force behind speech and thought. When
unknown, this subtle energy of the letters binds us and
forces us into thoughts and feelings that seem completely
out of our control. It allows our emotions to rise beyond
volition at the mere sound of a couple of words. It allows
our minds to create universes of worry, anger, fear and every
negative and destructive feeling. It makes us feel helpless,
with no way out of our predicament. Yet, when the same
Matrika Shakti is known and understood as the female
aspect of Universal Consciousness, she can make us masters
of our thoughts and feelings. She can make us masters
of our lives.

The term *matrika* is very significant. Every letter of the
Sanskrit alphabet is called a "little mother." This implies
that each letter has a certain power to give birth to a world
of ideas. Matrika Shakti, in the form of letters, arises within
Paramashiva, the Supreme Reality, and takes the form of
the Universe; in the same way the subtle letters arise and
give form to the individual's universe of thoughts and
perceptions. Just as at the macrocosmic level Supreme
Shakti descends and, through a process of self-imposed
contraction and limitation, creates a world in a dualistic
framework where time is perceived as linear and space
as three dimensional, so the contraction of the same Consciousness within the individual leads to a state of limited
experience and knowledge. This state produces the sense
of separation from all other beings, a sense of ourselves
and others being imperfect. "After all, we are only humans.
Nobody is perfect." Well, the scientists and seers of mantra
yoga do not believe so. The ancient Indian texts of both
Shaivite and Vedantic traditions are full of statements
declaring that all human beings are indeed perfect. It is
our own wrong understanding about our perfection and
limitlessness that makes us imperfect and limited. This
is brought about by ignorance of the power of Matrika
Shakti. According to Shaivism, everything that we experience
is nothing but a creation of our own consciousness. In

the *Pratyabhijnahridayam* it is stated: "Consciousness itself contracts from the level of pure awareness and becomes the mind" (Singh, 1980a).

The mind is contracted into the form of whatever we are experiencing or perceiving at any moment. It actually takes the form of our sensory experiences. For example, right now you are reading the words of this text. It is clear that, although the letters are on the paper, the experience of them is in you, specifically in your mind. In effect the whole world is being experienced inside you, in your mind. Sense data come through our organs of perception and are filtered through our memories, subconscious patterns, likes and dislikes, habits and built-in concepts. Then we project the result of our inner process outside ourselves and call it "the world." We go even further and call the world we perceive "an objective world," and we argue with anyone who does not perceive the world the same way we do. Of course everyone else does the same thing. As result, we get entangled in endless arguments to prove that we are right and everybody else is wrong. Since everybody feels the same way, we are all in a no-win situation.

Are we then hopelessly attached to the web of Maya, to the intricacies of Matrika Shakti or the power of speech and thought? Can we get out of this predicament? Shaivism declares that we are neither hopeless or helpless. The Eastern sages provided different practical means for getting out of the chaos that our minds are capable of producing. One way would be to become aware of the four levels of speech within us. We can observe the power of the words we are using as they arise through these levels and create images, thoughts and feelings. By controlling our thoughts, we begin to realize we can control our own reality. Every word and every thought is a mantra because each is a vibration of Consciousness. Using harsh, insulting words and indulging in negative feelings is using destructive energy against our own selves. The method of word awareness, mantra awareness, does not require us to sit for a long time in a remote place to practice. Rather it is important to practice it in our everyday busy lives as we go about whatever we do. These levels of speech are not theoretical, resulting from some abstract philosophical system foreign to us. This method utilizes our understanding of the levels of speech and develops awareness of those levels from our mundane experiences of the world. It is vitally important to realize that the words we use come from the very center of our being. If we choose to use this tremendous energy to hurt ourselves, then we have the license to do so. However, the big revelation of Eastern mantra science is that we have a choice.

The two great Hinduist traditions of Shaivism and its sister school of Vedanta are relevant for twentieth-century Western people because they address universal principles which not only can be studied in an abstract sense but also can be experienced in one's own being as the creative process. In Chapter 6 "The Mystical Experience," we examine various paths in the Eastern and the Western traditions and find that East and West emphasize different aspects of the creative process. The Eastern views agree on the identity of the individual consciousness with universal Consciousness, the identity of the drop with the ocean. For example, Vedanta emphasizes that the world is an illusion and *only* the Absolute is real, while Shaivism emphasizes that the Absolute is real *and* gives rise to everything else.

We can discover these creative levels within ourselves by becoming aware of the development of thoughts, from the level of the soundless sound to the level of actually spoken words. For this reason Eastern metaphysics is not just a deep philosophy; it is a practical system of knowledge, a *science of Being*. Here the word "science" is used in its original sense of a body of knowledge. The practical aspect of this science is to use one's own being as the laboratory.

When we plant the seed of an apple tree, we harvest only apples from that tree. When we plant seeds of negative thoughts and feelings, we can expect to harvest only negative fruits as a direct consequence of our choices. At this profound level of understanding sound as the creative process, we can really understand the concept of free will. Generally speaking, most people's lives appear to be the result of forces completely outside their control. But it is our lack of understanding of the creative power of words, thoughts and feelings that makes us feel powerless. This is why Matrika Shakti is called the Un-understood Mother. Another practical way out of the chaos of the mind is through mantra repetition. By this practice we can use the power of mantra sound to carry us back through the four sound levels to the source of all sound vibration, the soundless sound. In mantra repetition *the mind becomes the mantra* (Singh, 1979a). The mind begins to vibrate at the level of the mantra vibration, but since all mantra vibrations stem from the soundless level, mantra can lead us back to that level. Since mantras are composed of letters, which are the grossest manifestation of the soundless sound, the letters of the mantra provide the link between the physical and the soundless levels. Moreover, the mantra is pregnant with all the appropriate vibrations as we go to more subtle levels, until we reach the final destination, the soundless level. Mantras are ladders of involution with all the necessary vibrational steps available. This process of involution, the journey back to the source, has two components: the mantra and the mind. Like a musical piece and a musical instrument, initially they are different, but both are needed to make music.

When the mind finally vibrates at the level of the mantra, then everything—mantra, mind and the level of consciousness of the individual—become one: They are undifferentiated, pure Consciousness; unity, wholeness, without object or subject. Everything in the perception of the individual's world is unity. The mind in this state becomes an extraordinary instrument. It becomes capable of perceiving different objects through the senses, but it does not interpret them as essentially different. The great twentieth-century teacher of Shaivism, Swami Muktananda, once said that when he opens his eyes he first sees the blue light of Universal Consciousness, and behind that light he then sees the different people and objects. Such great beings perceive a reality beyond our ordinary perception. They do not lose the perspective of the world of phenomena; they still perceive through their senses. However, their perception is not covered by the veil of Maya. The word "phenomenon" is from the Greek and means "that which appears" as opposed to "that which is." It embodies the veil of illusion, of Maya. Enlightened beings do not live in Maya; they live beyond its veil. It is said that they have fun as they watch the tricks Maya plays on us. In our seriousness we get caught in our own dramas; in their lightness they don't. That is a characteristic of all great beings; they can be light like children. What they perceive is Reality, universal and eternal: universal because there is only one Truth, only one Reality, pure undifferentiated Consciousness; eternal because there is no time since Reality does not depend on time. Eternity is not a very long time, as many of us believe. Eternity begins when time collapses.

As the mantra is repeated with the tongue and mouth, it is said, the physical body is purified. Usually the energy of the mantra is felt vibrating in the tongue and mouth, the areas where this level of speech is focused. Then the mantra "descends" to the next level of speech. As the aspirant keeps practicing mantra repetition, the mantra purifies all the subtle bodies as it descends the levels of speech until it reaches the level of the soundless sound (paravak). Then the aspirant experiences intense bliss. In fact, a being whose speech has been purified to this level has the power to create through words. The *Brihadaranyaka Upanishad* says: "That speech, verily, is divine by which whatever one speaks comes to be" (Nikhilananda, 1975).

Mantras are capable of tremendous impact on an individual's consciousness because the vibrational levels innate in the sound of the letters are also in each individual. All four levels of the sound unfoldment exist in every human being and can be activated by mantra. Both mantra and the aspirant are indispensable ingredients in the process of involution. They need to come together in the process of involution, the cosmic play. Complementarity is necessary for wholeness.

Mantras have the power to create. In Genesis it is said, "And God said, Let there be light." The highest level of the practice of mantra is the experience that mantra is nothing other than awareness of the eternal "I" consciousness which vibrates within us. Practicing this awareness, after having understood the subtle power of sound, and the power of letters, can free us from bondage to Matrika Shakti. Some Eastern schools of thought, most notably Zen Buddhism, hold that the more meaningless a mantra, the more powerful it is in calming our minds. A meaningless sound does not create images and thoughts in our minds, so that the mantra can be a useful tool to save us from drowning in the waves of our overactive minds. In this case the mantra is used only at the gross level, but the real power of mantra lies in using them at subtler levels and in understanding them. As the secret of mantra begins to reveal itself to us, we can see how apparently meaningless sounds, because of their fundamental nature, have the ability to bring all the various levels of our being into harmony with each other as well as with all creation.

Mantras are not just mere tools for reducing stress, as they have often been used in the West. Mantra repetition has a much more significant scope and function: to align one's energy with the universal energy.

There are hundreds of thousands of mantras. Some Eastern traditions have different mantras for different functions and outcomes. Generally speaking in the East mantras are categorized into two kinds: ones that can be found in books and scriptures and ones that a spiritual teacher or master hands down personally, after having used them extensively. These latter mantras are very potent, and their beneficial results are felt in a very short time by the aspirant who practices the science of mantra. Though all mantras are potent because of their creative nature, their power is dormant. Repetition for a prolonged period is necessary for their power to manifest. Mantras that have been used by sages and seers in their journey back to the Source arise directly from the level of the soundless sound, and their power is at its full development. These mantras are called alive (*chaitanya*) mantras, alive because they are in their manifested form, as a tree becomes alive when manifested from its seed. Such a mantra can make the aspirant ready for the mysteries of the Universe, if he or she puts enough effort into mantra repetition.

Mantras can be constructed by sages based on their understanding and experience of the cosmic process of creation and the science of sound. An element of high significance in the Sanskrit language is the symbol of the point, which, when placed over a letter, produces the sound of *M*. The point is the symbol of the second level of sound unfoldment, and it indicates the entire universe coming together to form a point. Thus, according to the ancient seers, the point, *bindu*, represents the total unified nature of creation. A word that begins with the letter *A*, अ, and ends with the sound *M*, represents not only the complete process of creation, but also signifies the final union of Shiva and Shakti. In silence the lips are together and closed; to pronounce the sound *A* they separate, and they unite again to pronounce the sound *M*.

It is important to understand that when Eastern sages refer to inner sounds and mantras they mean the subtle aspect of the sounds that we produce with our mouths. The same is true about the letters of the Sanskrit alphabet. The sounds we produce with our vocal cords are only gross approximations of what the sages have heard in deep meditation states. The closest proximity to these sounds is what we may here term the "subsound," or the "metasound." As with the aftertaste of foods, there is a subtle subsound that carries the energy level of the inner sounds after the physical sound is gone.

AUM or *OM*, ॐ, is a special sound, a special mantra, that is not constructed but is self-existent, self-begotten. The sound *OM* is the primordial source of all creation. In an individual it is heard from within as the inner sound of thunder, which is the tenth and highest inner sound. The practicing aspirant can be absolutely certain, after he or she hears this sound from within, that his or her journey back to the level of unmanifest sound is close to completion. The real energy of the mantra manifests after we have pronounced the *A*, the *U* and the *M*. As we keep the lips closed in humming a long *M* at the end of the word, the metasound of all three letters is the closest approximation to the mantra *AUM*.

Another way to get a glimpse of the subtle sounds is

to try to "hear" them in silence. Actually, the great teachers of the East teach us that the sound *AUM* is the base, the foundation of every sound in the Universe (Yogananda, 1982). In other words, every sound, every noise in our cosmos includes the vibratory frequency of the sound *AUM* because this sound is the cornerstone of the creation of this Universe. They teach, also, that we can hear the sound *AUM* in every sound and noise around us. If we listen attentively to sounds consistently for long periods of time, then we actually hear the sound *AUM* in everything. Listen to the sound of thunder, the roar of the sea waves or the rushing waters in a river; listen to distant sounds like the traffic in a highway; listen to sounds of appliances, like a refrigerator. You will begin to distinguish the humming sound of *OM*. In this way we can maintain awareness of our inner state, regardless of what is happening in the surrounding world. This is how some yogis have acquired freedom from the physical world. They are living in the same physical world as everybody else, and yet they are not affected by it.

The concept and the effect of the metasound, soundless sound or unstruck sound has been well known and practiced for thousands of years in another great Eastern tradition, Buddhism, where the gong is used extensively for meditation. In Tibetan monasteries a huge gong is hung outside, and the trunk of a big tree is used as the "stick with which to hit the gong." The sound of some gongs can last for hours. The monks who work and live in the Himalayas get into a meditative state by following the metasound of these incredible gongs.

The science of mantra is universal. Mantras are part of most Hindu traditions including Shaivism and Vedanta as well as Buddhism. The power of sacred words, the profound significance of the sound or throb of Consciousness in the creative process, are not only gems of the philosophical systems of the East. They are also found in all the three great religions of Judaism, Christianity and Islam.

The ancient Hebrews believed that God reveals himself through *Memra*, a term analogous to the Greek *Logos*. The Memra of Jehovah was manifested to Abraham, Isaac, Jacob and Moses in the burning bush. The Memra revealed to Moses was summarized in the statement "I Am That I Am." It is found in the East in the same exact expression and is the content of the five pure levels of creation according to Kashmir Shaivism. Moses made the Memra into a concrete way of living expressed in the Ten Commandments of the Hebrews.

The ancient Greek philosopher Heraclitus used the same term "Logos," and similar ideas can be found in the philosophies of Plato and the Stoics. Greek-speaking Jews familiar with the writings of the Jewish philosopher Philo of Alexandria (15 B.C.—50 A.D.) believed that God mediates through his Logos (Dummelow, 1960).

In Islamic religious thought it is stated that: "The first thing that God created was the Primal Element, that is to say, the primal element of the entire Universe" (Palmer, 1974). According to the *Koran*, he created this of himself without any medium whatever: "And it was not the business of an hour, but even as the twinkling of an eye, or quicker still."

This concept is analogous to the *Spanda* (Dyczkowski, 1987) of Kashmir Shaivism, Spanda meaning the throb of Consciousness. Consciousness does not need any external medium to manifest the Universe. In Islam the Primal Element is God's world, and the Universe is the world of the Primal Element. By this alone the Voice of God is heard (Palmer, 1974).

In Christianity, the Gospel according to St. John[2] begins with the sentence: *"En Archi in o Logos kai o Logos in pros ton Theon, kai Theos in o Logos."* This translates into English as: "In the beginning was the Word, and the Word was with God, and the Word was God." Many believe that the Christian *Logos*, which is translated in English as "the Word," is the Christian equivalent to the Eastern "mantra."

Summary

The concept of soundless sound or unstruck sound is stated in a unique and explicit way in the philosophical traditions of the East. It is found also in the roots of many other philosophic traditions. It is the concept of the primordial creative power of potential sound, the seed from which all creation sprouts. The entire Universe, according to this tradition, lies unmanifested in the form of the "soundless sound" as a whole tree lies unmanifested in the form of its seed. In a series of unfoldments, the sound manifests itself and so does the Universe. These same levels of unfoldment of the sound are found in the human body and represent gateways to other realms of consciousness and awareness. The Sanskrit alphabet is the closest approximation to the inner sounds that the Eastern sages "heard" during meditation. Mantras are words composed of letters. Because of the creative power of the letters, mantras have tremendous power to transform the level of awareness of the aspirant. Mantras contain all the vibrational levels of consciousness necessary for the process of involution, the journey back to the source, which is pure Consciousness. Mantras, through recitation by the tongue and mouth, link the physical plane with subtle vibrational energies of the letters, thus providing all the steps in the ladder of involution. These steps are linked with the levels of sound unfoldment within the individual, so that through them one can access these levels of consciousness within oneself. The whole process of mantra repetition is unfolded in the mind. At the end of involution the mind vibrates at the level of the mantra. At the final destination, the mind, the mantra and the consciousness of the aspirant become all one: undifferentiated, unified Consciousness.

The concept and the workings of mantras are found in most of the major spiritual traditions of the East, such as Shaivism, Vedanta and Buddhism, as well as the three religions, Judaism, Islam and Christianity.

5
Mind and Metamind

Yoga is the control of thought waves in the mind.
Patanjali

We are dealing with our minds every moment, even when we are asleep or unconscious. But what is it we are dealing with? We know that our mind is a part of us, as our legs and arms are a part of us. We may even think that our body and our mind *is* us. We think of ourselves as men, women, black, white, tall, short, defined by all kinds of physical characteristics. We also take ourselves to be liberals, conservatives, scholars, illiterates, with attributes spanning the entire spectrum of intellectual development. People are different not only because they happen to have different bodies, but also because they have different ideas. But we grow and our bodies change. We read new books, are exposed to new ideas, new circumstances, and our thoughts change. We are living in a constantly changing environment and keep changing ourselves. Nevertheless, with passion and conviction every moment we identify with things that will surely change the very next moment, our body and our ideas. We feel secure only when we understand what our senses perceive, only when we put objects in the cosmos in little drawers with labels on each drawer. Whatever does not fit into a predetermined drawer we are eager to discard, along with the person who brought it to our attention and disturbed our short-lived sense of balance. After all, Socrates was executed, and Galileo was persecuted for not conforming with the labeling system of their contemporaries.

In our search for the ultimate Truth of the world and ourselves, the mind plays not only a vital role but an indispensable one. First we use the mind to see out, and then we look in, focus our attention within, to understand and interpret what we perceive. Nevertheless, we do not use the mind's full potential as the vehicle to help us arrive at our goal, understanding ourselves and our world. Furthermore, what we perceive as "mind" may not be all there is in us. Maybe there is a threshold that one needs to cross in order to fully develop and experience one's own true nature. Maybe we need to be able to go beyond what the mind can capture. Going beyond the mind does not mean that we lose our mind. It means that we expand our understanding not only beyond what our senses can capture, but even beyond what our mind can reach and hold.

What is beyond the mind? What is the source of the mind? Here we give that beyond the name "metamind" to indicate that which is beyond and yet primary to the mind. What is its nature? Is it possible that the metamind is the same as the subtle sounds culminating in the metasound, the level of unmanifest vibration of Consciousness?

The Brain

Western science does not give a clear definition of the term "mind." In most scientific disciplines the mind is treated in an unclear way, as an entity not completely separate from the physical brain. In many cases, reference is made to the brain/mind with no distinction between the two. The brain is the physical apparatus through which the mind functions, as the light bulb is the physical apparatus through which electrical current passes and light shines. It would seem that equating the brain with the mind is like equating the light bulb with the electrical current and the phenomenon of light itself.

To understand what the relationship between the mind and the brain is, we must understand *both* the mind and the brain. Trying to unveil the mysteries and intricacies of the brain has been proved to be difficult and extremely complex. It leaves us with more unanswered questions than occur in almost any other scientific discipline. Brain researchers started by looking for models of the brain, systems to represent how the parts of the brain work. One of the early models was the automatic telephone exchange. In the early 1920s scientists thought that the brain is a complex web of nerves that reaches every part of the human body, as telephone lines reach into every part of a city. This early model did not last long because it became apparent that the brain and the nervous system are far more complex than any telephone exchange humans can build. Besides, the way in which electrical signals are carried in telephone wires is very different from the way signals are carried by nerve fibers (Weizenbaum, 1976).

In attempting to find a metaphor for the human brain, researchers developed automata, that might "act" and "behave" like a human being. Then came the computer age. After numerous attempts to automate many human functions, researchers started looking for anthropic elements in modern machines. The computer was first on the list.[1] Human behavior was analyzed in terms of heuristic systems in which problem-solving leads to self-education. The human vision was reduced into "pattern recognition" and "image compression." Computers were given names, even referred to as "he." Researchers tried to explain human behavior in a way that would fit into a computer structure. However, these attempts did not mean that computers function like humans as physicist Roger Penrose (1989) aptly demonstrated. After all, there is really no similarity between the neurons in a human brain and their associated synapses—there are roughly 10 trillion synapses in the brain or more than the total number of people who have walked on the earth since the human brain evolved to what it is now, 100,000 years ago—and the simple yes-or-no binary type bytes in an electronic computer. Nevertheless, there may be insights to gain if computational science makes real progress in research involving neural networks and parallel supercomputers, since certain aspects of these may also occur in the brain. For example, it now appears that many tasks are simultaneously distributed in different parts of the brain, as is the case with parallel machines.

Generally speaking, models are limited in scope and function by their very nature. Models cannot reveal anything more than what is already known. They help keep track of the behavior of interrelated parts but contain no original information which was not put into their designs from the beginning.

The concept of localized functions in the brain was widely accepted for many years in neurosurgery. Researchers believed that specific centers in the brain correspond with the functions of the human body: movement, hearing,

Hologram

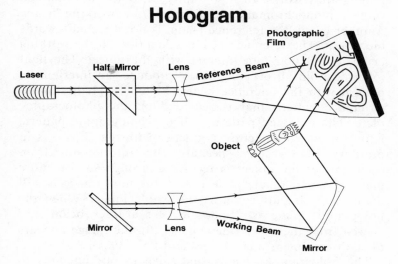

Figure 19. Schematic diagram of a hologram

vision, etc. Memory, they thought, works like a well organized library, with a complex cross-reference index. However, situations turned up that defied the localized concept of the brain. For example, people with severe brain damage from accidents were not handicapped the way localized theory predicted (Grof, 1985).

A decentralized concept for the brain started gaining supporters among brain researchers. In the mid-1960s a new paradigm emerged. Many scientists, among them Karl Pribram, introduced the "holographic brain" model (Briggs and Peat, 1984). This new model of the functioning of the brain was quite different from previous models. It did not try to simulate the brain by a machine. Also, a decentralized brain means that the various functions of the human body are not controlled and therefore do not depend on any one specific location in the brain, which required a completely new approach to the problem (Briggs and Peat, 1984).

The fundamental aspects of the holographic model of the brain are demonstrated in the way holographic photography works. In holography, an object is illumined with a monochromatic laser beam, the working beam. Another beam, the reference beam, is not directed towards the object. The reference beam is identical to the working beam, but it does not interact with the object. The light reflected from all over the object produces an interference pattern with the reference beam (Figure 19). It is this interference pattern that is recorded on the photographic plate. The recorded pattern, called a holographic pattern, is not in one-to-one correspondence with the object, as in ordinary photography, because the information from each part of the object is recorded throughout the entire plate. If a part of the plate is lost, the total image is still there, as each part contains the whole image. When the holographic plate is illuminated by a laser beam and viewed from the other side (Figure 20), the image appears to be three-dimensional (Briggs and Peat, 1984).

The holographic idea is suggestive in our attempts to understand the functionings of the brain. However, scientists still need to determine if the processes in our skulls are analogous to a holographic transformation.

One important member of our glandular system is the pineal complex of cells, located in the upper middle area of our brain. It seems to be the brain's ancient prototype. A major function of this structure, among many other important functions, is to govern a molecule called melanin.

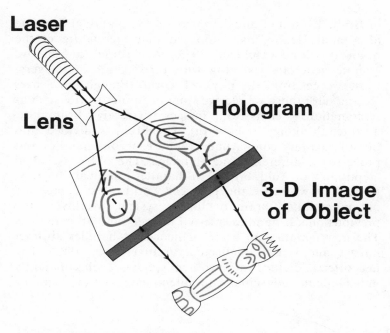

Figure 20. Production of a three-dimensional image by illuminating the holographic film with a laser beam

Melanin does extraordinary things: it acts like a transformer or translator of energies in our brain; it translates sound waves into light waves and vice versa; it transforms electric and magnetic energies into light and/or sound waves. All living forms have melanin. In our body melanin can be found in many areas, with heavy concentration in the brain, heart and genitals. It is also found in the skin, where it causes suntan. Some researchers believe that this molecule might be the link between mind and brain. Others feel that the light-sensitive molecule of melanin might be the holographic film in the brain (Pearce, 1985).

Research on the brain has not been the exclusive territory of neurosurgeons and research physicians. People from all branches of science have become involved: physicists, biologists, human development scientists, psychologists, to mention just a few. Paul McLean, chief of the Laboratory

of Brain Evolution and Behavior of the National Institute
of Mental Health, has proposed that the nature of the
brain is triune (McLean, 1973). According to him, we
operate generally speaking with three kinds of imagery:
those we get from the physical world, through our senses
(seeing out); those we receive from our inner world, such as
imagination, dreams; and images we receive from pure,
abstract thinking (looking in). The brain is divided into
three imaginary compartments, and each one handles and
processes a different kind of image. The oldest is called
"reptilian" or "old brain." It handles physical imagery;
through it we sense the physical world. Next comes the
old mammalian brain or limbic system, overlaying the
previous one. It handles internal imagery and all emotions.
The new mammalian brain or neocortex handles abstract
images and is our intellectual brain (Pearce, 1985). The
neocortex is divided into two hemispheres, each apparently
independently conscious and able to carry out the complex

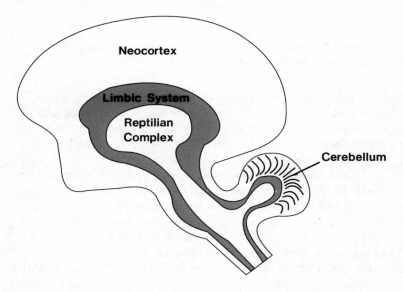

*Figure 21. Schematic diagram of the reptilian, old mammalian
brain or limbic system, and the new mammalian brain or
neocortex*

cognitive processes for which it is specialized. The left hemisphere is the main center for abstract semantic language and controls analytical functioning. The right hemisphere is primarily responsible for overall spatial construction, simple concrete language comprehension and nonverbal ideation.

The two hemispheres seem to operate in a complementary fashion: the functions of one seem to exclude the functions of the other, and yet both are needed for the brain to operate as a unit. Complementarity thus seems to operate at the most fundamental level in the physical hardware of our brains. This division of our brain according to the kinds of tasks performed may turn out to have a profound influence on the way we view the cosmos. Even though complementarity appears to be the fundamental principle on which the entire universe is based, we cannot be absolutely sure that it is nothing more than the reflection of the processes taking place in our brain. As quantum physics asserts, we cannot isolate external reality from the procedure through which this reality becomes known.

The brain may be viewed as a laboratory apparatus through which we can find out about our own reality as well as about what we may conveniently label as external reality (Wilber, 1982).

The Nature of the Mind (Western View)

Freud divided the human mind into three different sections: a. the id, or unconscious mind; b. the ego, or conscious mind; c. the superego. The id is the dark, primitive, instinctive part of our mind. Most of its contents are of a sexual nature, but not exclusively. It is the basement where we keep things from the past that we no longer use: urges, instincts, memories, past experiences. Everything in the unconscious belongs to us, and yet we do not want others to see it. We want to forget it. Therefore, we suppress it and do not allow it to come up. The content of the unconscious mind continually strives for expression, but the conscious mind prevents this. The ego is our conscious self, our personality. The superego is the repository of ideas, ideals, and the codes of morality imposed on us, during childhood, by our environment and without our own consent. One of Freud's greatest contributions was his realization that the more he tried to dig into his patient's unconscious mind, the stronger the patient would resist. He theorized that the resistance comes from the same forces which prevent patients from knowing the contents of their unconscious minds. Actually, he felt that these are the very same forces that abolished many thoughts into the unconscious mind.

Freud thought that the mind is divided into a number of different sections or compartments, each quite independent from the others and with very little communication between them. This idea is known as the dynamic conception of the human mind. All these different compartments belong to one of the three categories of unconscious mind, ego and superego (Gregory, 1987).

Freud was a medical man and was interested in diagnosing and treating illnesses. He thought that stresses from the conflict of interest between the unconscious mind and the ego are often the cause of illnesses. While feelings and thoughts from the unconscious struggle for expression, the forces of the conscious mind suppress them into "no existence." When the pressure becomes much too great, the patient becomes ill. If these hidden forces in the unconscious mind can be pulled back into the conscious mind, the illness is often relieved. This can be done by psychoanalysis.

Later Carl Jung, a student of Freud's, added the theory of the collective unconscious. It is a part of the psyche whose content has never been either conscious or in the contents of the unconscious mind, and therefore has not been individually acquired. The contents of the collective unconscious are essentially archetypes, a word derived from the Greek word *archetypon*. *Arche* means beginning, and *typon* means species or article. Therefore, archetypes are articles or species that existed before anything else, pre-existent forms. According to Jung, they have occurred in many cultures throughout history and have been recognized in other fields of thought. Researchers in mythology call them motifs; researchers in the psychology of "primitive" cultures call them representations collectives; students of comparative religion define them as categories of the imagination; other researchers call them elementary or primordial thoughts. It is interesting to note that the myths of each culture center on such archetypes. For example, the ancient Greek gods, in the light of these archetypes, appear as forces within nature as well as within ourselves. Thus myths have something powerful to teach us about the human psyche. According to Jung, these archetypes, as the content of the collective unconscious, are the same for everybody (Campbell, 1971). Jung himself summarized his thought (Campbell, 1971):

> My thesis, then is as follows: In addition to our immediate consciousness, which is of thoroughly personal nature and which we believe to be the only empirical psyche, there exists a second psychic system of a collective, universal and impersonal nature which is identical in all individuals. This collective unconscious does not develop individually but is inherited. It consists of pre-existent forms, the archetypes, which can only become conscious secondarily and which give definite form to certain psychic contents.

In the twelfth century, Averroes, a Muslim philosopher who lived in Spain, taught that some of our ideas are not necessarily our own but may be common to humanity. His view and Jung's implies that somewhere there is a pool of ideas, accessible to each of us. It is interesting to consider "where" this pool of common wealth is, and under what conditions we can gain access to it. In common everyday experience, we are not in constant free communication with it. Medical science has concluded that the seat of our awareness is the brain. Of course, our awareness is ours, and ours alone. So we expect it to be located somewhere in our bodies. However, since we all share the same collective unconscious it is not obvious to consider any part of our body as the seat of the collective unconscious. It is not like many different people having copies of the same book. It is like all people sharing the same book. The implications of this idea are beyond our normal perceptions and understanding of ourselves. Actually it revolutionizes both. We might, after all, not be as individualized as we think we are. However, in a way, the concept of the collective unconscious, as a part of everybody's reality, puts us all in the same boat. Most of us do not have the distinct experience of accessing this part of our psyche. Why do we not ordinarily use this personal and collective wealth? It may be that the creative process is a way in which we draw on the collective unconscious, that the "ah-ha" experience comes from this collective property. It seems from the stories of people who have suddenly gotten illuminating ideas that there are requirements for participating in the creative process. When one operates from this level everything comes effortlessly (Taylor, 1981). Sometimes answers arise in a very direct way, though usually they come symbolically and need interpretation. A typical example of this process is the well-known case of August Kekulé, the famous chemist who discovered the benzene ring:

> August Kekulé . . . was seized with the notion of a certain possible molecular combination not then extant. He pursued his new possibility with characteristic zeal and passion. He exhausted all resources; the answer eluded him. One day he sat down before his fireplace to get his mind off his obsession and drifted into reverie. And there before him, in a single second, appeared a ring of snakes with their tails in their mouths, forming a peculiar configuration. Eureka! He had his answer. . . . Kekulé had to take this dream-like metaphoric animal image and translate it into the language of chemistry. This gave the world . . . the benzene ring, the hexagonal molecular basis of all twentieth-century chemistry. . . . In an address to a scientific convention, Kekulé said: "Gentlemen, we must do more dreaming" (Pearce, 1985).

There are common characteristics in such cases: people work hard on their problem, be it personal or scientific. They think out and examine its every angle and keep working strenuously on the question. Then they leave the problem alone for a while. When they least expect it, the answer comes up. Often it takes strenuous effort to translate the insight from symbolic form into language that everyone understands. This process accounts for great insights and inventions that have changed our way of living, for the genius of Archimedes, Newton, Mozart, Kekulé and Einstein.

In Figure 22 we attempt to illustrate the steps of the creative process. This includes the primarily intellectual type involving creations such as new mathematical theories and new types of airplanes, as well as the artistic type involving such things as musical compositions. On the vertical axis is the degree of conscious creative awareness or creativity, labelling it C in arbitrary units. The scale plots the logarithm of C extending from high creativity states (positive C) to low creativity states (negative C). The average (say, zero level) refers to ordinary left-brain activity. The horizontal scale plots time in arbitrary units. As a person engaged in creative activity thinks of a problem and its solution, the C activity continues for some time hovering around the zero level or higher (we think of the problem and do tedious, preparatory work that allows the solution to present itself). As we go through many cycles

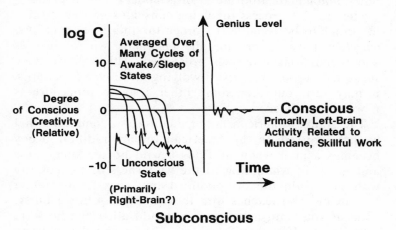

Figure 22. Schematic diagram plotting the logarithm of creativity involved in "solving a problem" as a function of time

of this activity, the process sinks back to the subconscious to negative values of log (C). We hypothesize that, although most conscious activity involves the left brain hemisphere in some way, as we continue to think of the problem and its solution, and particularly as we switch to sleep over many cycles of this activity, the process switches to the right hemisphere. We may, of course, go back to more and more cycles of conscious activity where the logarithm of C is hovering around the zero level but these cycles continue to deposit information in the repository of the subconscious mind, which is associated with the right brain. This hypothesis may eventually be testable by monitoring brain-wave activity, although it would require the isolation of brain-wave patterns associated with a particular creative activity.

Eventually the solution "presents itself," as happened to Kekule, and many others, in the ah-ha moment when the solution in its entirety becomes clear in a single moment. At that point creativity reaches its height. Perhaps then both hemispheres become coordinated into an undivided whole. Then the creative process switches back to "translating" the solution to ordinary forms, such as musical notes, mathematical formulas or a model of the airplane.

The creative process involving conscious awareness may in principle be testable. In order for this to happen, *we, ourselves*, have to become the *laboratory* where theories about conscious processes are tested. Although we have suggested a possible test involving brain-wave patterns, it may turn out that some other testable procedure is more appropriate.

The Native American father might know something that we have missed. In the American Indian tradition, a boy becomes a man when he finds a wild horse. After hours and hours of wandering in the wilderness of his country with no result, the disappointed boy goes to his father for advice, who teaches him the way to look for a horse: "Son, if you want a horse, you should allow the horse to come to you. You should feel like a horse, you should think like a horse, you should eat and drink like a horse, you should dream like a horse." And, the story goes on, one day after months of practicing his father's advice, the son opens his eyes and finds that a horse is next to him. Now, he is a man. Maybe this is the key: don't focus on the answer; focus on the problem. We must submerge ourselves in the problem, in every aspect of it, again and again, for as long as it takes to completely absorb it. We become the problem the way that the Indian boy became the horse. The process might not be exclusively intellectual. We are preparing ourselves for the answer to flow to us freely and effortlessly. Maybe that is what the Indian father meant when he advised his son to "allow" the horse to come to him.

Accessing the collective unconscious is a process that needs to be ignited. Firing desire in the heart seems to be the necessary spark. Without that the collective unconscious remains closed. Only very few obtain the privilege of knowing what is in there.

No general understanding has been reached on the important issue of mind-brain. Biochemist Paul Weiss, a Nobel laureate, concludes that all we can say about the brain-mind problem is that consciousness does not simply reduce to the sum of activities in the brain cells; the whole is definitely more than the sum of its parts. We do not know how the brain functions. We can only theorize about it. We do not and probably cannot all agree on the nature of the mind. We do not have the faintest idea of how our material body relates and interacts with our immaterial mind. There are many interpretations of the word "mind": scientists tend to interpret it in terms of matter and mechanistic systems; psychologists define it according to the school of thought they belong to (Goleman and Davidson, 1979). Philosophers have pondered this question for over two thousand years. René Descartes, philosopher and mathematician, believed that the body and the mind do not relate at all, do not interact. They are like two well synchronized clocks that work independently. Descartes' dictum "I think therefore I exist" is quoted as summarizing Western scientific dualism. Now old dualism has been abandoned, for the evidence to the contrary has been overwhelming through the years. Our material brain and body do react with our immaterial mind, but we do not know how.

If the seat of the mind is not the brain, as scientists in the West are beginning to suspect, then the concept of non-locality has to be reconsidered with reference to the brain and the mind (Walker, 1961). This concept first introduced in quantum theory is now appearing in a different field. Experience shows that when a concept or principle comes up in different domains, there is a good chance that it might be more universal than initially believed.

There is good evidence that something exists at the mental level beyond our ordinary, individual minds, and it can be tapped in the creative process. Jung called it the "collective unconscious," but we prefer the term "metamind." This term indicates that it is beyond and beneath—the source of the ordinary mind. Collective unconscious does not convey the idea of the source, which is most important (Blakemore, 1977).

Television provides an analogy of the entire system and process. The set is a receiver, hardware, and by itself cannot give us information about the show we are watching, the commercials, the time slot, the director, etc. All these are external to the way a TV works. Without the physical TV we could not receive any show, but without all the stations and their broadcasts, the set would display only static. Both the set and the broadcasting process require electromagnetic energy to work. In this analogy, the set represents the physical brain, the shows and commercials represent the activity of the mind, and the electromagnetic energy symbolizes that which allows the brain and mind to work. In pursuing this analogy further, the electromagnetic energy stands for the underlying "stuff," the metamind, needed for our mind to work.

The Nature of the Mind (Eastern View)

The Eastern traditions view the mind in a completely different way from the West. According to Swami Muktananda (1976): "The mind is the body of the Self," and also "the mind is nothing but a throb of consciousness." Swami Muktananda was a psychologist as well as head of a spiritual lineage. In Muktananda's tradition psychologists are sages, men and women of a rare wisdom, called Siddhas, Self-realized Masters. These are beings who not only have achieved high states of human evolution, but are able to propel others toward them.

Yoga means union, and the goal of yoga is to achieve union with the highest consciousness. Christianity expresses a similar idea in the term, "mystical union" while Buddhists call it "Nirvana." Although there are many different paths to this union, the Indian philosophies have a common concept that: God is already *in us* in the form of us (Muktananda, 1978). We all, with no exceptions, are made of the same stuff, and that stuff is energy, conscious energy. Some call it Supreme Intelligence, some Creative Intelligence, and others God.

In the philosophies of the East, it is stated that we all are this Cosmic Consciousness, even though we normally do not relate to ourselves as such. We identify with the boundaries of our bodies (Yukteswar, 1984). We understand ourselves as separate and different from everyone and everything else, as "skin encapsulated egos." We limit ourselves because we consider that we are limited. In the Eastern view, we practice yoga not to attain God, but to purify and control the mind, in order to experience the God already within us. We practice yoga in order to realign our understanding of ourselves, so we can experience our godhood, our own divinity.

Over 1500 years ago, Patanjali, a great Indian sage, wrote a series of aphorisms to explain yoga to his contemporaries (Prabhavananda and Isherwood, 1953). No other work before or since has succeeded so well in clarifying what yoga is, its aims, its methods, its powers, and the nature of the liberation it affords.

According to Patanjali, the mind is made up of three elements: a. *manas* b. *buddhi* c. *ahamkara.* Manas is the recording faculty which receives impressions gathered by the senses from the outside world. Buddhi is the discriminative faculty which classifies these impressions and reacts to them. Ahamkara is the ego-sense which claims these impressions as its own and stores them up as individual knowledge (Prabhavananda and Isherwood, 1953). Patanjali does not mean that the mind is divided into three different sections. He was referring to three different functions of the mind. Swami Muktananda clarifies this point when he speaks of the "movement of the mind" (Muktananda, 1981):

> When the mind is filled with thoughts, it is called manas.
> When it makes decisions, it is called buddhi, the intellect.
> When it takes on the feeling of "I"-ness, it is called ahamkara, the ego.

The purpose of yoga, according to Patanjali, is to accomplish the stilling of the modifications of the mind or thought waves. The entire system of Patanjali deals with the subject of stilling the thought waves of the mind (Hariharananda, 1983). He provided a classical metaphor for this concept. Our mind is like a lake. When there are ripples, thoughts, we cannot clearly see our image because the image is distorted. What we see on the surface of the water does not look like us. If we had never seen ourselves in a mirror, only on the surface of a rippled lake, we could not imagine how we really are. When the water is still with no ripples, we can see ourselves as we are. The same is true for the mind. The afflictions of the mind, the thoughts that constantly come and go, prevent us from experiencing who we really are. We identify with our thoughts and feelings and understand ourselves as such. Negative and limiting thoughts and feelings make us believe that we are limited. Our true image can be reflected only in a steady and thought-free mind which lets us experience our true nature, our own Self.

Emptying thoughts from the mind does not mean that we make the mind inert and dull. It does not mean that we become passive, mindless or stupid, or lose our personality, any more than a calm lake without ripples loses its identity and quality as a lake. We do not lose our mind if we clean it up from the unnecessary inner chattering that goes on all the time. On the contrary, we make our mind strong. As long as we identify with our thoughts, our mind is very weak, because it is scattered in many different directions.

A weak mind makes us run after sense pleasures against our best interest with no control, and in extreme cases it addicts us to food, alcohol, tobacco or drugs. But if we focus the mind in one direction, we can accomplish a lot because then the mind has tremendous power. The rays of the sun focused through a lens on one spot can start a fire. A mind free of its modifications is clear and can allow us to experience what is underneath: the metamind, the source of the mind.

The focus of the Eastern psychologists, the sages and teachers of yoga, has been totally different. They had a clear understanding of the mind and its limitations. They formulated their understanding from concrete experiences. Eastern psychology is scientific, but not in the sense of Western science. The apparatus, the field of study and the laboratory are all within us; in fact they are us. The Eastern masters of yoga were concerned with the metamind because they knew from firsthand experience that there is where the secret of the mystery of the mind is to be found. Friedrich von Schiller, German philosopher, put it aptly in his poem "The Sentences of Confucius" (Heisenberg, 1971): "The full mind is alone the clear, and truth dwells in the deeps." The "deep" here is the metamind, beyond the surface of ordinary awareness. The "full mind," far from being filled with the useless, ordinary inner chattering, reveals a vast underlying reservoir of awareness, but only when the thought-waves subside. At the core of the "deep," in the metamind, is where the Self resides. Here the emptiness becomes infinity. The true source of the mind is infinite, beyond space and time, without attributes. The Indian philosophers/sages term it the Atman, which in the West is translated as the "Self." The term is somewhat un-fortunate because it immediately brings to mind the personal, limited self, the ego. Unlike the self, the Self can never be studied as an object. We think of our egos, our feelings, our thoughts as objects of perception, but, truly speaking, we can never define the Self; we can only experience it. The Self is the ultimate Subject, the source of the objectified mind, the core of the metamind, self-luminous and purely subjective. The mind is none of these.

According to the philosophy of Kashmir Shaivism, in

the 36 steps of the unfoldment of the cosmos, the mind originates from the ego level. At this level all the unlimited attributes of Paramashiva have been constricted through the veiling powers of Maya, illusion. Paramashiva, now becoming the individual human being through a series of self-imposed contractions and limitations, becomes confined. Its eternal existence becomes finite and time comes into the picture. The individual human being is subject to birth and death. The omniscient Paramashiva becomes a human being with very limited and superficial knowledge that comes primarily from information and data perceived through the senses. The understanding is shallow. The omnipotent Paramashiva becomes confined to a restricted spectrum of activities; there is only so much that humans can do. And finally the omnipresent Paramashiva becomes bounded by space and time. No ordinary human can be physically present in two places at the same time. However, saints of all the major traditions, after they transcended their human consciousness, have exhibited the unlimited attributes of Paramashiva. There are numerous records, in all traditions of the East and the West, of saints being seen in different places at the same time. There are also records of sages who could materialize objects, fly, and do things considered "miraculous" for an ordinary human being.

In the West one particular function of ordinary mind has been glorified and made the basis of all knowledge and science: the logical, analytic, mathematical aspect. This seductive power of analytical thinking, with its associated immense scientific successes, is nevertheless limited. In the East this aspect of the mind is recognized as a limited functioning of buddhi, the intellect. It cannot be the answer to all our questions, because most of the time we are not in that logical, analytical frame of mind.

> The truth is that we are all inclined to flatter ourselves—
> despite our daily experience to the contrary—that we spend
> our time thinking logical, consecutive thoughts. In fact,
> most of us do no such thing. Consecutive thought about
> any one problem occupies a very small proportion of our
> waking hours. More usually, we are in a state of reverie—a
> mental fog of disconnected sense-impressions, irrelevant

memories, nonsensical scraps of sentences from books and newspapers, little darting fears and resentments, physical sensations of discomfort, excitement or ease (Prabhavananda and Isherwood, 1953).

How can we stop the ceaseless inner chattering, and make the mind strong? Patanjali gives the answer: practice and detachment. Here Patanjali means spiritual practices. There are many different spiritual practices to choose from, based on one's temperament. Patanjali considers the best exercise for the mind to be the development of a constant awareness of one's identity with the Truth, the constant remembrance of *I am That*, I am pure Consciousness. As one practices awareness of unity, little by little the modifications of the mind cease. However, Patanjali recognizes that not everyone has a mind strong enough to maintain this constant awareness. For this reason he gives a variety of techniques, so the aspirant can choose ones most suitable for him or her.

Among all the practices, a very useful one is mantra repetition. The scriptures say, "Mantra is God" (Singh, 1980a). Repeating a mantra eventually makes one aware of this as being true. If we are called "stupid" we get angry because we identify with the word. If we call ourselves "God," in time we will identify with God. If we do this for a long period of time, the mind merges into the mantra and becomes one with the Self.

One of the aphorisms in *Shiva Sutras*, the famous text of Kashmir Shaivism, says, "The mind is mantra" (Singh, 1979a). The mind in this case should be understood to be the mind which is turned within. It then becomes a throb or pulsation of pure Consciousness (spanda). In this sense the mind is nothing but mantra—the pure liberating power of God. As we saw before, we should not think of mantra as merely sound. In its pure sense it is the very light of Consciousness which illumines everything that the Consciousness reflects and takes the form of.

According to this view, the mind can be trained. Through specific, regular, consistent and persistent practice, we can direct our mind any way we want. Ultimately, this leads to control of the mind. In the West, we think of the mind as something almost uncontrollable and outside of us. When we have negative thoughts about other people, we feel that the thoughts were stimulated by the particular person and we are not responsible for them. This is absurd. Our thoughts are created in our minds and are ours and nobody else's. We have full and complete responsibility for them. We live with an absurd attitude about them because we do not understand the nature of the mind.

In the East thoughts are considered reflections of a state of mind. The mind's nature is to create thoughts constantly, as the ocean's nature is to create waves. There are no good or bad waves. There are no good or bad thoughts. There are only thoughts that bring us closer to the inner core of the metamind, and thoughts that take us away from it. Thoughts of love and friendship make us feel good because they bring us closer to their essence, which is pure, selfless love. Christ, too, taught selfless love.

Eastern yoga is not "positive thinking," which is an artificial attitude. The entire universe is based on duality. Life is full of pleasant and unpleasant situations, joys and sorrows, triumphs and tragedies. That is how this cosmos was created; it is based on duality. The coin always has two sides. One cannot have one without the other. This is another case of complementarity. Yoga does not aim to remove the unpleasant situations or thoughts. It aims to help remove the coin of duality altogether. This means that one can face both pleasant and unpleasant situations without being crushed by either. It means that when the mind is strong, neither calamities nor good fortune can create turmoil in the heart or chaos in the mind. A clear and calm mind is a prerequisite for an appropriate decision, no matter what is happening in the surroundings. This is the state for which Patanjali and yoga aim. A great Teacher once said that only in shallow water can a fish make big waves. Only in a weak mind can any situation create turmoil.

Patanjali considered spiritual practices, such as meditation, chanting, praying, going to church or temple, selfless work, important, but he considered the practice of nonattachment equally important. Spiritual practices without the practice of nonattachment can be extremely dry, frustrating and dangerous. Detachment is the exercise of discrimination. It means consciously choosing between what brings us closer to the inner Self and what does not. Patanjali considered the practice of detachment indispensably linked with spiritual practices. He put both in the same aphorism. According to him both are needed to still the modifications of the mind.

Trying to still the mind in a forceful and rigid way would be like trying to hold a wild horse still. The horse will react violently and there is no way that one can overpower it. Similarly, if one tries always to be "good" and not have any "bad" thoughts, one becomes very judgmental towards others and oneself. Nobody can avoid "bad" thoughts because it is the nature of the mind to produce thoughts. Trying to do so will cause resistance the way a wild horse will resist being kept still.

During spiritual practice failure is bound to come, particularly in the beginning. If we are attached to the immediate results of our practices, then we cannot take this kind of failure. Patanjali does not teach people to become puritant, dry, unhappy individuals. His system and yoga practice aim to make us free from the torture of the mind. Nonattachment is freedom from the bondage of desire, whether for food, material gain, or ambitions such as gaining fame or being constantly "good." Dropping attachments is not an easy task. It is accomplished gradually and is a slow process. Patanjali teaches that by not identifying with thoughts and emotions one becomes free from the afflictions of an impure mind. There is nothing wrong with the mind itself, but it is tainted by wrong understanding and desires. Through the mind we identify with the limitations of the physical body and consider ourselves bounded (Prabhavananda and Isherwood, 1953).

In the Eastern tradition there are no sinners; there is no judgment, because there is no sin except ignorance. If one practices nonattachment and stills the modifications of the mind, then the truth will be revealed from within. The darkness of ignorance will disappear. Nonattachment does not mean that we become indifferent or selfish, that our lives become dull and boring since the fire of desire has been extinguished. It means exactly the opposite, that one becomes freer every time an unnecessary desire is conquered. It means that one is able to love for the sake of love and not for selfish reasons. One loves another not because of beauty, intelligence, money, social prestige, etc., but for what that person is. Those at the Christ level of consciousness can love so-called "ugly," "poor," "dirty," "criminal" individuals as they are. That is the level of consciousness to which these practices lead us: the Christ within. It is only when one is free from all the unnecessary, ego-oriented, petty desires, that one reaches the ultimate heights: the Divinity within.

The mind is an instrument in this process, which cannot even be started outside the realm of the mind. In the Shavaite philosophy *Chiti*, the female creative aspect of God, descending from the plane of pure Consciousness, becomes the mind by contracting in accord with the object perceived (Singh, 1980a). But Shaivism and Patanjali held that the mind is pure, undifferentiated Consciousness which has contracted itself to assume the form of the object perceived. Western philosophers and psychologists have not been able to grasp the nature of the mind in its entirety.

Indian philosophies and yoga are characterized by practical guidance, as well as a philosophical approach to life. They are not mere thought creations. Spiritual practices and the practice of nonattachment are the keys to Patanjali's yoga. Most of the rest of the aphorisms are instructions and techniques on how to achieve the state of equanimity or the state of nonattachment. The *Mahabarata,* the *Bhagavad Gita,* Kashmir Shaivism, Vedanta and Patanjali all teach one how to become continuously and permanently happy, no matter what happens in the surroundings (Bahadur, 1979).

Most scholars of the Indian tradition accept Patanjali as an authority on yoga and a great sage. It is said that he codified ancient teachings and set them down as the *Yoga Sutras* after he mastered his own mind. These sutras are not religion but genuine psychology. Only those who have explored the mind and transcended it can explain what the mind is and understand how it works. Patanjali explains not only these, but also how the mind troubles us, how we can control it and the state of those who have done so (Hariharananda, 1981).

In the West, we tend to believe that the brain is the seat of the mind. The Eastern sages believe that the mind is centered in the heart, and in meditation that area becomes still. Swami Muktananda, in one of his talks about the mind, said that when people have terrible shocks, they get heart failure, not explosions in their brains! Whatever turmoil is created by thoughts is experienced in the heart (Muktananda, 1980).

Ramakrishna, another contemporary Indian Master, underwent an operation for cancer without anesthesia. During the operation he continued teaching and discussing with his students, who were present in the operating room. The doctors asked him how he was able to do this. He said that he withdrew his mind from the part of his body that was under surgery and did not experience pain. The heart is the main location of the mind, but the rest of the body is not considered mindless. The same view is held by the Buddhists. Their view about the nature of the mind is very similar (Gyatso, 1984):

> . . . the conventional nature of the mind is clear light, and thus defilements do not reside in the very nature of the mind; defilements are adventitious, temporary, and can be removed. From the ultimate point of view the nature of the mind is its emptiness of inherent existence. If afflictive emotions, such as hatred, were in the very nature of the mind, then from its inception the mind would always have to be hateful, for instance, since that would be its nature. However, that this is not so is obvious; it is only under certain circumstances that we become angry, and when those circumstances are not present, anger is not generated. This indicates that the nature of hatred and the nature of mind are different even if in a deeper sense they both are consciousness thus having a nature of luminosity and knowing.

The similarities between Buddhism and Hinduism, regarding the nature of the mind, are startling. Even though there are many paths and traditions, there is only one Truth.

When the mind turns within, it becomes tuned with the Self and reflects the Self's infinite power. The mind is instrumental in that search of Truth. Truth is not in the mind, but through the use of a mantra or creative contemplation, the mind creates and becomes the link with those levels of Reality where Truth is found.

When the mind turns outward, it takes the form of the perceived object. As long as the mind is focused on the outside world, it becomes many different things, some of them conflicting. It becomes restless. Lasting contentment does not exist. There is a story of a monk who had nothing, not even a blanket. One day he thought it would be nice to have a blanket. A little later someone gave him a blanket, but mice came and made holes in it. Then the monk thought that it would be nice to have a cat to chase away the mice. Somebody gave him a cat. A little later he thought that it would be nice to have a cow to give milk for the cat, who was chasing the mice. Before he knew it, he forgot his search for the Truth.

When the mind is focused inwardly it becomes capable of reaching other levels of awareness. Turning within means turning the attention from the external world to the inner world. A specific sound or image or feeling can carry the mind and the awareness of the aspirant to the end of the road, to the final destination, the experience of our Real Nature. Turning within has always been used in the process of the spiritual journey in the major religious traditions.

Summary

In the West, we are aware of the brain/mind system, but we do not really know how the brain works and do not fully understand the mind. There are different theories about the brain, one of the most recent being the holographic theory. This theory supports decentralization of the mind, but further research is needed before we can conclude that the brain does indeed function like a hologram. The nature of the mind seems to be a mystery to psychologists, psychiatrists and human developmentalists who deal with it. Though mind is characterized as "non-body," we can deal with its functions, intricacies and tricks. Different schools of psychology explain the mind in different ways. Sigmund

Freud's model contains three sections: the unconscious mind, the conscious mind or ego, and the superego. Carl Jung added the concept of the collective unconscious though some schools do not accept this concept. As of now, we do not really know how the brain works, and we do not know what the mind is or how it functions. The various theories mostly leave us with more questions than answers.

In the East, sages teach about the mind with a certainty that is startling by our standards. There are no theories about the brain, which is treated as a part of the physical body. The nature of the mind is explained in a very direct way through the understanding brought about by personal experience. Saints, sages and seers throughout the ages have experienced their minds as pure creative energy, God, who has willingly assumed limitations and become the contracted energy of the mind.

The mind is our worst enemy and our best friend. It is our worst enemy because, when focused on the external physical world, it tortures us by constantly giving birth to numerous thoughts and desires. It makes us happy or miserable; when we identify with the afflictions of the mind we ride on a roller coaster with no control of what is coming next. Further, the mind projects its inner state to the outer world and makes us perceive the world as independent of our inner state.

The mind is our best friend because, when focused within, it allows us to experience what is beneath and beyond it, the metamind, our true nature, our Self. When the modifications of the mind are stilled, then the metamind is revealed, and the light of pure Consciousness, which is the Self, shines through. The Eastern psychologists provide a step-by-step system for stilling the modifications of the mind.

Focusing the attention on our inner world of perceptions is a way of experiencing other levels of awareness in most traditions.

6
The Mystical Experience: Looking In

Again, the mystics of many centuries, independently, yet in perfect harmony with each other have described, each of them the unique experience of his or her life in terms that can be condensed in the phrase: DEUS FACTS SUM (I have become God).

Erwin Schrödinger

In all traditions and at all times there have lived certain strange beings. Outwardly they appear to be ordinary people. Some have families and jobs; some live as monks or nuns. Some live like beggars; others like kings. Some live as recluses in mountains, deserts or forests, away from cities. Others act like madmen, always intoxicated. Despite their outward differences and manners, they share the same inner state. Their gaze is always turned within. They live in the world, yet they are not of this world. They experience the Divine within themselves. God is not some far-off transcendent principle for them, to be known only after death. God is as real as their own breath. They live in God, experience God, and eventually merge into God.

These people are known by different names: saints, sages, philosophers, religious leaders, yogis, masters, great beings, perfected beings, God-realized men and women, prophets, mystics. Their contemporaries sense something different about them. Yet more often than not they are misunderstood. Some have been treated harshly, tortured or even put to death; they have been crucified, hung, burned, given poison to drink, all for the same reason. They lived in a state their contemporaries could not comprehend, even though they tried to show that there is something much greater than ordinary awareness.

Yet if it were not for these very saints and mystics who so unsettle us, there would be no religions to steady us when our control over our lives slips away. Religions are sustained because of the living experiences of the saints, because of their deep inner journeys of faith that allow them to find harmony and guidance from within. Without their lives and examples, religious institutions would be empty structures. Yet, the message of most religions has been misunderstood. In the hard task of translating a mystical experience into a trackable path, many truths of the inner transformation have been lost. Few of us trust venturing wholeheartedly into this transformational process; most of us look for safe paths to aim us toward it. So we get involved in establishing "right" and "wrong" paths and pointing up differences and divisions rather than the unity of the inner experience. From this mentality, religions have often developed into narrow self-justifying dogmas or sects that have done more to divide humans than unite them with central mystical truths. And so, "in the name of God" humans have pitted themselves against one another over differing dogmas.

Religions are divided, not because of the rightness or wrongness of dogmas, but because of ignorance of the common mystical experience underlying them. We cannot just follow a doctrine and overlook the inner transformational experience. The truth of all religions can be found only within, and for this to occur we must explore and know who we truly are. In most traditions the human subtle anatomy, the "world within," is described in veiled and poetic terms. What follows is a brief examination of the subtle anatomy of a human being according to specific mystical traditions. It will become apparent that, despite all the differences of expression among traditions, they hold some deep principles in common.

The Human Subtle Anatomy

Since the time of the Renaissance, the tendency in the West has been towards a primary emphasis on the physical body. Humans in the modern world tend to identify with the physical body as a unique expression of their individual personalities. Yet, the message from the East, and primarily from India, is that the physical body is only one aspect of our being. It is the body in which we live and have experience in the waking state, but the waking state is not the only state we experience. We all are aware of the dream state, but we do not associate any specific "body" with it. In the East, the dream state is associated with a subtle energy state. In fact, the Eastern sages describe four human bodies, each with a different state of awareness. These subtle bodies support one another and together support the physical body. We, therefore, as human beings are not just the physical body, just as the tree above the ground is not the entire tree. As the tree could not be alive or whole without its roots, the physical body could not be alive without the other energy bodies.

The reality we live in when we are awake can be called the empirical state, in which one experiences the world through the senses. Since food sustains the physical body, the Eastern sages named the body of this state the "food sheath." According to Muktananda (1980) in deep states of meditation the physical body appears as formless red light that is the same for everybody with no individual characteristics. Its size is the same as the physical body, and its seat is in the eyes. It is associated with the vibrational energy of the letter *A*.

The next state of consciousness is the dream state, and it is associated with the subtle body into which our consciousness is projected during sleep. This sleep state is illusory because dreams and imaginary objects disappear with the end of the dream fantasy. The sustainer of the subtle body is air. According to Muktananda in meditation the subtle body is experienced as small as a human thumb. Its color is white, its seat is in the throat, and it is associated with the vibrational energy of the letter *U*.

The next state is deep and dreamless sleep, associated with the causal body. Bliss is its sustainer, the sense of refreshment one experiences after a good night's sleep.

This bliss can become an obstacle of further development, and like the other sheaths, eventually has to be transcended. The size of the causal body is experienced in meditation as a human fingertip. Its color is black, and its seat is in the middle of the eyebrows. It is associated with the vibrational energy of the letter *M* (Muktananda, 1978).

The last state is the transcendental one in which the true nature of ultimate Reality is perceived directly. In this state Reality is not a mere intellectual understanding but a direct experience. This Reality is absolute: it contains no differentiation, no duality and no subject-object divisions. It is true unity and wholeness, undivided wholeness. The associated body is termed the supercausal body and in many traditions is called the soul. Achieving the transcendental state is the purpose of human birth. Once experienced in meditation, it transforms one forever. Its size is that of an extremely small seed; its color is blue. In India it is often called the "blue pearl" (Muktananda, 1978) and is the jewel of all spiritual experiences. Its seat is at the top of the head inside the luminous triangle of the "thousand petal" *sahasrara* or chakra, whose activation marks the end of spiritual journey (Plate VI). Saints in all traditions have been depicted with a halo around their heads representing the light of the sahasrara.

These subtle energy bodies cannot be seen or experienced in a normal state of waking awareness. In deep meditation they are experienced as pure light, with specific colors but no specific features. They represent different states of consciousness rather than physical entities. During meditation, the awareness of the aspirant is projected onto these states. Countless testimonies of sages and saints who have experienced these bodies reveal them as gateways to different "worlds" of reality, which the aspirant can visit and explore. That is what is meant by turning within. Turning the attention and focus of the mind inward to its source enables the aspirant to experience the absolute Reality while still living in the relative world of everyday life. For sages in all traditions, the external physical world, which human beings are trying to understand, measure and describe scientifically, is only a reflection of the Absolute. Unless one experiences the transcendent state, which is the foundation of all states, the other states of dream and physical reality can be easily misunderstood and misinterpreted.

The most important aspect of the human subtle anatomy is *kundalini*, a term found in most schools of thought of India (White, 1979). It is called by different names in other traditions: the Kon tribe of the Kalahari call it the *N-um*. The ancient Sumerians called it *Ningish Zeda*, which literally means the "Serpent God," and the Mayans called it *Kukulcan*. Kundalini means "the coiled one." It is the universal energy which in its outer functions sustains life in every individual, though its inner spiritual nature usually remains dormant. It cannot be found in the physical body. Often experienced in deep states of meditation, it appears as a brilliant, shimmering light energy. It is coiled 3½ times at the base of the spine in the subtle body, hence it derives its name. Often, as in Egyptian and Hindu art, it is represented as a coiled snake or a cobra, the king of all snakes. In its outer aspect, kundalini sustains us through all biological processes. In its inner aspect, kundalini is the same energy that brings about the creation of all worlds. In its universal function it is the Supreme Creative aspect of Universal Consciousness, Paramashiva, cosmic creative energy that becomes everything and anything in the manifold Universe. In our subtle body this energy lies dormant, waiting to be awakened in the aspirant for his or her return journey back to the transcendental state in the infinite light of sahasrara.

The concept of universal energy or Kundalini is found in all spiritual traditions, although often alluded to in apocryphal terms and under different names. In the Chinese tradition, the universal energy is known as *Chi*. In the Japanese tradition as *Ki*. In Christianity as the *Holy Spirit*. Different traditions, different paths, different cultures all refer in different ways to the same basic foundation of all creative energy.

The subtle energy bodies do not have veins and arteries, bones, blood and body fluids. They are pure energy circulating through millions of subtle channels called the *nadis*.

The awakened kundalini spreads through the nadis and purifies all bodies. As the bodies are freed from blockages, a new dimension of human perception opens. One becomes certain, beyond intellectual pronouncements, that all knowledge is contained within. This "turning within" or looking in is the seat of evolution for the human species.

The nadis, as they cross each other, form knots or junctures of subtle energy. These junctures are literally wheels of power, often described as lotuses because they resemble the lotus flower. In many traditions they are termed spiritual centers and in Sanskrit are known as the *chakras*. We have thousands of chakras in our subtle bodies. All of them are significant and have an important function to perform in our spiritual evolvement. There are seven major chakras, that are the subtle counterparts of our ductless glands. All seven of these chakras can be experienced in deep states of meditation. Their functions are veiled in symbolism. Various colors, shapes, animals, deities, mantras, numbers of petals are attributed to them; the intricacies of the chakras never end. Many works have been written on kundalini and the chakras, and the reader is encouraged to read some of them and explore the significance of the chakras (Avalon, 1974; Mookerjee, 1986; Radha, 1978; White, 1979).

One of the chakras is the *muladhara*, which is situated at the end of the subtle spine. Kundalini remains dormant in the muladhara until it is awakened, either through spiritual practices or by a Master who has the appropriate knowledge. Another chakra, the *anahata* chakra, lies at the level of the subtle heart. When the kundalini energy purifies this center, the aspirant experiences waves of love. The journey ends at the *sahasrara*, at the top of the head (Eliade, 1969; Muktananda, 1979; Radha, 1978). There the active energy of Universal Consciousness, often referred to as the female aspect, unites with the primordial Being, the male aspect of Universal Consciousness (Radha, 1978; Avalon, 1974).

Aligned along our subtle spine, the chakras represent milestones of spiritual development. They are stepping stones for the kundalini energy to climb, to purify, to open, to expand in its journey to the ultimate destination of complete spiritual unfoldment. Spiritual development is nothing other than this inner journey from the bottom of the spine to the top of the head. It is a journey without distance, all within! One need not move an inch to experience Absolute Reality within one's own being.

Turning within is also an eternal journey, for eternity is not a long period of time. It is no time, where time collapses. The physical body is subject to time: we are born, grow older and die as time goes on. Time, however, does not exist in the same way at other levels of consciousness. It becomes distorted at the subtle dream state, seems to disappear at the deep sleep state and becomes eternity at the transcendent state.

As the kundalini climbs the ladder of evolution along the spine, the journey becomes more and more refined and also more and more difficult and demanding. The temptations of the ego become subtle and harder to resist. Many begin the journey, but very few go far along the upward spiritual ladder. Even fewer reach the top. Complete, absolute impeccability in thoughts, emotions and feelings are needed for that. Nothing can be hidden; there are no secrets between the aspirant and his or her own inner energy, the kundalini.

When the journey is completed, the aspirant's inner state is completely transformed. How to facilitate that process is the subject of all mystical traditions, the true subject of all religions, and the intent of all great spiritual teachers throughout all times.

The Mystical Way

The meaning of the words "mystic" and "mystery" can be found in their common root, which in Greek means "to keep silence." The way of the mystic is to turn within. In closing the outer eyes, the mystic perceives an entire Universe within. Eventually the outer Universe is realized as one and the same with the inner: both are emanations of the Divine. When we open to full conscious awareness of the Divine, then closing the eyes and the withdrawing of the senses are not necessary for direct experience of Divinity within all.

Though mysticism is often identified with such areas as occultism—or fascination with astral levels, the levels near the physical level—and astrology, actually mysticism and occultism are diametrically opposite to each other. True mystics take pains to point out the differences between their experiences and occult practices dealing with lower level "astral" energies. Mystical knowledge is beyond fascination with the supernatural and manipulating power toward some end. It takes us to the inner Light, where we realize that God is acting through us and as us. It is beyond ego orientation.

Within mysticism, there are various traditions and paths which can be broken down into two main types: the mysticism of the transcendent or infinite Divine, and the mysticism of the personal form of the Divine (Avalon, 1974). All mystical traditions contain both of these elements, although usually one predominates (Eliade, 1969). Examples of the former are the system of Neoplatonism, as taught by the ancient Greek philosopher Plotinus, and the system of India's great sage Shankara. The latter type includes most Christian and Muslim mystical traditions. Some paths emphasize total merging with the Divine, while others emphasize knowledge or deep understanding of God. Despite the apparent differences, the ultimate goal of all mystical traditions is the same: union with the Divine within. That union takes the form of pure love, love for the sake of love only, love for the essence of all creation, which is perceived as emanating from the Absolute, God. Quite often we encounter a description of that union in terms of heightened human love, in the poetic terms of a lover and a beloved. Yet mystics point out that in that ultimate union there is no distinction between the subject and the object, between the lover and the beloved (Yogananda, 1952). There is true union, and only love remains. Mystics lose their own identity and identify with God, with Love. The union takes on an intensely personal, yet suprapersonal relationship. The infinite and the personal become one. Whatever path mystics follow to reach divine union, their descriptions agree on this ultimate union, the divine *ecstasis, nirvana, satori,* or *samadhi* (Underhill, 1956).

Since the inner state of a saint can be experienced only

in oneself and not vicariously through the mind, we have misunderstood much of what saints have tried to share. It is as though we were fascinated by footprints in the sand without the presence of the person who made them, not even knowing where the footprints lead. Saints have an expansive impact on our hearts, and that helps us stretch beyond our narrow way of viewing ourselves. Often the words of a mystic or a saint sound foreign because we cannot comprehend the state from which they sprang. Therefore, mystics and saints can be approached only with the heart and not with the mind. We often glibly identify with what we can understand of given saints and miss the depths of their presence. How can one identify with that inner state if one has never experienced it? It is not surprising that accounts of the lives of saints have been diluted. For example, Christians tend to identify with the human part of Jesus Christ and his suffering, rather than with his inner state of the "kingdom of God." They miss the real message of his inner-God realization and are fascinated by simply footprints in the sand. Yet Christian mystics have identified with the inner state of the Master, transcended human suffering and reached the kingdom within.

Obviously, it would take volumes to give a complete account of mystical traditions, of what writers Aldous Huxley, Ken Wilber (1984) and Fritjof Capra (1975) call the "perennial philosophy." Rather than attempting an in-depth analysis of specific mystical traditions or a comparative study, as Huxley, Underhill and others have done, we wish to show the universality of the mystical experience through examples from traditions that span space and time.

Egyptian Mysticism

The oldest known religious texts of Egypt are the Pyramid Texts which were found in the burial chambers of the royal pyramids of the Fifth and Sixth Dynasties. In the Pyramid Texts there are numerous references to Osiris, the deity of the Nile who represents the principle of perpetual return, death and rebirth. The annual flood cycle of the

Nile formed an integral part of Egyptian mythology (Lamy, 1981) and served as an allegory for the mystery of creation. For the Egyptians the great mystery was the passage from the invisible to the visible, from the One to the Many. Stemming from this tradition, we find a common description of the origin of cosmos at all the four initiatory centers: Heliopolis, Memphis, Hermopolis and Thebes. The first desire of the Creator, the Nun, the primordial ocean, was to know himself, and this manifested as an outward projection. The originating power of the Creator was symbolized by the heart and the outward motion of projection of an arm that is throwing (Lamy, 1981).

This outward projection expresses the whole eternal process of becoming, symbolized by the scarab. As in American Indian cosmology, for Egyptians animals became representations of important archetypal patterns which humans live out. As such, the scarab—with distinct stages of development from egg to larva to nymph, and finally to winged form—represented a reflection of human evolution with its physical and spiritual transformation (Lamy, 1981). The original state, the egg, is a reflection of the infinite potentiality of the universe contained within the Nun. This comes into earthly expression as a larva where the universal and the individual aspects are brought into an individual form. Then the larva turns within and gives itself over to transformation into a nymph, an allegory of the transformation that takes place when a human remembers the Divine within. The nymph finally emerges as a new winged form, as a human who turns within eventually becomes a new "winged" being, a God-realized person. How appropriate this allegory is for us! The freedom to live out our divine potential consciously is tantamount to developing wings to soar in the spiritual heights. To develop the allegory further, the scarab, when viewed from above, reminds us of the human skull (de Lubicz, 1977), which has long evoked awareness of both our mortality and our evolution.

Ancient Egyptians employed such symbolism to express many complex truths. On the day-to-day level, symbolism was used in all areas of Egyptian life. Their hieroglyphic method of writing, their sculpture, their painting, their architecture, like the Temple of Luxor (de Lubicz, 1977), all took on extended meanings through the symbols that adorned them.

In Egyptian mystical thought as expressed in the Pyramid Texts, the One can be defined only through its countless symbolically represented qualities which assume a myriad of names. These names represent the active cosmic powers, the *Neters*, which express themselves eternally as the universe unfolds. The ancient invocations addressed to these powers or divine attributes trace the entire process of cosmogony (Lamy, 1981).

Beginning with Heliopolis, Creation arises as Atum— which means both All and Nothing—and Atum "projects himself" from the primordial background of the Nun. In one version of the myth, Atum creates himself by the projection of his own heart, and he brings forth nine elementary principles, the Great Ennead of Heliopolis (Lamy, 1981). In the Pyramid Texts the Great Ennead doubles and becomes the generative power that creates the universe.

For the Egyptians numbers represented the creative principles of the universe, and this belief undoubtedly found its way into ancient Greek Pythagorean cosmogony. The basis of all Pharaonic mathematics is in the process of halving (Lamy, 1981):

> I am One that transforms into Two
> I am Two that transforms into Four
> I am Four that transforms into Eight
> After this I am One.

Thus for the Egyptians, as for the Pythagoreans, numbers were not just abstract entities; they represented the fundamental creative principles of the cosmos. This sacred perspective of numbers was also used in a practical way. For example the Golden Section was used in the construction of temples (de Lubicz, 1977) and was later used in Greek temples.[1] For the Egyptians the Golden Section represented the natural principle of the laws of equilibrium. In all aspects of Egyptian life, sacred knowledge resulted in practical application.

Continuing in the mythic tradition, at Hermopolis we find the description of the Nun as the primordial environment, the initial waters, characterized by spatial infinity, darkness and void. In Egyptian cosmogony we find striking parallels to Genesis, but here the Nun is understood as the eternal source of everything rather than only the initial process of creation of the universe. At Memphis creation is taken one stage further (Lamy, 1981). Ptah the divine blacksmith—the equivalent of the Greek god Hephaistos—gives substance to the primordial fire. What existed in seed form as the Ennead of Atum becomes a concrete expression in Ptah. Then from Thebes, taking this yet another step, Amun, the "hidden one," assumes paramount importance. From this springs the eternal Trinity as Amun, Re and Ptah (Lamy, 1981):

> Three gods are all the gods: Amun, Re, Ptah who have no equal. "He whose name is hidden" is Amun, whose countenance is Re and whose body is Ptah. Their cities on earth, established in perpetuity, are Thebes, Heliopolis, Memphis, for eternity, Amun-Re-Ptah, Unity-Trinity.

For the Egyptians, as for the Christians and the Hindus, the Trinity had great significance and represented the Divine. In Egypt, the numerical value of number 1 was 3: Trinity makes the One whole. Egyptian mysticism, including the ideas about the Trinity, found its way into ancient Greece. It is well known that Greek philosophy profoundly influenced the early Church, and one finds common elements in Egyptian, Greek and early Christian mysticism. Also, Egyptian mysticism was closely related to the ancient Hebrew religion and particularly the mystical component of the latter, the *Kabbalah*. The parallels in these ancient traditions point to the universality of the eternal principles. There is, however, a case for a common source of many mystical traditions in ancient Egypt: the ancient Hermetic philosophy[2] taught by Hermes Trismegistus, also known as the "Master of Masters." *Trismegistus* means "three times great." Many learned ones came from different lands to study with Hermes, including, according to tradition, Abraham. Hermes was so revered that he was deified by the ancient Egyptians, Greeks, and Romans, as Thoth in Egypt, Hermes in Greece, and Mercury in Rome.

Egyptian cosmogony and the process of creation expounded in the writings of Kashmir Shaivism such as the *Pratyabhijnahridayam* are strikingly similar. Essential to both systems is the concept that the universe springs forth from the undefinable Absolute—Paramashiva or Nun—by a process of division and outward projection. Most importantly, in both ancient Egypt and ancient Kashmir, these descriptions were not considered abstract statements but represented creative principles found within us—the basic universal message of mysticism.

In ancient Egypt mystical principles were often expressed in cryptic form in objects of everyday life, such as the architectural structures of the pyramids and the Temple of Luxor. In Egypt, in India and in Gothic Christianity, the temple was a book that revealed mystical teachings to the initiate. Both numbers in Egypt, representing the creative principles, and Sanskrit letters in Shaivism, representing the various levels of the creative process, demonstrate ancient understandings of how consciousness operates in a human being. As in India, the sages of Egypt knew of the inner divine energy, kundalini, and also represented it as the cobra. In the Pyramid Texts there are numerous references to lotuses, representing the inner subtle energy centers or chakras. The Egyptians, like the Shaivites, understood the emanation-projection aspects of the creative process. All this attests to the universality of the mystical experience which spans space and time.

The Egyptians considered that there is a divine plan which continuously unfolds, realized through time by successive kings, the guardians of the ancient tradition (de Lubicz, 1977). The Pharaohs were considered divine, not in the secular way of the Romans but as embodiments and guardians of the mystical knowledge. Even though we do not know the lives of the Pharaohs in detail, there is no doubt that some of them, like Amenophis III, the builder of the Temple of Luxor, were ancient sages.

Hebrew Mysticism

The ancient Hebrews worshipped a single God, the God of the Old Testament. Over and over in that collection of religious texts one finds reference to the mystical experience of the divine presence within among the ancient patriarchs of Israel, the prophets and sage-kings. Moses, Elijah, Ezekiel, King David, King Solomon are some of the greatest mystics of the Hebrew tradition. Judaism states that Moses received the Torah, the Law, both in written and oral form at Mount Sinai. Moses ben Nahman, Bible commentator and Kabbalist who lived in Spain in the thirteenth century, wrote that the Torah was composed of the names of God, and that by further division of its words one could find more esoteric names (Ponce, 1973). Thus, at one level the Bible can be interpreted in the usual Rabbinical tradition, and at another level in an esoteric, mystical way.

An even more striking statement about the creation of the written Torah was made in the seventeenth century by the founder of the Hasidic movement in Poland and Russia, Baal-Shem Tov. He proposed that the Torah existed originally as an incoherent array of letters, and that the coherent writing came into existence at the time that the events described took place (Ponce, 1973). We find here an interesting account of the power of sound in the form of letters. According to the Kabbalists, the Hebrew mystics, historical events are not predetermined by God. The creative principles represented by the letters in the Torah are predetermined, but the universe unfolds in a universal dance. Moreoever, the Hebrew mystics regarded the creative power of the vowels in the Hebrew alphabet as the feminine, creative aspect of God, strikingly like the Hindu understanding of the power of the sound in the form of letters.

The Kabbalists were mainly concerned with unraveling the mystical message of spiritual life, and the Kabbalah is full of mystical knowledge. It is not a single book or recollection of books like the Bible and the Koran, but a system of thought, a system of life expounded in many different works written at different times. To begin with,

Kabbalistic tradition held that the Creator God of the Bible is a limited God, subordinate to the higher, limitless and unknowable En-Sof (Ponce, 1973). It also held that the universe was created as result of complex operations by the emanated attributes of the En-Sof, the ten Sefiroth, who are a bridge connecting the finite universe with the infinite En-Sof. As in Kashmir Shaivism, the emanated attributes of the Divine are to be found in every individual. The task for every Hebrew mystic was to reverse the steps in all the Sefiroth back to the Source within. Many Kabbalists considered the *Sefer Yetsirah* or *Book of Creation*, written between the third and sixth century A.D., as the foundation of Kabbalistic study. The contents of this book were allegedly revealed to the patriarch Abraham and preserved by word of mouth for many centuries. This work is concerned with the ten Sefiroth, represented as numbers, and with establishing the Hebrew alphabet as the foundation of all things (Westcott, 1960).

> The twenty-two letters and sounds comprise the Foundation of all things. There are three mothers, seven doubles and twelve simples. These three Mothers are *Aleph, Mem* and *Shin*—Air, Water, and Fire.

Air was assigned to the letter *Aleph* because it is an aspirate, pronounced with silent breathing. *Mem* is the prototype of the mutes, letters with no sound, pronounced by pressing the lips together. The silence indicated here is typified by fish; hence the element of water was associated with *Mem*. The letter *Shin* is the prototype of the sibilants, letters which are pronounced with a hissing sound, and it is represented by fire. These three letters represent the three divisions into which all letters of the Hebrew alphabet fit, and they were called the mothers of the alphabet (Ponce, 1973). There is a striking similarity to the creative principles contained in the letters of the Sanskrit alphabet. Even the terminology is the same: the Sanskrit term matrika, which denotes the inherent power of the letters, literally means "little mother."

The 22 letters of the Hebrew alphabet represent 22 qualities that we have to embody in order to be able to start the process of involution. The 21 consonants with the vowel *Aleph* are the outer expression of God. It is interesting to note that there are no written vowels in the Hebrew alphabet. As in the Shaivite tradition, the vowels represented the inner aspect of God and the consonants the outer aspect. Similarly, in the Christian tradition Jesus of Nazareth was the outer expression of God, while his inner state, the Christ consciousness, was the inner aspect of God or Logos.

Each Hebrew letter has a name, but only for the sake of pronunciation. The meaning of the name has no connection with the quality or principle that the letter, as vibrational energy, represents. The names of the letters represent common objects. For example, the name of the letter *Ghimel* means "camel," but it is like our saying *g* as in goat (Ponce, 1973). Many commentators on Hebrew linguistics have arbitrarily extracted symbolism based on the meaning of the name of the letter as esoteric interpretation. But an interpretation based on the name of the letter is subjective. Only the principle of the letter has to do with objective reality.

Each Hebrew letter has a numerical value. This is also encountered in the Greek and Sanskrit alphabets. Each Sefiroth had a corresponding number between 1 and 10 associated with it. Like the Egyptians and Pythagoreans, the Kabbalists believed that the attributes of the cosmos and God are represented by numbers.

En-Sof, the primordial God, is the ultimate source of the universe. Even before the creation of this round of evolution, heaven and earth, God had *inistence*[3] (as opposed to existence), which means that there was prior creation where nothingness was to be found. In the inistence aspect of God there is no thing—no objects, no thoughts, no feelings—only bliss, total complete absolute bliss. But En-sof desired more of itself, which is the Light, and the Light engendered desire for more Light. At this stage Light was not only created; it was emanated.

From the involutionary process of the inistence came the *existence*, through the Spirit, the creative aspect of the universe. It is represented as the Tree of Life and the ten Sefiroth are its components. The Tree of Life can be seen as equivalent to the chakra system of the Tantric philosophy (Ponce, 1973). The middle pillar of the Tree is known as the Shekhinah, which Kabbalists considered as God's presence in every human. That presence is feminine. At the very top of the Tree is the absolute, undifferentiated Self, also known as Adam Kadmon. It is that primordial Being that decides to manifest itself as the world in the process of evolution. That objective Self is the I AM revealed to Moses on the mountain. Evolution can be reversed and become involution as kundalini rises to the top of the head. We are never far from the primordial Being, the Adam Kadmon, which is nothing other than everlasting bliss. This is the bliss that we all yearn to find in our lives, for it is our true Home. However, the more we become a part of this earth, the more we forget about our origin, the primordial Being within.

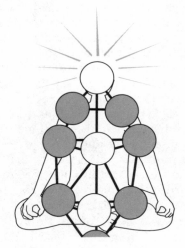

Figure 23. The ten Sefiroth of the Tree of Life, creative principles or attributes of the Divine found in man

The Tree of Life represents four bodies: the intellectual, the astral, the emotional and the physical. Through the use of these bodies we can perfect ourselves and "bring heaven to earth." The Kabbalists believed that it is the task of every human to seek perfection. Most of us know nothing of our perfection and dwell only in the physical, emotional and intellectual world. We have no idea that we are divine mind, divine feeling, divine love. It is only after knowing the I AM presence within that we begin our return journey Home, our involution. As humans we are the products of a cosmic evolution. Our aim is to become no-thing through involution.

There are striking similarities between the Kabbalah's teachings of the creative principles, the power of the letters, the mystical knowledge of humanity as the microcosm of the universe and other mystical traditions. This can only mean that all ancient traditions approached the same universal Truth, the archetype of the creative process itself.

As all great religions, Judaism was based on the lives and teachings of mystics and sages. Some, like the mystic Baal-Shem Tov, approached God through devotion. Others, like the Kabbalist writers, sought God through inner or spiritual knowledge. The two paths of love or devotion and of knowledge are found in many traditions, so it should not surprise us that we also find them in mystical Judaism. In the end when the human again becomes Adam Kadmon, the primordial divine Being, love becomes knowledge and knowledge love. Mystics like Baal-Shem Tov give religion its meaning. Central to the Hasidic revival move-ment, which he initiated, is the concept that God is present in all things. According to Baal-Shem Tov, once we under-stand this, we understand that all evils in the world result from our faulty view of things and not from the things themselves.Hasidism was open to everyone and the Hasidim worshipped God through joy and celebration (Ponce, 1973).

The Christian Saints

Christianity is not simply an extension of earlier Neo-platonic and Hebrew thought. Although profoundly influenced by both, it nevertheless was a new phenomenon, undoubtedly due to the personality of Jesus. The word "Christ" is derived from the Greek *Christos* and means "the Anointed." To his disciples Jesus was a Master, a

spiritual teacher, a rabbi. His teachings have survived in
the hearts of Christians for two thousand years. His message
was that all humans are the children of God and could
become like him. In the Christian tradition the inner
Divinity can be experienced when the Holy Spirit is activated.
The Holy Spirit might be interpreted as kundalini. In the
East it has been known for thousands of years that the
easiest way to awaken the latent spiritual energy is through
a Master. Jesus was a Master who had become one with
Godhead (the Father of the Hebrew tradition), and even
after his departure his disciples received inner awakenings
in the Pentecost. Other traditions confirm and give credence
to the message of Christ, pointing to the universality of
his message and to the common spiritual experiences of
people from different traditions (Ranade, 1983).

There are countless saints in the Christian tradition,
men and women who followed the teachings of Master
Jesus and reached the "Christ within." Both Catholic
and Eastern Orthodox traditions revere the teachings of
the saints because their lives provide an eternal example
on the potential of the human spirit. Their lives and teachings
are manifestations of the Spirit in the community of
Christians. Saints like Francis of Assisi and Teresa of
Avila were reformers who devoted themselves to the betterment of their fellow men and women.

St. Francis was born into a rich and noble family of
Assisi, Italy. As a young man of the thirteenth century—
like other young nobles of his time—he drank, sang and
caroused until one day he suddenly realized the meaning-
lessness of it all. He turned to the monastic life, rejecting
all of his riches, and founded the Franciscan Order of
monks. He identified with his Master Jesus so completely
that he developed stigmata, the markings of the crucifixion.
He considered all creatures his brothers and sisters and
became a living example of the power of love and humility
(Ranade, 1983).

St. Teresa of Avila lived in Spain in the sixteenth century.
She felt the urge toward the monastic life when she was
young and suffered because of her strong attachment to her
family and friends. She became a living example of the

power of meditation and wrote many books on the inner journey that describe her experiences and the stages of her silent "contemplative" prayer. As she progressed, the presence of the Divine within opened to her. She described in beautiful words a powerful experience of initiation or spiritual awakening and her many visions of Christ. St. Teresa was a lover of God, and for her Christ was a living presence within, in real form and in words. She spoke of the soul as a garden (Ranade, 1983):

> It has always been a great delight to me to think of my soul as a garden, and the Lord as walking in it. Our soul is like a garden, out of which God plucks the weeds, and plants the flowers which we have to water by prayer.

Her ecstatic experiences and raptures were misunderstood by ignorant contemporaries, but she never doubted the Divine Presence within her. Her descriptions of the parts of the "inner castle" are similar to descriptions of the inner energy centers by the Eastern sages. Not only was she a saint who was guided from within and who reached the highest spiritual levels; she was a very practical person. She stressed that real spiritual progress comes through selfless service and love even more than from contemplation and isolation.

Meister Eckhart, another Catholic saint, had a constant awareness of God as present in everything, "even a fly." He lived and preached in Germany and Holland in the thirteenth and fourteenth centuries and was an accomplished theologian, a great preacher and able administrator. Even though rigorously trained in Aristotelian logic, as were all Church scholars of his time, he quickly broke through all mental constructs to the inner kingdom.

> There is a Citadel within us, the Little Spark, which is greater than either the highest intelligence and understanding God has of Himself, or the highest love which God is. Even God cannot look into this final Citadel of my soul as He exists in any of His forms or mode—not the Father, nor the Son, nor the Holy Ghost. All these Gods must leave outside to look inside my Citadel. Here in this Citadel God is neither creating nor created, and in this inner part, my soul and God are the same (Pearce, 1987).

Meister Eckhart is describing the goal of all spiritual practices and experiences. His "Little Spark" is the blue pearl described by Swami Muktananda, and the "mustard seed" of Jesus Christ.[4] It is the form the soul assumes in every individual, the individual Divine Spark or Fünkelein of Universal Consciousness. It transcends any awareness of object or subject. Mystics, consciously or unconsciously, turn within to have a vision of the blue pearl and eventually merge with it. This experience grants them the vision of the greatness of human beings.

Meister Eckhart stated over and over that his authority derived from within, not from any external Church. He was seen by some of his contemporaries as a threat to the Church, and he was finally brought to trial before the Inquisition. He did not live to see what followed: complete banning of his books and attempts to erase his message from the minds and hearts of the simple folk who loved him so dearly.

The Eastern Orthodox Church did not undergo the upheavals and extreme forms of religious prejudice witnessed in the West (Meyendorff, 1962). From the early years of Christianity, a mystical tradition was preserved and accepted much more openly by Orthodox Church authorities, and it provided a continuous way of spiritual life. Beginning with the "Fathers of the desert," monks like St. Anthony the Great—who lived in the first centuries of the young Christian Church—provided powerful teachings that spread beyond mere monastic life to all the faithful.

The *Philokalia*, "Friend of the Good," is a collection of mystical works dating from the early years of the Byzantine Empire. Written over many centuries, the works that make up the *Philokalia* were compiled by monks of Mount Athos in late medieval times, probably after 1350, put in final form in the eighteenth century and published in 1782 (*Philokalia*, 1957). The late medieval period was a time of mystical revival in both Catholic and Orthodox Churches, as well as in India where sages like Jnaneshwar and Kabir lived and taught. In these particularly trying times as the temporal power of the Byzantine Empire was waning, mystics like Nicolaos Kavasilas lived and taught the "quiet" life while carrying out activities and duties in the everyday world. *Philokalia*, in the words of St. Nicodemos, contains "the treasury of the washing away; the guardian of the mind; the mystical teaching of the noetic prayer; . . . the tool of becoming divine." In the monastic tradition the "washing away" refers to removing the impurities of the mind to reveal the soul within. The "noetic prayer" of the Eastern Orthodox mystics is similar to the "contemplative prayer" of the Catholic mystics and the "meditation" of the sages of India, China and Japan. The goal of *theosis*, "becoming divine," was known and accepted by the Orthodox mystics as the ultimate goal of spiritual unfoldment. The noetic prayer, also known as the "Jesus prayer," was practiced by the monks of Mount Athos and was passed on from teacher to disciple. It was seen as a tool to gradually purify the mind. One particularly well known form is: "Kyrie Iesou Christe Theou Ie eleison mai." It translates as, "Lord Jesus Christ, Son of God, have mercy on me."

Initially, the noetic prayer was to be repeated with the lips and gradually to descend to the heart level and then to the navel region. Its repetition was to become gradually subtler until *theosis* occurred, the union of the soul with the Divine. The Hindus also held that inner unfoldment occurs as the sound of a mantra descends to more refined levels.

The mystics of the Eastern Church knew that there are different types of individuals and prescribed different ways for disciples to accomplish the inner journey according to their temperaments. They taught four "paths" or "means of approach." The sages of Kashmir, from a totally different tradition, described in different language concepts almost identical to those in the Orthodox tradition (Singh, 1979a): 1) *Shambava Upaya*, identifying with the highest Truth through the use of will power. This is accomplished by a subtle alertness or awareness without using the mind. 2) *Shakta Upaya*, using the mind to contemplate the nature of the individual, the nature of the meditative process and tools of the latter such as mantra. 3) *Anava Upaya*, the path of action, using such practices as rituals and breath exercises to still the mind. 4) *Anupaya*, the "pathless" path, recognizing one's true nature as result of a single word, look or gesture from his Master. The mystics of Kashmir Shaivism and the mystics of *Philokalia* knew that the only obstacle between us and the inner Self, the only obstacle to theosis, is the mind. Like the treatises of Kashmir and Patanjali's sutras, *Philokalia* is nothing other than a collection of works expounding how to purify the mind so that the seeker can unite with the Christ within.

The Ecstatic Sufis

Sufism is considered to be the mystical aspect of Islam, though it is also associated with other traditions. The term "Sufi" is derived from the Arabic word *sufi*, "wool," referring to the dress adopted by the dervishes, the masters and teachers of Sufism (Palmer, 1974). This mystical system reconciled philosophy with revealed religion. The first principle of Sufism is "I am the Truth," a statement found in the Koran. The principal writers of Sufism are the lyric poets, who aimed to elevate people spiritually through personal experience of the Divine. Sufism is primarily based on the principle of the initiation into mystical knowledge when the teacher sets the disciple on the inner journey.

As in the writings of St. Teresa, many Sufi poets refer to the longing for God in terms of human love, as the union between the lover and the beloved. For many Sufi mystics, every sound was taken to be heavenly music, a message from the beloved God. Along with sound and music, ecstatic dance formed a central focus for many Sufis, expressed beautifully in the poems of the poet-saint Jalaluddin Rumi (Schimmel, 1975). Dance became a central form of expression in the Sufi Order of the Whirling Dervishes.

For the Sufi mystic, the ultimate goal was merging of the beloved with the lover, *fana*, "extinction." This merging was expressed eloquently by Rumi: "Like the flame of the candle in the presence of the Sun he is really non-existent" (Schimmel, 1975). In the final form of fana there is no object, no subject, no beloved, no lover. Yet for Sufis, this love for God could not exist were it not for God seeking the aspirant. As Rumi said: "Not a single lover would seek union if the beloved were not seeking it." Meister Eckhart expressed a similar idea.

The Sufi saint Husayn ibn Mansur al-Hallaj, who lived in Baghdad in the tenth century, continuously expressed the central message of many mystics from many traditions, *Ana'l-Haqq*, "I am the Absolute." The politicians and learned scholars of Baghdad were afraid of the simple teaching that everybody is really the Divine and, as with Socrates, Jesus Christ and Meister Eckhart, saw it as a threat to existing institutions. Hallaj was put to death in 922 A.D. Tradition has it that he was so immersed in Ana'l-Haqq that even after he was cut to pieces by his executioners, every part of his body kept uttering that message.

The Sufis used mantras, vehicles to turn within, as did the Hindus, Buddhists, gnostic Christians and the mystics of *Philokalia*. The main Sufi mantra was "*La Illaha Il Allah Hu*: There is no God but Allah (the Absolute)." Meditation was known and practiced by the Sufis. Jalaluddin Rumi poetically expressed the value of "Mystical Silence" or meditative silence (Ranade, 1983):

What follows is hidden, and inexpressible in words.
If you should speak and try a hundred ways to express
　　it, it is useless; the mystery becomes no clearer.
You can ride on saddle and horse to the sea-coast, but
　　then you must use a horse of wood (i.e., a boat).
A horse of wood is useless on dry land,
It is the special vehicle of voyages by sea.
Silence is this horse of wood,
Silence is the guide and support of men at sea.

In Sufism philosophic knowledge was direct and intuitive. This was perhaps expressed best by Dhu'l-Nun, an early Sufi mystic who lived in Egypt. This intuitive knowledge or *gnosis* as the early Christians called it, is not different from love for the Divine. Dhu'l-Nun reiterated in many of his poems that the two are one, and divisions between the path of knowledge and the path of love ultimately disappear.

The Sufis revered Muhammad, the Prophet, the vehicle

who brought divine knowledge and founded Islam. The importance of his role was expressed by Muhammad Iqbal, who declared, "You can deny God, but you cannot deny the Prophet" (Schimmel, 1975), mirroring the Christian statement that the Father is known only through the Son. In both traditions the Transcendent is inaccessible without the Immanent or personal form of the Divine; the former is difficult to reach for most people and without the latter can be meaningless.

Many great Sufi saints were women, like Rabia, the first saint of Islam, and Fatima, the wife of Ahmad Khidruya. The latter guided her husband in his religious life and freely discussed spiritual matters with the well-known Sufi and scholar mystic Bayezid Bistami. The Sufis attributed a place to women not found in other Muslim sects. As Rumi stated, "she is not created but creator," meaning that the creative activity of God is revealed through women. It is probably for this reason that the Sufis loved Mother Mary and considered her, as do the Christians, to be the immaculate mother of the divine Light.

Nowadays many consider Islam as a rigid religion which denies other religions. Nothing could be further from the truth. The Sufis in particular, as all Muslims, respected and revered the prophets and the saints of the Hebrew and Christian religions. In India there were saints who transcended religious differences between Hindus and Muslims, such as the poet-saint Kabir who lived in the fifteenth century and Sai Baba of Shirdi who lived in the nineteenth and early twentieth centuries. They both taught Hindus and Muslims alike and are revered by followers of both traditions.

The Indian Sages and Saints

Indian philosophies are believed to be among the most ancient in human history. Some of them span the entire spectrum of philosophic knowledge, from the materialistic to the monistic (Eliade, 1969). Here we examine briefly two of the most sublime philosophies of all times, *Vedanta* and *Shaivism*.

The ancient scriptures of India, the *Vedas*, are believed to have been divinely revealed, as were the Law of Moses, the Old Testament, the Gospels and the New Testament, the Koran and the Sutras of Kashmir Shaivism. There are four kinds of Vedas: the hymns and prayers, the procedures or the rituals, the spiritual interpretations of the rituals and the teachings of the ancient sages about God, the Self and the world (Eliade, 1969). The section at the end of the Vedas is called the *Upanishads* and provides the source of Vedantic philosophy. The word *Vedanta* literally means "end of Vedas." There have been many attempts through the ages to interpret the Upanishads. The first known interpretation is called the *Brahma Sutras*, and many Indian sages have written commentaries on it. There have also been different schools of commentaries on Vedanta. The school of the sage Shankaracharya, known as the "non-dual Vedanta," is the most widely known and considered by most scholars as the official Vedanta. Shankaracharya was a great sage and reformer. At a time when people in India were confused about religious beliefs, his teaching and living example spread this profound system of non-dualistic philosophy.

Vedanta is a monistic philosophical system. It is the path of knowledge, although all the great Vedantins such as Shankaracharya were also *bhaktis* who, like the Sufis were filled with love for the Divine. Vedanta is not dry knowledge but knowledge put into practice (Eliade, 1969). Liberation of the individual soul comes from the knowledge of the identity between the Self and Absolute Reality. In addition to the Upanishads, Vedanta philosophy accepts the authority of two other important works, the *Brahma Sutras* and the *Bhagavad Gita*, and its philosophy is expounded on these scriptures.

Shankaracharya's famous statements summarize the essence of non-dual Vedanta: 1. Brahman (the Absolute) is Reality; 2. The world is an illusion; 3. The individual Self is nothing but Brahman.

According to Mircea Eliade (1969), an authority on the history of religions, when Shankaracharya wrote about the "Real" and the "unreal" or illusory, he referred to the

impermanency of the world. Some scholars and followers
of Vedanta are confused about this point and proclaim that
the world is non-existent. Shankaracharya's position is,
nevertheless, very clear: "Real" in Vedanta is defined as
anything that is eternal, and only Parabrahman, the Absolute,
is recognized as such. Everything else is unreal in the sense
that it does not last. In Vedantic terms, because the world
changes and does not last, it is called an illusion. As Swami
Muktananda put it, "The world is real in every sense because
God is real." This statement recognizes that not just the
individual soul but the entire universe is identical with
the Absolute. Vedanta states that Brahman is *Sat-chit-ananda*,
Absolute Existence, Consciousness and Bliss or Contentment. In its essence, therefore, Vedanta is identical to
Kashmir Shaivism, the other great monistic philosophy
of India. The latter holds Reality or *Paramashiva*—literally
meaning "Supreme Shiva"—to be Existence (*prakasha*)
and Awareness (*vimarsha*), which is nothing else but pure
Bliss. However, the two systems differ in the way one applies
the fundamental principles to one's life. Vedanta emphasizes
that we should inquire about the nature of Reality. We
would then conclude that Brahman is "not this, not this,"
neti, neti: nothing in the phenomenal world is the Absolute.
Kashmir Shaivism, on the other hand, emphasizes that all
things, this and that and everything else in the phenomenal
world, *are* the Absolute. The two approaches are different,
but the end result is the same: identification of the individual
with the Divine. "I am Brahman (*Aham brahmasmi*); This
Self is Brahman (*Ayam atma brahma*); Brahman is Consciousness (*Prajnanam brahma*); That thou art (*Tat tvam asi*)."
   Kashmir Shaivism is perhaps the most complete monistic
philosophical system. It is also called the *Trika* system, or
the philosophy of the triad, because it explains the relationship between the Lord of the Universe, the Universe
and the individual soul.[5] Shaivism sees everything, as the
expression of the one fundamental principle, Paramashiva
or Supreme Consciousness. It is not a mere philosophical
school, for it expounds a way of living, a practical means
to identify with the Absolute. Since though one cannot
achieve this identification simply with the mind, Kashmir
Shaivism emphasizes *anugraha*, the grace of the Master.

Grace, as we saw, is the fifth action of Paramashiva. It is eternal and is not confined to a few individuals in particular physical forms, a central point of Shaivism. Shaivism is rich in great scriptural and philosophical works. Maharashtra is one of the principal linguistic and cultural provinces of India. There, in late medieval times, lived a number of ecstatic saints (Ranade, 1983). They taught, revived an awareness of the divine among the people and were immersed in love for the divine. Their poetry is very moving, for only through poetry could they express their profound state. Eknath, Akkamahadevi, Tukaram, Jnaneshwar, Janabai, Namdev, Sautamali, Kurmadas, Mirabai—one cannot find any other period or place in human history where so many great beings who followed the path of love appeared. Their message was profoundly simple, and they taught it through their own lives: God is nothing other than love; an individual is nothing else than love. They felt profound love and gratitude for their spiritual teachers and expressed it in moving poetic words. What they felt for the divine, they felt for their teachers at the core of their being. In all religious traditions the saints are personifications of love. Their simple message constitutes true religion: true Christianity, true Judaism, true Islam, true Hinduism, true Buddhism, true Taoism, the true religion of the Inner Self.

The Mystic and the Scientist

The great mystics often teach philosophy, primarily the practical knowledge of the science of the Self, how to experience one's own true inner nature. This basic approach is found in all traditions. In this science, one is both the observer, the observed and the process of observation. The fact that the subjective inner journey can be corroborated objectively by the experience of others should appeal to anyone who appreciates the beauty and objectivity of natural sciences. Physicist Erwin Schrödinger said:

> You are struck by the miraculous agreement between humans of different race, different religion, knowing nothing about each other's existence, separated by centuries and millennia, and by the greatest distances that there are on our globe.

One thing can be claimed in favor of the mystical teaching of the "identity" of all minds with each other and with the supreme mind (quoted in Wilber, 1984).

In this passage, Schrödinger showed that he profoundly understands the basis for objective verification that exists in all mystical experiences. Even though the science of the Self differs radically from the natural sciences in methodology, focus and object of inquiry, both are "objective" in the general sense of the word. One cannot validate the other, and yet both, in a complementary way, can be taken to reveal the fundamental aspects of the Universe and ourselves. A scientifically minded person can find out about what "science cannot touch," to use the words of Schrödinger, by exploring his or her own inner depths. Biologist and Nobel laureate George Wald holds, as physicist Wolfgang Pauli did, that matter and mind are two complementary aspects of the same reality (Wald, 1984). Wald points out that consciousness cannot be localized anywhere in the physical body. He argues that the mind is primary over matter, and that in some sense the universe is a knowing universe. The two ways of knowing matter and mind— physical science and the science of the Self—are complementary ways to approach undivided wholeness.

The physicists who developed quantum and relativity theories were interested in metaphysics, and a number of them wrote extensively about going beyond physics. Heisenberg, Bohr, Einstein, Schrödinger, de Broglie, Jeans, Planck, Pauli, Eddington were not only concerned with the physical world; they were interested in what lies beyond it (Wilber, 1984).

These physicists knew both the limitations of science and the direction for getting beyond science. Erwin Schrödinger put it aptly (Wilber, 1984):

The scientific picture of the real world around me is very deficient. It gives a lot of factual information, puts all our experience in a magnificently consistent order, but it is ghastly silent about all and sundry that is really near to our heart, that really matters to us.

In the words of Werner Heisenberg (Wilber, 1984):

> The space in which mankind develops as a spiritual being
> has more dimensions than the single one which it has
> occupied during the last centuries.

In another time of revolution in science, the Renaissance
when classical physics was developed, philosopher-scientists
like Kepler, Galileo, Newton, Descartes, Spinoza, Bishop
Berkeley, Leibniz were interested in the metaphysics of
"natural philosophy" and wrote extensively about it (Durham
and Purrington, 1983). The mystery of the cosmos has
always attracted such thinkers, taking them beyond the
ordinary (Jeans, 1931). Even since the quantum revolution
scientists like Rupert Sheldrake and Edward Fredkin
are going beyond the bounds of today's science. Sheldrake
considers fields transcending space and time as carriers
of information; Fredkin considers information in a computational sense to be the primary stuff of the cosmos (Wright,
1988). Physicist Henry Margenau (1984), in considering
the relevance of oriental views to modern science, looks at
mind as a field. Could we conclude that the writings of
these and many other scientists are related to the mystical
traditions of all cultures? In the sense that these men have
realized the limits of science and at the same time have
seen the need to extend it in parallel to the perennial
philosophy or mystical tradition, the answer has to be yes.

One can then be both a mystic and a scientist, and in
fact most of the great scientists are mystics of a sort. They
are deeply convinced of the order, simplicity and beauty
of the physical universe, and this vision gives them a sense
of the underlying wholeness of the universe. Similarly,
all religions deal with the order, simplicity and beauty
within us. In a real way then, as Einstein put it, "a legitimate
conflict between religion and science cannot exist," because
"science without religion is lame, religion without science
is blind" (quoted in Wilber, 1984).

Yet, natural science and true religion are not the same.
They cannot even validate each other. Nevertheless, they
complement each other wonderfully. The physicists who

built quantum theory knew that in the dialogue between scientists and nature something universal and simple is revealed: though science deals with objects and the multiplicity in the physical universe is fundamental to any scientific point of view, yet scientists have intimations of the ultimate unity of the cosmos. So far, science has not managed to achieve a unified vision of the cosmos while excluding the role of consciousness in the physical universe. The mystics tell us that we will never be able to comprehend ultimate unity unless we search inside ourselves for that unity. Find it inside, they tell us, and you will find it everywhere. The plurality that we perceive is only an appearance; it is not real. This is the basic message of mysticism. Scientists of the caliber of Schrödinger, Einstein, Heisenberg and Bohr understand this basic message very clearly (Wilber, 1984).

Summary

Mystical traditions describe ultimate Reality in strikingly similar terms. Whether the Nun of the Egyptians, the En-Sof of the Hebrews, the Father of the Christians, the Allah of the Sufis, the Tao of the Chinese, the Brahman of the Vedantins or the Paramashiva of the Shaivites, Reality is the same: eternal, infinite, attributeless, primordial, dynamic, throbbing, ever-creating, ever-preserving and ever-destroying. The static aspect is often portrayed as male, and the dynamic as female, in contrast to what we Westerners usually assume.

Mystical traditions also agree remarkably well that Ultimate Reality manifests the Universe by a series of steps involving separation and projection. The Continuum from which the Universe arose contains no distinctions; all distinctions arise as a result of a series of projections into pairs of opposites. The Universe is manifested through complementary relationships, but eventually in the infinite sea of Consciousness all complementary relationships merge back into unity, and the object merges with the subject. One cannot describe the primordial matrix, for it can be known only by what it is not, no-thing, not in the sense of an absolute vacuum, but of absolute fullness containing no objects.

Many traditions emphasize that the creator God cannot be the highest because creation implies a separation into distinct parts, in the sense that there is a creator—subject—and a created—object. The Kabbalists insisted that there has to be something higher than the creator God of the Bible, and they termed it En-Sof. The Shaivites likewise viewed the Ultimate Reality, Paramashiva, as "above" even the first five pure creative steps, above the first creator God, Ishwara. Similarly, the Hopi Indians accepted that the act of creation was carried out by a creator God who emanated from the Absolute (Waters, 1969).

The first act of creation is separation. It is described in lucid terms in the first five pure levels found in Shaivite philosophy. The act of creation involves the inherent power of sound, the letters of the alphabet and words. In both the Hebrew and Shaivite mystical traditions, the letters are classified as feminine or masculine. The overall creative process is said to proceed from the feminine aspect of the Absolute, and in mystical traditions—Kabbalistic, Indian, even gnostic Christian—feminine Divinity is worshipped as well as the male God. Traditional religions tend to separate the Divine into two and then emphasize one—usually the male aspect—over the other. In all religions, despite tendencies to de-emphasize the Goddess, the worship of the Goddess remains, in the worship of Mother Mary in Christianity.

The Absolute is without attributes of any kind. Separation into objects of perception occurs in the creative process itself. The separation into male and female energies is the primal archetype of all separation. To retrace the steps back to the origin requires complete acceptance of both feminine and masculine aspects. Until that happens, religions will need continuously to justify the unjustifiable, the unnatural imbalance between the two aspects. Ever since the female stopped being the Goddess, the Fall of Man has continued.

The above statements would be meaningless if they did not derive from experiences of the mystics throughout

the world. Mystical statements cannot be verified or understood by intellectual processes, but those who have had
a mystical experience are convinced of the truth revealed.
For revelation is not distance, coming from "above" or
"below." Rather, revelation proceeds from the depths of
humans and is put into words by humans to attempt to
describe what is basically indescribable. Mystical experiences validate each other because they are similar,
even though individual mystics may be different from each
other. A mystic is not a solipsist, isolated in a narrow,
closed universe of his or her creation. A mystic is one in
union with everything, particularly the innermost part of
his or her humanness. There, the human is revealed to be
what it really is: pure Divinity itself. This pure state transcends all boundaries, including the boundary of the body.
It is always there and remains ultimately. It transcends
religious differences. There are many paths, but only
one Truth.

Mystics broke through to the ground of Godhead and
live continuously in mystical states of pure contentment. If
one human can do that all humans potentially can. Mystics
of all traditions emphasize that they are not unique. The only
thing different about them is that they are continuously
aware of the Divinity inside them, while most other human
beings are not. Because the message of saints and mystics
is so simple they may not be understood by their contemporaries; they may even be mistreated, though they
usually come to be revered. It seems that the complete
disregard for mysticism and what is true religion—the
religion of the inner Divinity—not the ritualistic religion
widely practiced today—is a relatively new phenomenon
(Eliade, 1959).

The fact that saints come from all social classes and
walks of life, all nations, all races and both sexes points
to something basic in human nature, the fundamentally
simple message, "you are That." But the message is not
given merely verbally. The men and women who break
through to the ground of the inner Self and become established in continuous awareness of their Divinity teach
others primarily through the example of their own lives.

The way that the Infinite becomes the bounded individual self is mysterious. Kashmir Shaivism describes how, through Maya and the 36 levels of the creative process, the unlimited powers of the Infinite become limited. Nevertheless for most of us this is still a mystery. For this reason great beings have provided the practical means for us to reverse the process and go back Home. The practices include selfless service for the common good, contemplation and meditation and generally practices which purify the mind. For when the mind becomes pure, the inner Self shines through. That experience is very real, as Schrödinger would put it, in fact more real than anything else. And that real experience is nothing else than pure love. Mystics try to portray pure love in poetic language, for how can one give discourses on love (Jampolsky, 1979)? Books cannot capture it, philosophy cannot convey its real essence, even though every human being experiences it in some degree. To experience it, one can only sink into it and come to realize that love is God.

7

Undivided Wholeness: The Quantum, the Universe and Consciousness

As here, so elsewhere.
Shiva Sutras, *Part II, 14*

"Holism," signifying the view that the universe is an undivided whole, is a word that is particularly popular nowadays, although it often acquires nebulous meaning. It is usually understood to imply that in some way the parts of something are really a whole. However, a more specific meaning is needed, and holism must be used carefully, or we may either state the obvious or jump to unsubstantiated conclusions. What are the parts? What is the whole? Questions like these used to belong to the realm of philosophy and metaphysics. Recent progress in physical science, and particularly quantum physics, is beginning to make these questions accessible to experimental evidence in a meaningful way.

Einstein's formidable challenge to quantum theory, formulated in the EPR thought experiment, has now been tested in the laboratory, and the evidence turned out to be different from what he would have thought. Bell's theorem and the experiments designed to check its predictions challenge our usual assumptions about physical reality. Not only is quantum theory vindicated in its predictions vis-à-vis other models of the universe which conform with common sense; even more surprisingly the evidence indicates that whatever we mean by the term physical reality, that reality has to be non-local.

The implications of this vindication of quantum theory have not been appreciated by the general public or even by most practicing scientists. We clearly need a new vision of the cosmos that is somehow holistic. Here again, unless one is more specific, the vision of wholeness can be taken as stating the obvious.

The architects of quantum theory were aware of these problems. Einstein himself was painfully aware of what quantum theory implies about our usual way of looking at things (Howard, 1989):

> Further, it appears to be essential for this arrangement of the things introduced in physics that, at a specific time, these things claim an existence independent of one another, insofar as these things "lie in different parts of space." Without such an assumption of the mutually independent existence (the "being-thus") of spatially distant things, an assumption which originates in everyday thought, physical thought in the sense familiar to us would not be possible. Nor does one see how physical laws could be formulated and tested without such a clean separation.

Einstein continues his point in another passage:

> However, if one renounces the assumption that what is present in different parts of space has an independent, real existence, then I do not at all see what physics is supposed to describe. For what is thought to be a "system" is, after all, just conventional, and I do not see how one is supposed to divide up the world objectively so that one can make statements about the parts.

Einstein was bothered not just by the possibility that God plays dice, but by the more disturbing possibility that the entire game is not real, in the sense of having permanent, independent existence. Einstein is arguing against exactly what Bell's theorem implies and recent experimental evidence has shown to be true. To use Henry Stapp's terminology (1989) "faster-than-light influences" are implied in a worldview where the failure of local microrealism is a fact of nature. Somehow, the two parts of the whole—in

the Bell experiments the two separated particles—remain
a whole even after they have been separated by large distances, and that wholeness is really outside of space and
time. What is in crisis then is not quantum theory but our
usual views of what seem to be "separate parts" of what
remains, after all, a whole.

If we have to revise our usual way of thinking, where
then is the crisis? In our usual way of thinking! We saw
that a view of the universe where non-locality is taken as
a fact may explain some nagging problems in cosmological
models. The new worldview of wholeness in physical theory
will have to feature a generalized principle of complementarity in all fields of study. From our experience in
microscopic theory and our observations, two factors seem
to always be there: *complementary views* and an *undivided
wholeness*. Wholeness, obviously outside of space and
time as the Bell experiments indicate, is wholeness over
all scales, in *both* space and time. "Microscopic" and
"macroscopic" are just convenient labels.

This is where we leave physical theory, for the vision of
wholeness is truly holistic. This vision cannot be achieved
unless we include in our views of the universe the conscious
actions and thinking processes responsible for these
views—in other words, ourselves. If holism is a valid world
picture, Consciousness cannot be left out. As the architects
of quantum theory were painfully aware, physical theory
does not presently say much—and probably cannot even in
principle say much—about our own consciousness. What is
then the relationship between us as individuals, universal
Consciousness—call it metamind, collective unconscious,
the inner Self, God or what you like—and the physical
universe? For clues we turn to the perennial philosophy,
not to make some nebulous connection between Western
science and Eastern yogic science to prove that one validates
the other, but because this philosophy, more than any
other human activity, concerns itself with the issue at
hand—the relation between individuals, Consciousness
and the cosmos.

Wholeness and the Physical Universe

The failure of local theories, which conform to our everyday view of the world, and the vindication of quantum theory have ushered in the era of non-locality in physics. There is also abundant evidence from other branches of physics and biology pointing to non-locality. To make matters more interesting, mathematics itself seems to be limited in a fundamental way in providing a complete picture of the Universe. This should not be surprising; if wholeness is the fundamental property of the Universe, we wouldn't expect any tool, no matter how "abstract" or "pure," to provide us with the whole picture.

In 1930, the young mathematician Kurt Gödel proved a very strange theorem known as Gödel's Incompleteness Theorem. He proved that *mathematics is open-ended*, that there can never be a final system of mathematics. Every axiom-system in mathematics will eventually run into a problem that it cannot solve. The mathematician Rudy Rucker explains the profound significance of the Incompleteness Theorem (Rucker, 1982):

> The implications of this epochal discovery are devastating. The thinkers of the Industrial Revolution liked to regard the universe as a vast preprogrammed machine. It was optimistically predicted that soon scientists would know all the rules, all the programs. But if Gödel's Theorem tells us anything, it is this: Man will never know the final secret of the universe.

That is, we will never know the final secret of the universe if we insist that a complete picture of the universe, as an object different from ourselves must be obtained mathematically. Gödel's theorem still does not say anything about Consciousness, only about the limitation of any mathematical description of the physical universe. However, mathematical language is still a *language*, invented by humans. It may be the most universal language, but it is still a language. Its letters are the numbers, and its syntax and grammar are mathematical relationships. Niels Bohr and Werner Heisenberg were very aware of the limitations of language in general and struggled with this problem in their formulation of quantum theory:

> . . . the chief profit we can derive in these problems from the progress of modern science is to learn how cautious we have to be with language and with the meaning of words (Wilber, 1984).

Bohr more than any other physicist was aware of the limitations that language imposes on any picture of the universe. He was known to spend hours or even days on reworking and clarifying a single sentence in his articles.

That letters, words and language can provide limiting views of what we are trying to convey was understood by the ancient philosophers of the East. A Shaivist sutra makes the profound statement "Limited knowledge is bondage" (Singh, 1979a). This does not state that limited knowledge is "wrong," only that it binds us—by making the unreal appear as the real. The bondage arises because we identify with the concepts inherent in words and sentences, we identify with the inherent power of the letters, the matrika shakti, without understanding that power. The same is true of the numbers. There is an inherent power in numbers and their relationships with which we identify and, as a result, we believe in a perfect, mathematical universe. These views are not wrong, only limited and therefore binding.

One could ask how the idea that some mathematical model would eventually succeed in explaining how the Universe came about? Certainly, the Pythagoreans, who are credited as the first to have believed in the mathematical structure of the Universe, had notions of the numbers totally different from ours today. We take numbers as simply secondary to or representing the physical quantities to which they are assigned. The Pythagoreans, on the other hand, believed that numbers contain or represent the creative principles of the cosmos, the Ideas. They also believed that the geometrical figures represent the forms they correspond to[1] (cf. Warner, 1958).

We today, like the Pythagoreans, believe that the structure of the physical universe is deeply related to the structure of the mathematical universe. Unlike the Pythagoreans, we believed the universe could be completely understood in terms of mathematical models, not that numbers hold the secret to the creative principles of the Universe. Ours was a modern product of the Age of Reason. However, quantum theory and Bell's theorem have shattered all clock-like classical views of the cosmos, and Gödel's theorem has shattered all views of the cosmos resting completely on mathematics. Now we have a choice of being either pessimistic because science cannot disclose ultimate Reality, or taking the optimistic view of accepting a holistic view of the Universe. A holistic view must include us, all that is artistic, all that belongs to the realm of feelings and thoughts, the stuff of the heart, not only the stuff of the mind. Holism must include all that cannot reasonably be fitted by any mathematical model. In other words, any modern view of the Universe will have to include Consciousness in a primary way.

According to Heisenberg, who was quoting Heinrich Hertz (Wilber, 1984):

. . . a natural science is one whose propositions on limited domains of nature can have only a correspondingly limited validity; that science is not a philosophy developing a worldview of nature as a whole or about the essence of things.

Wholeness is manifested through the mathematical beauty and harmony of the physical universe, and yet it cannot be simply defined or constrained by either of them. Western science is being forced to look hard and seriously at what was accepted in the ancient systems of yogic philosophy: the ultimate wholeness that pervades the cosmos. Today, we don't have to assume wholeness based solely on the kind of intuitive sense that Einstein had. Physical nonlocality, which hints at an underlying wholeness, has been unequivocally confirmed in the laboratory with tests of Bell's Theorem.

Wholeness can be witnessed in the most dramatic visual ways in the Universal Diagrams which plot common properties of all characteristic objects in the physical

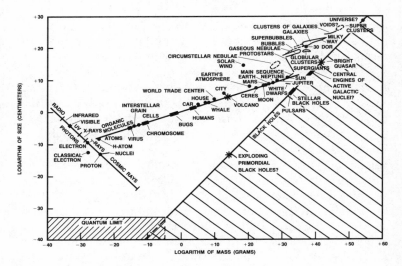

Figure 24. Mass versus length diagram depicting most known classes of objects in the universe

universe (Kafatos, 1985, 1986; Kafatos and Nadeau, 1990). These plots do not result from some theoretical picture; only the observable properties of known classes of objects are plotted. Because many orders of magnitude have to be included, one has to plot the logarithm of the corresponding physical quantity. These diagrams are very compact. In Figures 24 and 25 two such diagrams are shown. In the first one, the masses and lengths of known classes of objects in the universe are plotted. It is immediately obvious that the plots are not scattered, that objects seem to fall nicely into distinct relationships.

Running through most of the central regions of the diagram is a unique line on which cells, bugs, humans, in fact all living entities are located, as well as most familiar objects, from atoms and molecules to planets and most normal stars. All objects on this line have a common property; they have the density of matter, which is the density of water. What we call the density of water is truly the density of atomic matter. If we take physical water to represent this density, then the conviction of the ancient philosopher Thales of Miletos that the primary substance of the cosmos is water is borne out by this diagram. There are other regions in this diagram which are beyond our normal perception. To the left of the water line one finds a line running diagonally from larger sizes and smaller masses to smaller sizes and larger masses. All objects on this line travel with the speed of light or very close to it and are "photon like." All quanta of light are found here. At the bottom left-hand corner of the diagram we find another shaded region labeled "quantum limit." Here not only would objects be beyond the horizon of observability, but physics breaks down completely and any description becomes impossible. This is the region of Planck vacuum fluctuations, where space and time themselves cease to exist.

In the upper right-hand corner of the diagram we find objects with densities less than the density of atomic matter, from a fraction of a gram per cubic centimeter to the unimaginable vacuum of intergalactic space with densities near 10^{-31} grams per cubic centimeter. Here we reach the horizon of present-day observability of the large scale of the universe. Nevertheless, this diagram gives a hint that still larger aggregates of matter can exist, perhaps larger than the observable universe, although we wouldn't know what to call them.

Finally, below the density of water we find very dense objects, the white dwarfs, dead stars with densities millions of times greater than water and the pulsars, and another class of dead stars with densities hundreds of trillions times denser than water. At the other end of the scale we know that objects of such unimaginable density exist: the nuclei of atoms. We don't know of objects between the sizes of nuclei and pulsars which are as dense as they are, but in principle they could exist: chunks of nuclear matter. Objects below the line labeled "black holes" are denser or more compact than a black hole. Therefore, inside the shaded region below this line, any object would be beyond the horizon of observability and not really a part of our universe.

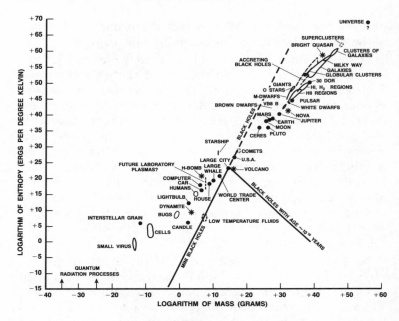

Figure 25. Universal Diagram of mass versus entropy radiated within the lifetime of objects of various classes

An even more puzzling diagram is shown in Figure 25. It shows a plot over almost 90 orders of magnitude between the masses of known classes of objects and the entropy they radiate within their lifetimes. Entropy is a thermo-dynamic quantity measuring the amount of disorder that results in any physical process, and here we show the entropy radiated away by different objects. Everything in the universe radiates photons, including us. (We radiate roughly the equivalent amount of 100 Watts, but mostly in the infrared.) Enfolded within this entropy is the total lifetime, the amount of radiant energy and the surface temperature of the objects shown. We do not know why a combination of these three quantities results in a tight linear relationship between entropy and mass. The basic scales of these diagrams are determined by our physics at the most fundamental level, by the very values of the constants of nature: the charge of the electron, the speed of light, the gravitational constant, Planck's quantum of action, etc. However, why an object's life span as observable in its particular form depends on these constants is a total mystery. The linear relationship shown is tight; the three orders of magnitude some objects stray from the average curve is very minute on the global scale of roughly 80 - 90 orders of magnitude in both axes. The most successful physical theory, quantum electrodynamics, predicts quantities to one part in 10^{15}. This diagram shows a relationship that is good to at least one part in more than one 10^{80}! Such diagrams can even be used for limited "predictions" of where specific objects might be found.

However, it is the global interrelations, the wholeness among different classes of objects, that is most striking. For example, the entropy radiated away in a single volcanic eruption is marked by the point "volcano." When we take into account that single volcanoes don't erupt just once, we would expect a volcano to erupt thousands to tens of thousands of times in its lifetime, which would bring it closer to the average relationship. Such a prediction in retrospect turns out to be reasonable in light of what is known about continental drift and the tectonic motion of plates. Predictions of this kind are amazing because we can make them by just looking at the appropriate diagram and considering that objects in the universe fall close to the average line; no detailed knowledge of a specific scientific field, like geology, is needed, only knowledge of the overall properties of the objects examined.

It is easy to overlook an important point. The plots in these diagrams are of specific objects, which means they have been observed. Without innumerable acts of observation recorded by scientists in different fields, these plots could not exist. As quantum physics has shown, our universe is, after all, a participatory universe. Our observations are a part of the whole.

To illustrate how these diagrams may actually change as our awareness of the cosmos expands, imagine that we try to draw a diagram of masses versus sizes as an ancient philosopher might have attempted to do it. We can imagine that Archimedes might have attempted that because he was aware of the rough sizes in the solar system and even the distance of stars. Archimedes used observation and experimentation in the same way a modern scientist would use them: to test hypotheses as well as to discover how nature behaves, and therefore to construct new hypotheses. In the "Sand Reckoner," Archimedes performed a calculation that is amazing even by today's standards. He managed to compute the number of grains of sand that could fill the entire universe! In his calculation he used all the elements of analysis that a theoretical physicist of the twentieth century would employ. Not only is the analysis correct, but the number that Archimedes obtained is very close to the amount of matter we believe exists in the observable universe! One may consider this just a coincidence until one realizes that the probability of obtaining that number purely by chance is exceedingly negligible.

For this calculation Archimedes invented a totally new number system that enabled him to manipulate very large numbers (Harrison, 1981). He reasoned in the following way: The size of the universe, according to Aristarchus of Samos, was much greater than the size of the solar system. Archimedes probably assumed the Golden Mean ratio and applied it to find the size of the universe. Hence, the universe is as large compared to the size of the solar system as the solar system is compared to the Earth. Since Aristarchus had computed the size of the solar system, and since Eratosthenes had measured the size of the Earth, Archimedes was able to calculate the size of the universe, the "sphere of the fixed stars" as the Greeks called it. In modern units, this turns out to be about one light-year. Even though we now know that not all stars are located at the same distance from us, it turns out that the closest stars are at a distance of only a few light-years—a value similar to that obtained by Archimedes. He then calculated the size of a grain of sand and computed that the universe could hold a number of grains which, our modern system of powers of ten, translates to one followed by 63 zeroes, or 10^{63}. If we wanted to convert the number of particles of sand to the number of protons in the universe we would find that each of Archimedes grains could hold 10^{17} protons. The total number of protons in Archimedes' universe would then be about 10^{80}.

Of course the observable universe is not one light-year in radius but roughly 10 billion light-years. Also, the average density of matter in the universe is roughly 10^{31} less than the density of sand (a few times 10^{-31} gr/cm^3). Sir Arthur Eddington, a modern cosmologist, wondered how many protons would fit in the universe and by a series of theoretical steps obtained 10^{80}. This number is similar to that for the average density of matter in the universe. Our modern, observable universe contains as many particles of matter as the Archimedean universe could hold if it were completely filled with sand! Somehow Archimedes, using the wrong size for the universe, computed the same number Eddington and modern astronomers have obtained after careful observations of distant galaxies. Mere coincidence? One wonders. If predictions like Archimedes' number and the total age of Brahma are born out by modern science, we may wish to entertain the possibility that purely intuitive contemplation can yield right answers. This was, after all, Pythagoras' belief, and it is mirrored in modern times by scientists of the caliber of Einstein and Eddington.

As far as we know, Archimedes never plotted a diagram such as that shown in Figure 26. If he did, it would have looked something like the one shown here. As we saw, Archimedes knew how to handle large numbers and he could have plotted the appropriate exponents in his system of numbers, much the way we plot the exponent in the powers of ten system. He knew the size of the solar system and estimated the size of the universe to correspond roughly to one light-year. At the other end of the scale he certainly knew the size of terrestrial objects, and although he did not know how large atoms are—Democritus postulated only that they would have to be extremely small—he knew that they would have to be smaller than any visible object. When we compare Figure 26 to Figure 24 one thing is strikingly obvious. We have increased our knowledge of objects in the universe immensely in the last two thousand years, particularly in the last fifty years, and the mass-size diagram has become much richer.

In a way these diagrams indicate the *expansion of our knowledge about external objects*. The increase of knowledge about the physical universe since antiquity results in more *intricate patterns* in any physical variable that we choose to plot.

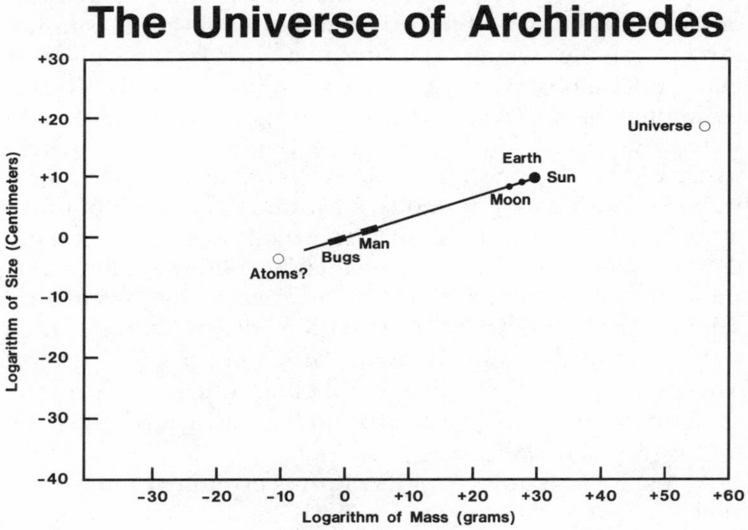

The Universe of Archimedes

Figure 26. The mass-size diagram as might have been drawn by Archimedes

The previous discussion leads naturally to the old question of the relationship between object and subject, a question which has been addressed by practically all ancient and modern philosophical systems of thought. We saw that Bohr himself struggled with it and ended up viewing complementarity as a fundamental aspect of the cosmos at every level. As we saw, complementarity has to be featured as the basic structuring principle in any view of physical reality. The Universal Diagrams illustrate graphically the emergence of complementary relationships giving rise to the appearance of known objects in that they show what is observable—everything outside the black hole and quantum limit regions—and what is not observable—everything inside these regions.

A generalized principle of complementarity is necessary in any picture which incorporates the wholeness evident all around us. This is because all complementarities boil down to the most fundamental complementary relationship known to us, that between the subject and the object (Kafatos and Nadeau, 1990). Among those aware of this need are Niels Bohr, Immanuel Kant, the ancient yogic philosophers, and the philosopher Alfred N. Whitehead. Whitehead (1929) saw no basic contradiction between philosophy and science (Prigogine and Stengers, 1984):

> Thus, for Whitehead the task of philosophy was to reconcile permanence and change, to conceive of things as processes, to demonstrate that becoming forms entities, individual identities that are born and die . . . he demonstrated the connection between a philosophy of relation—no element of nature is a permanent support for changing relations; each receives its identity from its relations with others—and a philosophy of innovating becoming. In the process of its genesis, each existent unifies the multiplicity of the world, since it adds to this multiplicity an extra set of relations. At the creation of each new entity "the many become one and are increased by one."

When Prigogine expounded the basics of Whitehead's philosophy as given in the passage above he beautifully illustrates the unfoldment of complementary relationships among objects. This step-by-step increase of our knowledge is graphically illustrated in the Universal Diagrams. Whitehead formulated a theory of time that involves subjective and objective sides. The subjective side assimilates past experiences and brings the present into the past. In this way it creates irreversibility, so that what has happened cannot be undone. The subjective can never be known as an object because the subjective always precedes the objective manifestation. Science only examines the objective side, what appears to be stable, although in reality stability and reversibility are special cases of an ever-changing flux that is brought about by subjective experience.

Any physicist or philosopher who has struggled with

the meaning of wholeness has touched upon the idea of complementary constructs—even though the specific term "complementarity" is often left out. David Bohm made a serious attempt at formulating a new physics of wholeness, evident in his "implicate order" (Bohm, 1981). The ordinary, external or "explicate order" is implied in the underlying implicate order, even when it has not manifested as a physical reality. Bohm goes on to state that the implicate order itself is implied in an underlying order of pure potential, which in turn springs from an infinite pool of insight-intelligence. This movement from the more implicate to the more explicate, which Bohm calls the "holomovement," features complementarity as the unfolding principle.

As the ancient sages realized, all opposites merge at the level of the core of the metamind or pure Self, as we saw at the top levels in the 36 steps of the creative unfoldment process in Shaivism. In more modern terms one could say all complementary relationships end at the level of pure insight-intelligence. In fact, Bohm's holomovement is a physical analogue of the unfolding of sound from the level of unstruck sound, insight-intelligence—the implicate order—to the spoken or audible sound—the explicate order.

The dream of Einstein and all theoretical physicists is the unified field. A graphic illustration is attempted in Figure 27. Particles are pictured as bumps in the underlying "stuff" of space-time as waves on the surface of the ocean. As two particles interact, the underlying continuum changes and the peaks move in different directions.

The problem with this unified field idea is that space-time itself may not be primary. Physicists have looked hard at the underlying "substance," but every time the "metastuff" seems to melt away. This metastuff cannot be described by any mathematical model, and it is not observable in the physical sense. At the metastuff level, physics collapses, because there one reaches the ultimate horizon of knowledge where objects cease to exist as external objects of perception. Physics is then forced to go beyond its own boundaries. At that level allegorical descriptions such as the Eastern image of the eternal dance of Shiva become more appropriate. Many scientists are optimistic that one day, hopefully soon, they will understand the fundamental field of the universe, even though experience from physical science to date indicates that *process* may be more fundamental than *substance*. In the end only the dance itself seems to make any sense, as the Greek philosopher Heraclitus asserted more than two thousand years ago.

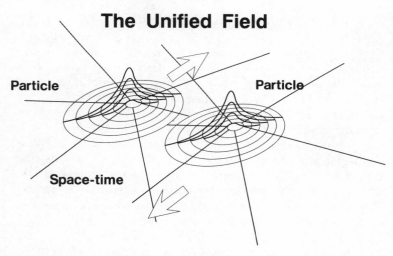

The Unified Field

Particle

Particle

Space-time

Figure 27. The unified field visualized as space-time changing locally to appear as interacting particles. The problem with this view is that space-time itself seems to be secondary.

Heraclitus of Ephesos (Burnet, 1930; Warner, 1958) was in some ways as modern a thinker as Blake, T. S. Eliot, Hegel, Marx or Bertrand Russell. Heraclitus is original and unique among the ancient Greek philosophers because he concluded that unity exists in variety. There is no fundamental substance to the universe; what is fundamental is process, the "fresh waters that are ever flowing," to use his own language. According to Heraclitus opposite tensions attuned to each other bring about this physical universe. Humans too are subjected to the "strife" of the opposites. In many ways Heraclitus is closer to the sages of the East than any other ancient Greek thinker. For example, he taught his students that "it is wise to listen not to me but to my

Word and to confess that all things are one." The "Word" of Heraclitus is not mere inquiry. It reminds us of the Word of St. John and the paravak, or supreme vibration, of the Hindu philosophers. When Heraclitus says to listen to the Word and not to him, he gives the message of all spiritual teachers in the East and the West: go beyond the mere human form.

One further example of the underlying wholeness of the cosmos comes from biology in conjunction with physics. The eyes of all species are most sensitive in the "water window," the yellow-green part of the solar spectrum. It is precisely in this range that the sun puts out most of its radiation. This, plus the gravitational constant, G, are primarily responsible for the structure of the Sun. Also, the atmosphere of the Earth allows radiation to reach the ground in this same spectral range. The reason is that the water window is determined by atomic constants like the charge of the electron, e, and Planck's constant, h, which fix the absorption properties of molecules in the atmosphere. Now why should the macroscopic constant, G, be so finely tuned to the microscopic constants, e and h? One may assume that this tuning is not by chance, and that the presence of life has to be brought into the picture.

Various versions of this relationship form what is known as the anthropic principle. To conclude that the presence of life, in this case the properties of the eye of living species, requires this connection is to attempt to find cause and effect in wholeness. But wholeness does not allow any notion of cause and effect, which are classical constructs, as they imply separation between what causes and what is caused. This is a fundamental problem for some versions of the anthropic principle and the related *Large Number Hypothesis* of Dirac (1937). The concept of complementarity may offer a better approach to these ideas, for within the conventional physical framework they make no sense. If, however, they are taken as constructs that complement ordinary physical theory, then they do make sense: The existence of life must be included in any attempt to understand the physical universe, although physics in principle cannot be used to understand the presence or origin of life. In other words, the physical universe and life both exist, and the two imply each other within a complementary relationship in an undivided wholeness. But they don't "cause" each other. The Universal Diagrams which show the presence of animate as well as inanimate matter graphically illustrate the wholeness, even though these diagrams do not, and cannot, provide an explanation of wholeness in the scientific sense of the word.

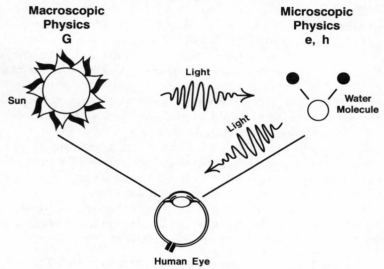

Figure 28. An illustration of the anthropic principle. Macroscopic and microscopic physics are connected through the existence of the eye. This demonstrates the fundamental wholeness of the Universe.

In trying to understand wholeness with the aid of physical theory alone, we have reached an impasse. Wholeness is implied with abundant evidence from physical science, and at the same time wholeness cannot, by definition, be understood by purely scientific means. The dilemma can be put quite simply: A holistic view of the universe by necessity has to include the conscious acts of the observers; thus wholeness implies that Consciousness be included at the most fundamental level; but since though Consciousness is undivided and can never be examined as an object of inquiry, it follows that science can say very little about wholeness and Consciousness other than acknowledging their existence. Science may be able to make some simple scientific predictions based on the requirements of wholeness, as, for example, those made by using the Universal Diagrams, but such attempts hardly conform to the usual rigorous scientific methodology.

Perhaps we shouldn't expect analytical proofs, in the usual sense, to provide much insight. Undivided wholeness is not subject to analysis through breaking it up into parts. We cannot keep dividing the whole and hope that somehow this will lead to the secret of wholeness. *The reductionist approach of science is very successful to reveal the properties of the parts, but not of the whole.* As long as science keeps the separation between object and subject intact, it can at most provide hints of the underlying wholeness. So far, the only principle we have found that seems to operate in all human endeavors is a generalized principle of complementarity. As such, it must truly be a fundamental process in our dialogue with Nature and with ourselves.

Erwin Schrödinger struggled with the apparent division between object and subject, which is only apparent because in reality wholeness always persists (Wilber, 1984):

> The same elements compose my mind and the world. This situation is the same for every mind and its world, in spite of the unfathomable abundance of "cross-references" between them. The world is given to me only once, not one existing and one perceived. Subject and object are only one. The barrier between them cannot be said to have broken down as a result of recent experience in the physical sciences, for this barrier does not exist.

Nevertheless, Schrödinger was painfully aware of the inadequacy of science to deal with "the whole display," with wholeness:

> Most painful is the absolute silence of all our scientific investigations toward our questions concerning the meaning and scope of the whole display.

If logical, scientific methodology reaches a dead end, how can we proceed in our quest for wholeness? Schrödinger goes on in another work to propose that pictorial analogy may be the only valid method to follow in the pursuit of wholeness (Wilber, 1984):

We intellectuals of today are not accustomed to admit pictorial analogy as a philosophical insight; we insist on logical deduction. But, as against this, it may perhaps be possible for logical thinking to disclose at least this much: that to grasp the basis of phenomena through logical thought may, in all probability, be impossible since logical thought is itself a part of phenomena and wholly involved in them; we may ask ourselves whether, in that case, we are obliged to deny ourselves the use of an allegoric picture of the situation, merely on the grounds that its fitness cannot be strictly proven.

If a barrier between subject and object does not really exist and if pictorial analogies are needed to proceed further, where is the problem? It exists in the mind, as long as the mind refuses to use any part of itself other than the strictly analytical part. The mind is capable of thinking pictorially, of constructing images which bring us closer to direct perception than abstract thinking can. Schrödinger's exhortation to use that part of our mind is identical with what the yogic philosophers have been saying for thousands of years: go beyond the mind, beyond the usual thinking faculty. The image of the dancing Shiva seems absurd in a scientific sense, and yet it conveys a fundamental insight of how Consciousness works better than any analytical methodology.

Wholeness and the Individual

The vision of wholeness becomes a reality in the individual when he or she no longer perceives the external objective existence as separate from individual subjective experience. Consciousness itself *is* wholeness and can be experienced as such only when all boundaries between the perceiving subject and the perceived objects have ceased to exist. This forms the foundation of mystical experience. It is

described beautifully in the following passage by Erwin
Schrödinger, a "hard scientist," but it could have been
written by one of the ancient mystics (Wilber, 1984):

> Hence this life of yours which you are living is not merely a
> piece of the entire existence, but is, in a certain sense, the
> whole; only this whole is not so constituted that it can be
> surveyed in one single glance. This, as we know, is what
> the Brahmins express in that sacred, mystic formula which
> is yet really so simple and so clear: *Tat tvam asi*, this is you.
> Or, again, in such words as "I am in the east and in the west,
> I am below and above, *I am this whole world.*"

The last sentence can be found almost verbatim in the
Bhagavad Gita where Lord Krishna, the Teacher of Arjuna,
explains the identity between the individual, the Lord
and the entire world. Schrödinger's statement is analogous
to the sutra from Shaivism, "as here, so elsewhere." Wholeness, by definition, is the same everywhere and at all times.

Schrödinger goes on: "For eternally and always there
is only now, one and the same now; the present is the only
thing that has no end." This is the vision of undivided
wholeness, the content of pure Consciousness-in-itself, with
no perceiving objects. Or rather, the vision where all objective
experience has merged into pure awareness, the pure Subject.
Gurumayi Chidvilasananda, a modern Master of meditation, calls this pure awareness *Purno-aham Vimarsha*, the
perfect I-Consciousness, also known in Shaivism as Spanda
(Singh, 1980b), the dynamic throb of creative power. This
perfect I-ness or I-awareness is the innermost core of ourselves, the core of the metamind, the unstruck sound or
Logos, the level of insight-intelligence of Bohm. It is the
thought-free mind or "full mind" of Confucius, the "kingdom
of heaven" of Jesus Christ, the witness-consciousness of
the yogis, the state or *turiya* of meditators, the inner Self
of all, the goal of all mystics and experience of Masters
and great beings. Though beyond description, it can be
experienced in the inner heart and is within the reach of
everyone. Yet most people aren't aware of it because it
forms the very foundation of everything else. It can never
be perceived as an object by the senses because it illumines

the senses themselves and also the mind and intellect through which we are trying to comprehend it.

The inner Self can be pictured as the continuous thread running through garments, the gold in ornaments, the light illuminating objects in what would otherwise be a dark room. The mind needs such pictures, but when one is in the state of pure awareness there is no place for pictures. The experience is direct, all-encompassing and without boundaries. We become aware of our fundamental identity with the Universe and cosmic Consciousness. The first aphorism of the Shiva Sutras of Kashmir Shaivism is (Singh, 1979a), "*Chaitanyam Atma.*" The Self is Consciousness. The inner core of ourselves, the inner Self, is identical with Consciousness, the universal principle and foundation of the Universe.

How does the phenomenal world arise if everything is identical at the most fundamental level? Sir Arthur Eddington describes it in the following words (Wilber, 1984):

> These airy fancies which the mind, when we do not keep it severely in order, projects into the external world should be of no concern to the earnest seeker after truth. . . . But the solid substance of things is another illusion. It too is a fancy projected by the mind into the external world.

Shaivism says the same thing: Consciousness *projects* the external world. The 36 steps of creation are a projection from the inner to the outer realms. Consciousness becomes progressively more dense and at the same time more limited, until the physical universe is manifested. The projection operates by means of unfolding separations into seemingly opposite, though truly complementary, aspects which are needed for the creative process to complete itself. The process of division into complementary aspects can be seen in all steps of creation, from the initial motion towards separation in the first five pure levels, the first *tattvas*, all the way "down" to the level of the earth.

These steps of the creative process are universal. And if each individual is truly a microcosm of the cosmos, then we should be able to witness the creative steps in our own activities. The Universe is then continuously undergoing the creative process—which of course includes all five acts, such as creation and dissolution—in a universal sense as well as in countless individual beings. The creation of the Universe as well as the creative process in an individual are like the creation of a piece of art. For example, an artist conceiving an artistic work goes through the first pure levels of creation. At first, the two levels of creation are totally unseparated and might be considered as occurring simultaneously. At this two-in-one level the first throb of creativity begins to manifest itself, and the static *I* and the dynamic *AM* are one and the same. The terms Shiva and Shakti are used to correspond to the I and the AM but are really as inseparable as the two sides of a coin.

At the third level a desire to create arises. Here the I predominates in the relationship *I (am) This*; I want to create (something). At the fourth level, the objective side of the process becomes more defined and *This* predominates. The object begins to be known and emphasized, but still it is not separate from the perceiving subject. At the fifth and final pure level of the creative process, both *I* and *This* are emphasized equally and are in perfect balance. Here the power of action begins to manifest. In all these five steps the subject and the object, the static and the dynamic aspects of the perceiving consciousness, remain one. No object has yet been created; no separation has taken place.

Beyond the fifth level the creative process continues through the remaining 31 steps until the object is finally completely separated as a physical entity from the consciousness that conceived it.

The various levels of the creative process are contained within any creative throb or spanda of activity. The reason we are normally not aware of them, particularly the first five pure levels of creation where unity is unbroken, is because all these states essentially take no finite time to be completed. For example, when we first open our eyes in the morning we undergo these first pure levels in an instant. They occur before we perceive ourselves or the bed on which we slept or the bedroom, before we have any sense of time—"Oh, I am late for work"—or any feeling—"I had such a nice sleep." A scientist goes through the same five levels when he or she first feels the urge to create a scientific theory.

All steps of creation proceed from That which is absolute, undifferentiated Consciousness, Paramashiva. Here all attempts to grasp That, to describe That even in holistic allegorical terms, fail. Sages in all traditions state from their experience that Consciousness has two aspects, the static and the dynamic. At this level the complementary relationship does not cause any differentiation, and all complementary relationships have to reduce back to this primal level from which everything springs. The old philosophical argument of whether the primary substance is being or becoming, static Being or active process, is resolved in the merging of what are usually considered opposites. Consciousness is *both*; one can never separate the two. In Shaivism the terms *prakasha*, which literally means light or being, and *vimarsha*, which means awareness, are sometimes equated with *Sat-chit-ananda*: *Sat* means Being; *chit* means awareness or Consciousness; and *ananda* means bliss. Thus *Sat-chit-ananda* = *prakasha* + *vimarsha*. Absolute undifferentiated Consciousness is Being, awareness of Beingness, and the bliss that arises from that awareness. These three aspects of God are found in all traditions, often disguised by special terminology. Again, we have to be aware of the limiting condition that results through the use of any terms, even the most sublime ones. For example, the Christian terms "Father," "Son," and "Holy Spirit" convey a similar message: the Father or pure Being can be known only through the Son or embodied awareness in a process in which the Holy Spirit, divine energy or bliss, is indispensable. The use of everyday terms like "father" and "son" often bring emotional baggage with them. Even the term "bliss" is loaded. *Ananda* is not any ordinary bliss, not even the bliss of sublime spiritual experiences. It conveys the notion of completeness or contentment. Consciousness is complete in itself; it needs no outside support or medium to manifest anything.

Why does absolute, undifferentiated Consciousness, complete in itself, create countless beings, some of them, like minerals, inert; others, like plants or lower forms of

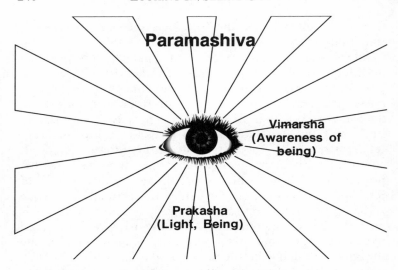

Figure 29. Allegorical picture of Paramashiva as always consisting of prakasha and vimarsha

life, active but unable to think; and still others, like humans, with the capacity to think? Why are we born to be mostly unaware of who we truly are and unaware of the world around us, to be mostly unhappy, incomplete or even miserable and rarely happy and content? What kind of God creates this world full of passions, wars, famines and other miseries? These questions are similar to the question, Why is water wet? Rather than asking why, we can choose to use our free will to find out who we really are; and stop blaming some outside agency like our parents, our teachers, our country or God. We will never know the "why," but we can find out what we can do about our situation.

If we insist on knowing the why we have to remember that the world consists of opposites and persists because of their existence. Heraclitus is quoted as saying that those who are praying for all evil to disappear are really praying for the destruction of the world. The opposites stand in complementary relationship to each other. Take one away and the other disappears as well. Without the opposites, without complementary relationships, there would be no world.

After the first creative throb, spanda, manifests itself in the ocean of undifferentiated Consciousness. Consciousness becomes progressively more bound and contracted through the various steps of creation. This contraction is just an appearance because the universal Shakti, the power of Paramashiva, remains pure, infinite, untainted and eternal. The first aphorism of the *Pratyabhijnahridayam*, the philosophical text of Kashmir Shaivism that outlines the creative process, states (Singh, 1980a):

> *Chitihi svatantra visva siddhi hetuhu.* Supremely independent universal Consciousness is the cause of the manifestation, maintenance, and reabsorption of the Universe.

Universal Consciousness is totally free to do anything and everything including creating all possible worlds, all possible opposites. If Consciousness would create only "good" things, then it would be limited and limiting.

The second aphorism from the *Pratyabhijnahridayam* answers the question of how creation occurs:

> *Svecchaya svabhittau visva unmilayati.* Of Her own free will, Consciousness unfolds the Universe on Her own screen.

The screen onto which Consciousness projects the Universe is also Consciousness. Bishop George Berkeley and Sir James Jeans, a twentieth-century cosmologist, concluded that the objectivity of objects arises from their subsisting "in the mind of some Eternal Spirit." If their statement is to make any sense, we have to take it to mean that mind and matter—contrary to what Descartes declared—are non-dual: mind is matter and matter is mind. Shaivism says the same thing. To put it differently, since all objects exist in the field of pure Consciousness, "in the mind of some Eternal Spirit," we all are thoughts of the primal Being. As such the Universe is not really different from Consciousness. And since the nature of Consciousness is the light of Being and the awareness of Becoming, the Self or Consciousness shines through the Universe.

These statements are made in an allegorical sense which, as we saw, may be the only way to approach wholeness. Eddington underlies the importance of what he calls "intimate" language (Wilber, 1984):

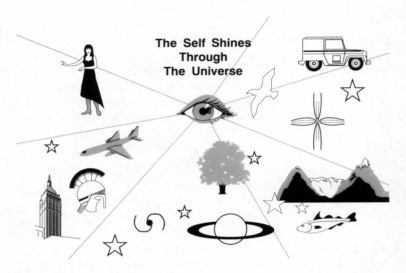

Figure 30. The allegory of the light of Consciousness shining through the physical universe

We have two kinds of knowledge which I call symbolic knowledge and intimate knowledge. I do not know whether it would be correct to say that reasoning is only applicable to symbolic knowledge, but the more customary forms of reasoning have been developed for symbolic knowledge only. The intimate knowledge will not submit to codification and analysis, or, rather, when we attempt to analyse it the intimacy is lost and it is replaced by symbolism.

This passage illustrates complementarity in another aspect: The direct knowledge that springs from Consciousness is intimate, what the yogis would call "direct experience." Descriptions of that intimate knowledge lose the intimacy. Ordinary knowledge of objects of perception and direct knowledge without any content or experience of Consciousness in itself replace each other.

From Evolution to Involution

How can we reach that inner core which is pure Existence, Awareness and Contentment? Without practical means these sublime statements on the nature of Reality are mere philosophical pronouncements. Yogic philosophy is, however, extremely practical. It is objective for it can be taught and learned and in this sense is scientific. It provides not just theoretical understanding but also practical means to accomplish our identification with the inner Self. In this the usefulness of mere intellectual understanding, the usefulness of any book including this one, comes to an end. Individuals seeking their true nature eventually must take responsibility for the search and decide whether they really want to experience and know the Self.

Shaivism gives a surprisingly simple answer to the question of how to reach our inner core: *reverse the process*. Universal Consciousness unfolds the universe through the process of evolution, of creation. To reach the inner Consciousness, we have to reverse the process. We have to *change evolution into involution*, back through the 36 steps until we reach the first 5 levels and merge with the Consciousness within. There are many procedures suitable for this, depending on one's physical, psychological and mental nature, one's past, one's tendencies and desires. Yet they all boil down to nothing other than *inner awareness*. That awareness takes on progressively more refined forms as we reach deeper and deeper levels of our being. This process is also known as meditation, although this term is often loaded with metaphysical baggage.

Simply put, meditation is turning within, focusing our attention into pure awareness. Patanjali and other philosophers of the East insist that we always meditate, in that *we always focus our attention on something*, tasks, objects, feelings, etc. Without meditation in this general sense all activity would be impossible. However, meditation on the Self requires a particular focusing. As we do this, we are carried progressively through various inner levels and begin to become aware of a variety of inner worlds, an inner universe far richer and less limited than the outer one.

Between the in-breath and the out-breath one discovers the space of absolute stillness (Muktananda, 1978). As our mind slows down our breath also slows down, and we begin to perceive the vast expanses of the inner heart from which arise all breaths and also all thoughts. As we concentrate in a state of inner awareness, we begin to perceive thoughts as arising out of a vast ocean of pure awareness. In the same way that one cannot count the waves in an ocean—they come and go all the time—one cannot count all the thoughts. They just arise for no reason, without a causal agency. The types of thoughts may depend on our state, what we ate, if we are agitated, etc., but their existence cannot be explained. As we ponder this, we realize that thoughts are nothing more than variations of the mind, as waves are variations of the surface of water. Below this surface, which we call "thinking mind," lies a vast ocean of awareness, the metamind, and at its very bottom is the ocean of pure awareness. Who can really count the waves of the ocean, our thoughts or even the different worlds and universes?

This inner journey is impossible without stilling the mind. As expounded in Patanjali's *Yoga Sutras*, this is the primary goal of yoga (Eliade, 1969). We find other philosophical and at the same time practical ancient texts which give us insights on how to achieve this. Two particularly sublime works are the *Bhagavad Gita* and the *Yoga Vasistha*, both texts in which the Master or spiritual teacher reveals the inner journey to the disciple. The importance of using the mind is stressed over and over in texts on how to reach the inner Self. One has to *use the mind to go beyond the mind*. The mind has to be trained with one ultimate focus, merging with its Source from which it receives the light of Consciousness.

The *Yoga Vasistha* (Venkatesananda, 1984), an important philosophical work, consists of 29,000 verses written sometime between the sixth and fourteenth century A.D. It is a practical discourse on the nature of Reality and the means to realize it. The discourse takes place between Rama, the disciple and the sage Vasistha, his teacher. In one of its verses we find:

> It is by the action of consciousness becoming aware of itself that intelligence manifests itself, not when consciousness apprehends an inert object.

And in another verse we read:

When objects as well as the experiencing mind have become tranquil, consciousness alone remains.

These verses describe concisely what meditation is. Quite often we think of meditation as something that we do: sitting down, watching a candle, repeating a mantra, stopping our thoughts. But meditation is much simpler. It consists in merely remaining in one's own Self.

The Function of the Teacher

The importance of the Teacher is expounded in scriptures and traditions of all traditions. We find it in a particularly illuminating form in the text of the *Bhagavad Gita*, (Nikhilananda, 1978), a work of sublime teachings and downright practicality, as applicable in the twentieth century as in ancient times. Lord Krishna, a divine incarnation, step by step reveals to Arjuna the secrets of the inner journey. The scene takes place on the battlefield of Kurukshetra just before the final great battle of the epic *Mahabharata*. The warrior Arjuna signifies the spiritual warrior and disciple, and Krishna, the charioteer, is his spiritual guide. All the important paths of yoga are described in the *Gita*: knowledge, selfless action, love, meditation.

The importance of fixing one's mind on the Self is stated again and again: "Fix your mind on Me only, your intellect in Me, then you shall no doubt live in Me alone hereafter." By "Me" Krishna means the outer spiritual Teacher, who is indispensable in revealing the Master within, but "Me" also refers to the Master within, the inner Self of every being. One experiences the internal background of Consciousness when attention is fixed on an external Master and gradually one turns to the inner Master. This ultimately leads to freedom from the bondage of a limited mind with all its afflictions.

We in the West are used to learning from others. We seek experts to teach us self-development, accounting, self-defense, driving, etc. Yet in learning about the inner journey we feel we don't need a guide. But a guide is indispensable for the inner journey through what appears to us to be unmapped territory. The skillful experts in the inner journey are the ones who have successfully completed the journey and can safely and surely lead us back Home. The term "guru" means "the one who shines light onto darkness," that is, a Master who brings forth the light of knowledge and dispels the darkness of ignorance.

These Teachers of the perennial philosophy are special individuals. They look like human beings and in many respects act like us. However, what makes them different is the level of consciousness at which they live. They are always in touch with their innermost being: *they know who they are.* We operate on the premise that we are different from each other. We identify with our bodies and our concepts and label ourselves as men, women, black, white. We pursue happiness but never seem to achieve it in a permanent way, even if we become wealthy or famous. The Masters of the inner knowledge live in a completely different awareness. They are aware of their bodies, but their consciousness is not bounded by their bodies. In other words, their "I" awareness does not mean for them their particular body with its particular characteristics. Their "I" awareness expands to the entire Universe, both inner and outer. It includes their body and their mind; it includes all humanity; it includes the sun and the stars, the trees and the animals, the rocks and everything that exists. They operate from a space of oneness. Everything for these Masters is God. "Do you really see God in that tree?" a reporter once asked Swami Muktananda. "No," Swami Muktananda said, "I see God *as* that tree."

The Masters see oneness; they see perfection. They point to our own perfection and in this way help us walk back to our perfection. We are like little kids crossing a road; holding mother's hand makes the task easy and safe. We follow the guidance of someone who has walked the path.

The disciple learns by following the example of the Master and from the Master's ways. In the inner knowledge formal lectures or classes are not of much use. No duration of the studies can be specified in advance. The disciple observes everything the Master does or says and contemplates and decodes the Master's behavior. Sometimes this seems contradictory until one realizes that the teachings are directed at different disciples with different temperaments and levels of understanding. There is a story of Master Ramakrishna scolding one of his disciples for defending him against someone who spoke ill of the Master. On another occasion he scolded another disciple who did not defend him in a similar situation. Ramakrishna knew what he was doing: he was teaching and guiding both disciples in performing right action according to their needs. The first disciple needed to conquer his anger, the second needed to overcome his fear and be able to stand up against others.

It is the Master's function to bring into the disciple's awareness all the knowledge that lies already within him or her. That is why classes and lectures are not important. Once, there was a noble young man in Japan of the old days who wanted to learn sword-fighting. One day he arrived at the house of the most famous sword-fighting Master. The Master accepted him, assigned him a house chore and told him that they would never discuss sword-fighting. The young man was confused but he did not dare to ask questions. In those days people thought more than they spoke. So, the student went on with his chores, wondering how he was going to learn sword-fighting. From time to time, as he was busy doing his work, his Master would appear out of nowhere and attack him. In this way, little by little, the apprentice learned sword-fighting without ever holding a sword. The basic belief of Masters is that all knowledge is inside us. This function is to bring this knowledge into the disciples' awareness and allow them to grow into it in an organic way, rather than feeding them useless information and techniques.

The importance of the Teacher has been recognized since antiquity in both East and West. Much of what forms the foundation of Western civilization sprang from the teachings of the ancient philosophers to their students or disciples. In Athens knowledge was imparted in the form of discussions and questions between the Master and students, as in the *Symposium* of Plato, which describes Socrates teaching by discussing the relevant issues with his disciples.

When Socrates said, "One thing I know, that I don't know anything," it was not an empty philosophical statement. He proved time and again through his impeccable reasoning that the inner Truth cannot be grasped in words or theoretical statements. Socrates was not creating philosophical arguments for the sake of arguing. He was after the Truth, and his "midwifery" method was meant to lead his disciples gradually to inner development.

As the interest in philosophy increased in Athens and other Greek cities, need of a more formal arrangement became evident. Schools and academies like those of Plato, Aristotle and others, were formed. In Plato's Academy the Socratic dialectical method was used and disciples gradually began to grasp the timeless order of the Universe, the transcendent "Ideas" and "Forms."

Probably more than other ancient Greek philosophers, Plato and Pythagoras influenced the development of science in the Western world. Pythagoras was a mathematician, philosopher and founder of an important philosophical-religious-political movement. With him philosophy entered a new sphere and became a way of life rather than an isolated activity. Pythagoras, it is said, compared people's lives to the three classes of those attending the Olympic Games: those who came to buy and sell; those who competed in the games; finally, the highest class, those who watched. In Greek the word for "watching" is *theorein* from which the word "theory" is derived. It means "seeing God." Disciples of the Pythagorean School had to keep complete silence for five years to prepare for this *theorein*, what is called in yogic sciences the "witness consciousness." Pythagoras' School was called *Homakoeion*, which literally means "to listen together," because the primary form of learning was attentively listening to the words of the Master without talking.

The disciples lived a life that would eradicate the three reasons for their downfall: desire for sense pleasures, desire for wealth and desire for being above others. Pythagoras taught through the use of aphorisms or compact statements for the student to contemplate. After five years of study, the disciple was ready to be admitted to the School. He or she (Pythagoras, in contrast to the ancient tendency to treat women as second-class citizens, admitted women to his School) then concentrated on the study of numbers and geometry. Pythagoras taught a coherent view of the universe based on numbers, in which harmony of the numbers was reflected in the harmony of the heavens of the cosmos.[1] However, he was not concerned with the study of the universe for its own sake but because it led to spiritual elevation, to the ecstasy of the spirit. "Ecstasy" is from the Greek *ekstasis*, which literally means "standing apart," that is, standing apart from ordinary bodily consciousness.

The School of Pythagoras in Krotona consisted of a theological school, a political science school, a medical school and a physico-mathematical school. Thus his school was the first university as well as the first monastery in the West. The Pythagoreans were the first to study mathematics seriously, and consequently the development of mathematics, astronomy and physics is attributed to them. Without Pythagoras modern science, which is clearly embedded in the language of mathematics, could not have developed. The origins of Western science as well as philosophy can be traced to the ancient school of Pythagoras (and later Plato), a school which was more concerned with ecstasy than with nature.

It is said that Pythagoras himself studied under the guidance of the Egyptian high priests. In ancient Egypt and later in Rome, temples were centers where knowledge was kept and transferred to initiates. We find a similar situation in Judaism and also in Christianity, in which priests were also teachers. The temples and churches were not just places of worship but places where the aspirant was "called" to attend and partake in the knowledge of the Spirit, as the Greek word for "church," *ekklesia*, indicates. In the early years of the Church a need arose for centers where the disciples could study and contemplate without worldly distractions. Gradually, particularly in the Middle

Ages, monasticism became accepted as a spiritual path, and the monasteries served the purpose not just of contemplative life, but also as centers of learning, the way universities serve today. The monastic way of life, in which a seeker studied with a Teacher, was, of course, practiced and revered for centuries in the East.

In Buddhism the function of the Teacher is indispensable for the upliftment of the seeker. In the Zen Buddhist tradition, the Zen Teacher gives the disciple a strange statement or *koan*. This is intended to stop the rational faculty, to still the mind and to let the light of the inner Self shine through. In many ways Zen is very simple, as the simple gesture of the Buddha who, when asked to talk about God, simply lifted a flower, indicating that the Lord is in everything. One of Buddha's disciples, Kashyapa, understood the gesture of his Master and immediately received enlightment. It is alleged that this is the way that Zen Buddhism originated.

In Zen there are many shining examples of the teacher-disciple relationship, as there are in Sufism, Hinduism and other religions. Dogen Zenji, a Zen Master of thirteenth century Japan, for many years looked for his spiritual teacher. He travelled to many places and ended going to China, a hazardous trip in those days. There he met his Master Ju-Ching, who initiated him into spiritual life. Dogen went on to become a great sage and a Master himself. He established Eiheiji, the "temple of eternal peace," near Kyoto, an active monastery even today. He taught that the Buddha nature cannot be manifested unless one practices. His life was a constant teaching to his disciples to relive what he taught, as all great mystics do (quoted in Ishwarananda, 1987):

> When you practice with a teacher and inquire about dharma
> clear the body and the mind, still the eyes and ears, and
> just listen and accept the teaching without mixing in any
> other thoughts.

Nowadays, teaching is rarely done on a one-to-one basis but in large classes. Studying has definite time limits. There are competition and grades in education today.

None of these elements was part of the interaction between the Master and the disciple or student in the past. However, despite the changed role of the teacher today, it can be traced to the ancient concept of the Master.

The value of a Master is not measured by the number of followers, ashrams, monasteries, centers, schools, books or material gain. It lies in his or her aim and ability to make disciples Masters; to make us like him or her. This is the true function of the Master and it is his or her glory.

Summary

Undivided wholeness in the cosmos is evident in a variety of ways and forms, such as the way seemingly unrelated objects obey common relationships and the way biology and physics are integrated through the miracle of existence and life. Ultimately, wholeness though, must be experienced and, therefore, understood not by studying the outer objects, but by turning within. From evolution to involution, the process takes us back to the inner Source. To proceed along this path, the function of the spiritual teacher is indispensable. As in ordinary life, someone who has traversed the path and knows the process can guide us through to the ultimate foundation of our own being. This process is an individual one and ultimately has to be experienced by each for himself or herself.

8

The Physics
of Consciousness

Without going outside you may know the whole world.
Without looking through the window you may see the
ways of Heaven.

Lao Tsu

A new paradigm of wholeness is emerging from Western
physical theory. No longer can the observer and the observed
be considered unrelated at the fundamental level. As John
Archibald Wheeler points out, the observer is a participant
because the act of observation cannot be separated from
what is being observed. In the quantum world one cannot
presume even in principle that one knows exactly what is
going on nor that physical properties always exist in a
physical system when no observation is taking place. Even
in the classical world, as chaos theoreticians have shown,
the laws of nonlinear dynamics require the unpredictability
of the evolution of a system, even though the equations
themselves can be solved. Deterministic predictability
belongs to the science of the past.

Finally, whatever is meant by the word "reality," it is
clearly non-local and not independent of the observing
process. The world of quanta is probabilistic by nature.
Physical attributes of quanta cannot be determined in a
precise way; only the probabilities of these attributes can
be determined a priori. Seemingly, "God is playing dice,"
and we, the observers, seem to be part of the game. Moreover,
in the quantum domain, the reality of solid matter and
the apparent permanence of particles dissolves into a

dance of ever-changing quantum interactions. What is real is the process, not the substance.

Bell's inequality has been tested in the laboratory. As long as the statistical predictions of quantum theory are valid, as proven time and again in the laboratory, we have to accept that quantum theory presents a worldview radically different from local realistic theories. Additionally, we have to accept the wholeness paradigm which emerges from quantum theory. No matter what view of reality one accepts, non-locality across space and time is a fact of the universe. Human beings are part of the game, part of the process, part of the dance.

Furthermore, non-locality seems to extend beyond the quantum domain. Researchers have found correlations linking the tiny dimensions of an atomic radius to the measurements that can be made in macroscopic laboratories. Apparently, non-locality may even extend over billions of light years, to the boundaries of the observable universe. If these correlations are correct, the universe is globally whole at the most fundamental level. In this case, inquiries into what kind of physical universe we inhabit cannot be divorced from the procedures we carry out to explore the nature of the universe.

Since wholeness is the paradigm emerging from physical theory, one also has to accept its underlying principle— complementarity. This principle extends to all fields of intellectual activity. However, complementarity is not merely the recognition that opposites exist. It is the recognition that any split between opposing views or theories, any discord over the act of observation or any other "strife"— to use the word of the philosopher Heraclitus—actually reveals underlying wholeness. All pairs of opposites are part of the game. Both members of a pair have to be brought into the picture if one is to make sense of the whole. The two parts of any complementary relationship should be thought of as antiparathetical rather than antithetical. The word "antiparathetical" is of Greek origin. It is composed of three words: *anti*—against; *para*—next to; and *thesis*—position or place. These three words express exactly what the term complementarity should convey—the relationship between opposite theories or constructs which, nevertheless, "stand next to each other" to provide completeness. The word "antithesis" conveys a static aspect; whereas the word "antiparathesis" is dynamic. Antithesis is a state, while antiparathesis is a process.

The human mind may be uncomfortable with these views. By nature the thinking mind demands that opposites remain opposite, that no wholeness emerges. The mind demands to know exactly what is going on everywhere at all times. The cosmos, on the other hand, does not seem to have any problem with wholeness through complementarity. The cosmos just is.

To understand and resolve the issue of complementarity we need to understand how the mind functions and what is the nature of consciousness. And here we rapidly reach the boundaries of Western science. Science cannot even decide *what* the mind is, *how* it functions or *where*, if anywhere, in the physical body it is located. Quantum theory has opened the door to the unfathomable realm of consciousness; yet science says little about the nature of consciousness, apart from merely acknowledging its existence.

For these reasons many scientists choose to ignore the whole issue of consciousness and insist that it is secondary to the random physical processes of the quantum world. However, to deny the issue of consciousness is to do what the ostrich does. Because we don't understand consciousness, we want to make it disappear. In the words of biologist George Wald, many scientists are embarrassed by consciousness. Yet the physical processes going on under our eyes are intricately interwoven with the act of observation. As Bohr said, we are participators—"actors in the drama of existence." Following Gödel's theorem, it is clear that a mathematical model of the cosmos cannot be complete in itself. Taking this a step further, if we insist that the cosmos has to be understood in terms of mathematics, Gödel's theorem forces us to conclude that such an understanding will be incomplete. Since any ultimate understanding is by definition incomplete, it paradoxically, cannot be ultimate.

Even if we could somehow achieve a complete mathematical view of the universe, we have to ask how such a view could be obtained. Where would the mathematics to provide such a description come from? The source of the mathematics is, of course, the mind. If we insist on a complete mathematical understanding of the universe, we would be forced to admit that *such an understanding is in our minds!* The protagonists of the quantum view knew these problems very well. However, they could do little beyond acknowledging that they exist.

What to do about consciousness remains, then, an embarrassing problem for science—not just in physics or biology, but in all of science. As George Wald put it (Wald, 1984):

> How could one possibly locate a phenomenon that one has no means of identifying—neither its presence or absence— nor any known parameters of space, time, energy exchange, by which to characterize merely its occurrence, let alone its content? The very idea of a location of consciousness is absurd.

Wald also quotes Wilder Penfield, the Canadian neurosurgeon, who, when asked to identify the location of consciousness, said, "I'll tell you one thing: it's not in the cerebral cortex." Somehow *the non-locality revealed by Bell's theorem parallels the non-locality of consciousness.*

Inherent unpredictability, both quantum theory and chaos theory tell us, is a fact of nature. Also, complementarity, wholeness and acknowledgement of the existence of consciousness are the tangible products of the quantum revolution, even though quantum theory or, for that matter, any scientific view of the cosmos, can do little beyond pointing out these profound concepts. The next step requires that we consider the observer and the observed as an undivided whole—that we stop viewing the observer and the observed as different. This cannot be accomplished through the scientific process, which works precisely because of the separation between the observer and observed. Thus we must either turn to the perennial philosophy, which deals with this issue exactly, or revise scientific methodology.

To state that science and the perennial philosophy say the same thing would be like trying to force two complementary views into one. It simply cannot be done. One possible way to revise scientific methodology is outlined in this book: accept the successes of science but, at the same time, attempt to see whether statements from the perennial philosophy have relevance for everyday experience. We can check the validity of these statements in a variety of ways, without restricting ourselves to the laboratory. Some of the effects are so subtle, after all, that it is not even clear that scientific instruments could detect them.

Physics and the sciences in general are based on a body of knowledge that has been obtained by constructing theories and testing them experimentally in an effort to understand the universe. Since the Age of Reason, the subjective aspect of human beings has been viewed as irrelevant to this task. Only recently with the rise of quantum theory has the observer been brought into the picture in a limited way. Quantum theory recognizes that the action of observation alters the state of the observed system. Yet it does not deal with questions about the nature of the observer: Who are we observers? Where do we come from? Why are we here? How do we relate to the physical cosmos? Physical science is but a few hundred years old; it itself is expanding as our understanding of the cosmos grows. It is time its horizons expanded further.

The perennial philosophy concerns itself with the nature of consciousness. Since an individual can only experience his or her own consciousness, the perennial philosophy is concerned with the individual. When the ancient sages wrote and taught about the natures of consciousness, the individual and the universe, their words were not mere intellectual pronouncements. They were meant to be experienced, for the teachings reflected their own experiences. When they wrote and taught about how universal consciousness gives rise to the objective universe, they were not concerned with the physical universe per se. If what they said applies to the physical universe, it is because the physical universe is an aspect of the undivided wholeness.

Their primary concern was the ultimate Subject which experiences the objective universe, not the objective universe itself. Their focus was looking in, not seeing out. In the process, the ancient sages reached profound conclusions about the Universe and the creative process. Since all they said derived from their own experiences, it follows that we too can experience the truth of these statements about the creative process. If that turns out to be the case, the perennial philosophy can provide answers to questions that are beyond the reach of ordinary physical science. The physical sciences, on the other hand, can use the perennial experience to expand its own horizon, in a way that could not be accomplished if it stayed within the confines of science alone. The answer to the question of how the creative process works can be found in the experience of the process within each individual.

The perennial philosophy, the sages keep emphasizing, is simple and always the same. For this reason, its statements about what is permanent, or Real in the sense of eternal, may sound almost trivial. However, profound truths are often simple. It is said that a sophist once criticized Socrates, "But, Socrates, this is a bore; you are always saying the same about the same." Socrates replied, "But you sophists, who are so clever, perhaps never say the same about the same" (Heisenberg quoted in Wilber, 1984). Perhaps this consistency is the difference between knowledge of the eternal—the knowledge of sages like Socrates—and ordinary knowledge—the knowledge of the sophists.

The perennial philosophy is a body of eternal knowledge that has been obtained through self-awareness, the ultimate end of any act of observation. Direct experience of the nature of one's self leads to Self-realization, to knowledge of one's own true nature. The science of inner awareness, or meditation—the "looking in" process—is not an exclusive product of any specific human cultures. It is practiced in both East and West, North and South. The study of mysticism, the "turning within" or "quieting down" of the mind, reveals an amazing commonality of experiences that transcend space, time or culture. Meditation is truly universal. The terminology may be different, or the subject may be veiled in cryptic language yet, time and again one finds common elements in the meditative experience. In meditation, the object of observation, the observer and the act of the observation are one. Knowledge of the physical cosmos is included as part of the study of oneself. The perennial philosophy deals with the act of Creation in general, human beings considered an integral part. Scientific experiments are subject to interpretation. The same is true of perennial experiments, which are in essence *objectively studied subjective experiences*. Scientific experiments in laboratories are set up so that they can be repeated; they are considered valid only if the results are consistently reproducible. In a similar way, spiritual experiences reveal common patterns. Individuals from different cultures, at different places and times and for thousands of years, have experienced the same general awareness, the same types of visions, and have ended up with a similar understanding of themselves. Physics studies the relationship between objects in the physical cosmos at every level—the microcosm, the everyday level and the macrocosm. These relationships seem to obey immutable "laws." In the same way, the *perennial philosophy*—the science of mind and of going beyond the mind through meditation—studies the principles of laws operating at all levels of Existence. These laws constitute the "physics of Consciousness." The practices which lead to Self-awareness can be taught, and they culminate in meditation, in transcending the mind. The universal principles behind a spiritual experience constitute the perennial philosophy. In turn, the perennial philosophy is identical to the physics of consciousness—the way human consciousness, as a part of the whole, operates.

The physics of consciousness obeys universal principles, which are self-evident and which apply at all levels. These principles do not constitute external laws, separate from the consciousness of the observer. If they did, undivided wholeness would be only an empty statement. Undivided wholeness is real precisely because of the universality of these ancient principles (see *The Kybalion*, 1908). We have expounded these principles throughout this book, often without identifying them as such. At this point it is appropriate to state them in a formal way. The seven principles discussed below cover most of the field of undivided Consciousness. They are a starting point, as well as an ending point, of the search for wholeness. Some of these principles apply to the physical realm as well as to other realms; others are appropriate only in the realm of metaphysics.

- *Being*

  The foundation of physical, mental, psychic and spiritual existence is the Absolute. Its nature is Existence and Awareness of Existence, or Being, Awareness and Bliss. Although it is given different names—God, Universal Consciousness, Self, That, Brahman, Paramashiva, Universal Mother, Father, the Tao, Allah, or the Void— it is indescribable and beyond sensory experiences, although it forms the foundation of all experiences. It constitutes the first level in the processes of evolution and involution of the Universe. It consists of a static, potential aspect (Shiva) and a dynamic, creative aspect (Shakti).

- *The Master Teacher*

  Because Absolute Being is beyond sensory experience, one cannot perceive it by ordinary awareness. Its most important actions, which can be witnessed throughout the universe, are five-fold: emanation, sustenance, dissolution, concealment of the true nature and revelation of the true nature. The latter is often termed "grace," and this constitutes the function of a spiritual teacher or Master. Only through this fifth action can Absolute Being be revealed to the individual. The teachings of the Masters have left an eternal influence on humanity. Some of the teachings have become established religions, such as Judaism, Christianity, Buddhism, Islam or Taoism. Others did not become religions but broad secret traditions instead. Nevertheless, Masters brought the essence of the old teachings back to people; they brought inner awareness to the seekers of Truth, students of the perennial philosophy. Through the spiritual quests of these extraordinary beings, the fire of inner knowledge is rekindled and remains alive. To help us turn within, the Masters' function is unique and indispensable.

Eventually, a student of the perennial philosophy realizes the true Master within the innermost core of his or her own being.

● *Flow and Rhythm*
As Heraclitus stated, everything in the Universe flows. Universal consciousness manifests countless worlds at all levels of existence through its own true nature, which is creative throb, spanda. Vibrations repeat themselves, and this is why cyclic changes, such as the eternal cycle of birth and death, take place. The mind itself is a throb of consciousness. Knowing this, the student of perennial philosophy is not attached to the vibrations of the mind but rather focuses on the creative process which underlies the mind. This focus constitutes inner awareness or meditation.

● *Complementarity*
Complementarity is central to all levels of Existence, from the pure levels of the creative process to the earth level of existence. Complementarity is the secret of creation, and thus it is no surprise that it plays a central role in the physical universe. Consciousness projects itself on itself by assuming pairs of opposites. These opposites seem to be in eternal strife, but the task of the student is to go beyond opposites to understand the underlying unity of all.

● *Correspondence*
As above, so below. As here, so elsewhere. There is always correspondence between the phenomena of the various planes of existence. Without correspondence, chaos would reign. Scientists could not assume universal physical laws, and thus science would be impossible. Without correspondence the student could not hope to find universal principles working within him or her as well as everywhere else. Without it, one could not unlock the secrets of the universe.

● *Cause and Effect*
The law of cause and effect is self-evident at the ordinary physical level and is the cornerstone of classical physical science. In the perennial philosophy, cause and effect implies that one should accept responsibility for one's

own reality. Most humans view themselves as the products of outside causes rather than as the creators of effects, or, in other words, of their own reality. One can reach the innermost core of one's own being only if one goes beyond all causes and effects. That this is possible is evident from the fact that causality in the classical sense is not relevant at the quantum level.

● *Abundance*

There is a never-decreasing abundance of energy in the Universe. Even at the physical level, abundance can be seen in the vast reservoirs of energy of the quantum vacuum. Abundance implies that the individual is boundless and as one unfolds, this becomes a true experience of living. In the individual, abundance does not imply physical wealth, although it can include this. Rather, it implies awareness of the ever-increasing mystery of Existence.

These principles ultimately reduce to the first one: Being. The conclusion of many sages is that the secret of the Universe is very simple. *The Universe just is.* This principle is nevertheless very profound. It allows us to take ourselves lightly and not be crushed by the weight of our own beliefs, our limitations, or the weight of our own minds. When a student of the physics of Consciousness realizes the nature of his or her own Being, he or she identifies with ultimate Being. In its transcendent aspect, this is called Shiva, the Absolute. In its immanent aspect, it is called Shakti, the universal Power that emanates, sustains and reabsorbs, but also hides and reveals. It is because of Shakti, Universal Consciousness, that all knowledge, physical and metaphysical, is possible and that spiritual knowledge is sublime. Shakti becomes the Universe, in fact, is the Universe. It becomes the individual who henceforth forgets his or her real, eternal, nature and identifies with external objects and concepts. When Shakti wills it, the aspirant is taken through the inner realm to the castle of the heart and beyond, to the ultimate merging of subjective and objective experience. Then one experiences, as the ancient sutra of Kashmir Shaivism states: "*lokanandah samadhi sukham—*The bliss of the world is the bliss of Enlightenment." The world is no longer perceived as different from the bliss of transcendental contentment, of Enlightenment. The external objects and subjective experience merge, and one lives in the world with the awareness that everything constitutes undivided wholeness.

We try to find the ultimate, eternal perfection in the outside world because Shakti is always within us, transcendent, luminous and eternal. We can never find perfection because in its outer form Shakti is ever-changing. The scientist tries to find the ultimate truth about the physical universe and projects the infinity and beauty within onto the outer universe. But without inner knowledge, external knowledge ultimately seems pointless.

We are both the field of knowledge and the knower of knowledge. In the West we tend to identify objectivity with consensus among scientists. But why should mathematical description of physical interactions be more objective than the common experiences of countless human beings? Both, after all, are securely based on a common foundation: our own consciousness.

To try to understand the mind is of paramount importance, not just because physical science is a product of the human mind but, more important, because as the sages tell us we need to experience the source of the mind, the inner Self, if we are to live happy lives. Knowledge in the perennial science of the mind is identical with experience. Science, like art, is a human activity that must be experienced. In spite of what scientists usually say, the desire to experience first hand the ultimate unity of the cosmos is the driving force behind scientific endeavors. This experience is felt at the highest realms of the intellect and is ultimately the reward of the scientific process. Scientists do science for enjoyment, in the same way as yogis do yoga.

This enjoyment goes beyond the familiar pleasure of the senses. The Greek philosopher-sages—Socrates, Plato, Aristotle, Epicurus, to name a few—knew this. True scientists, such as Einstein and Bohr, like the philosophers of ancient Greece, keep searching because of an inner conviction that ultimate simplicity is at the heart of the Universe. Bohr was right: at the physical level God plays dice, and we cannot even in principle know everything about the objective universe. Yet Einstein was also right; God does not play dice. Although Einstein was referring to the physical realm, at the core of our being there is ultimate simplicity, beauty and knowledge, and we can know this with certitude. There, God does not play dice. There Being is simply Being. Then one perceives Shakti in its true nature, and the Universe is seen as nothing but the ever-blissful play of Consciousness,[1] ananda. Anyone who has turned within to the core of his or her being has tasted this joy. Sages tell us that bliss is the very nature of our consciousness, which is Being, Awareness of Being, and Bliss.

For the physics of the Newtonian paradigm, the chasm between science and the perennial philosophy was impossible to bridge. In the probabilistic ocean of quanta, the chasm is still there, but quantum theory, by asking certain questions, provides the foundations to create a bridge. We no longer feel that science and perennial philosophy are two entirely different, conflicting domains. We see them as complementary aspects of human activity, forming a continuum in our efforts to understand the universe and ourselves.

If a chasm remains between the cosmos and the individual, it is like a dark line in the continuous optical spectrum. It exists only in our minds, in our understanding. Maybe rather than a bridge we need to jump into the void and allow our minds to drop concepts and ideas, the security of our instruments, and to experience our own undivided wholeness. Such a leap of faith is an individual issue. It cannot be taught in schools and universities. It cannot be done collectively. It is a matter of individual choice, readiness and decision. But, the testimony of the sages and the ages is that the leap from faith to wisdom is possible and infinitely worthwhile.

We can keep looking at the external cosmos searching for ultimate meaning. We can keep looking at the stars and galaxies, at the protons and electrons. But we can never observe, capture and graphically represent Wholeness as something separate from us ourselves. Wholeness is undivided; Wholeness is experiencing ourselves as the Universe; so that seeing in and looking out become identical and Consciousness and the Cosmos are not different from each other.

Notes

Introduction

1. For more information on Reiki, the Usui system of natural healing, contact the authors at: Institute for Computational Sciences and Informatics, George Mason University, Fairfax, VA 22030.

1. The Universe of Newton and Einstein

1. Waves are either transverse or longitudinal. Ocean waves, seismic waves on the surface of the earth and light are all transverse waves for which the medium vibrates in a direction perpendicular to the direction of propagation. Light itself consists of vibrating electric and magnetic fields perpendicular to each other and to the direction that light moves. Sound waves, on the other hand, and "push-pull" seismic waves are examples of longitudinal waves in which the wave propagates parallel to the vibration of the medium.

2. Michelson and Morley's experiment consisted of measuring the times required for light to travel two separate routes, one along the direction of the motion of the earth, the other perpendicular to the motion of the earth. To their surprise, Michelson and Morley detected no difference in the time light required to travel these two routes. Einstein eventually explained the results of this experiment by concluding that light travels with the same speed irrespective of the speed of the light source. See also Holton and Brush (1985).

3. Einstein's fundamental assumption was that the laws of

physics should hold independently of the motion of the observer, even when gravity is present. Einstein reasoned that gravity should be transformed away, and this is formulated by the principle of equivalence. Consider a space capsule far away from any stars or planets, so that it feels no gravitational pull and all objects inside the capsule float in space. Now imagine that the engines of the capsule are turned on and it begins to move through space with accelerated motion, the acceleration being equal to that of a falling body here on Earth. If one could observe the interior of the capsule from the outside, this observer would see that when an object is released inside the capsule, it moves upwards with a constant velocity equal to the instantaneous value that it had when released. Since the capsule is moving with an accelerated motion, the floor of the capsule will move in the same direction as the released object, but with increasing velocity; the floor will catch up with the object. The astronaut inside the capsule, on the other hand, will see the object "falling to the ground." Einstein reasoned that there would be no difference between what an astronaut inside the capsule saw compared to what a person sees when an object is released from rest near the surface of the earth. Applied to light, the same reasoning leads to the conclusion that light appears to be falling down in the presence of gravity.

4. The first part of the above statement is described analytically by Einstein's field equations of the general theory of relativity and the second statement by the geodesic equations (Weinberg, 1972). These equations cannot in general be solved exactly, not even with a computer.

5. For example, since light moves along curved spatial paths, one could try to detect these curved light paths in the vicinity of a massive object. In particular, during a total solar eclipse the positions of stars near the rim of the occulted sun should appear shifted from the positions of the same stars at night when the sun is not visible. The prediction was tested in 1919 by Sir Arthur S. Eddington during a total solar eclipse and found to be in good agreement with Einstein's general theory of relativity.

6. For comparison, the speed of escape from the surface of the Earth is a mere 11 km/sec, about 1/30,000 of the speed of light!

2. The Case for Wholeness

1. A simple way to build a black body is to take a styrofoam box, open a small hole and let light fall in. Since the hole is small, radiation will be unable to escape right away but will bounce against the sides of the box a large number of times, reaching thermodynamic equilibrium with the sides.

2. When the intensity of black body radiation is plotted as a function of wavelength, a bell-shaped curve results. Its characteristic maximum depends only on the temperature of the black body.

3. Planck's constant h consists of the units of action or angular momentum. It is the product of energy, measured by a unit called an erg, times time, with its unit of a second.

4. The photoelectric effect was discovered as a by-product of experiments which, ironically, provided conclusive evidence that the classical electromagnetic theory of light is valid. When the photoelectric effect was finally explained by Einstein, it showed precisely the opposite result: the inadequacy of classical notions to account for this phenomenon.

5. See Rutherford (1940). In his own words: "It was almost as incredible as if you fired a 15-inch shell at a piece of a tissue paper and it came back and hit you. On consideration, I realized that this scattering backwards must be the result of a single collision, and when I made calculations I saw that it was impossible to get anything of that order of magnitude unless you took a system in which the greater part of the mass of the atom was concentrated in a minute nucleus."

6. See Gribbin (1984), Herbert (1987) and Pagels (1982). These works provide a good, serious introduction at a popular level to the intricacies of quantum theory.

7. Many experiments have been performed to test Bell's theorem and its predictions, Bell's inequalities. Aspect and his co-workers have carried out the most important test so far. See Aspect, Dalibard and Gerard (1982).

8. The views of Bohm have evolved over time from the original so-called "local hidden variable theories" to the "implicate-explicate" order ideas.

9. Virtual quanta, for example, surround an electron in a hydrogen atom, interact with the "real" electron and cause shifts in the energy states of the atom. These shifts can be precisely measured in the laboratory, and their values agree with the predictions of quantum physics.

10. Three Planck quantities, length, time and mass, can be written in terms of three fundamental constants of nature: $\hbar$ Planck's quantum of action divided by 2π; G, the gravitational constant; and c, the speed of light (Misner, Thorne and Wheeler, 1973). The values are: $L_P = \sqrt{\hbar G/c^3} = 10^{-33}$ cm; time: $t_P = \sqrt{\hbar G/c^5} = 5 \times 10^{-44}$ sec; and mass: $M_P = \sqrt{\hbar c/G} = 2 \times 10^{-5}$ gr.

11. This is exactly the point of physicist John A. Wheeler. He has stated time and again that until we understand "vacuum physics" we will not have progressed very far in our understanding of nature.

12. In supergravity the theoretician searches for the ultimate symmetries provided by all possible values of one parameter, the spin. Supergravity predicts the existence of 65 fundamental particles, such as gravitons, quarks and electrons, and 98 carriers of the interactions, such as photons and Ws. It is hard to accept a theory that predicts so many particles, the vast majority of which have not yet been observed or are impossible to observe.

13. There are a number of good books on the most recent attempts at unification. For a general introduction to unified field theories see Trefil (1983); for grand unification see Davies (1984); for super-strings see Peat (1988); for symmetries in physics see Zee (1986).

3. A New Vision of the Universe

1. Biology is a "historical" science since in principle the path taken by evolution could have been different. Physics, on the other hand, at least at the microscopic level, is governed by physical laws that do not allow for a different world. When one takes into account the "coincidences" of fundamental constants, then "anthropic" arguments may require an intimate connection between biology and the cosmos, in which case the argument on the differences between biology and physics may not be valid (see Harris, 1991).

2. In physics, microscopic laws are time reversal invariant: if the arrow of time is changed, the process is still valid. This is not the case with macroscopic laws, which are generally believed to be time-irreversible because of the second law of thermodynamics. This is the law of the increase in entropy—the quantitative measure of disorganization of a physical system—that gives time its arrow in the macroscopic world. However, even in quantum systems, every measurement process includes an element of irreversibility. Prigogone has shown that entropy can be extended to microscopic phenomena. Thus reversibility and irreversibility can be seen as complementary constructs.

3. Hubble discovered an effect that distant galaxies seem to obey: the more distant a galaxy, the more its spectral lines seem to be shifted to the red part of the spectrum. If one interprets this shift as due to the so-called Doppler effect—which arises when a moving source of light is observed—the conclusion is that the more distant the galaxy, the faster it appears to be receding from us.

4. These two assumptions are also known as the "cosmological principle." No observer in any region of the universe is in a privileged position. Perfect cosmic equality applies to all observers.

5. To the criticism of those who pointed out that this violates the principle of conservation of energy, Bondi, Gold and Hoyle

replied that even in the big bang theory one has to deal with possible creation out of nothingness: what was prior to the big bang?

6. The specific value and large size of 311-trillion-year cycles is interesting to ponder. How would anyone in ancient times even grasp the magnitude of such numbers?

7. The interpretation which allows for the observing apparatus and the quantum system to be connected via superluminar connections is different from the standard Copenhagen Interpretation and Von Neumann's "all quantum interpretation." Herbert (1987) terms this interpretation "neorealist," although it would go counter to Einstein's theory of relativity.

8. In the delayed-choice version, *after* the photon has traversed the double slit a decision is made whether to record the photon on a photographic plate (which implies that the photon "went through both slits") or to record with a counter "through which slit the photon went." "In that sense," says Wheeler, "we decide after the photon has passed through the double slit, whether it shall have passed through only one slit or both."

9. For example, the ratio of the electromagnetic attraction between an electron and a proton to their gravitational attraction is about 10^{40}. Also, the ratio of the radius of the universe—the largest conceivable object—to the size of an elementary particle if 10^{40}. Why should these two seemingly unrelated ratios be so close in their value, particularly when that value is such a large number? Physics has no answer to this puzzle, which prompted Dirac to speculate that it is not a coincidence.

10. In Bohr's own words: ". . . we learn from the quantum theory that the appropriateness of our usual space-time description depends entirely on the small value of the quantum of action compared to the actions involved in ordinary sense perceptions. Indeed, in the description of atomic phenomena, the quantum postulate presents us with the task of developing a 'complementarity' theory the consistency of which can be judged only by weighing the possibilities of definition and observation" (see Kafatos and Nadeau, 1990).

11. The reason for this is that all atoms would have their electrons at the lowest energy state; there would be no electrovalent or covalent bonds between atoms, no quantum jumps of electrons between levels, no crystal structure and no biological molecular structure such as DNA. In the world of classical physics the only shapes that can be readily understood are those where gravitation, magnetism and electricity are the dominant forces: spheres for stars, discs such as the solar system or the galaxy where gravity and angular momentum operate, etc. Classical physics cannot explain the particular shapes of these bodies which arise because of interatomic or intermolecular forces.

12. In biology a mechanical description of the way an organ works requires that it be described as an isolated physical system. However, such isolation precludes describing the organism as "living," since the concept of life always involves the interaction between an organism and its environment (see also Folse, 1985, and Lockwood, 1989).

13. There are four problems: 1) New structures appear which cannot simply be explained in terms of the growth of structures which are already present in the egg at the beginning of the development. 2) Many biological organisms are able to regulate themselves, so that even if a part is removed or a new part added, the system continues to develop in a way that a normal structure is developed. 3) Regeneration, i.e., the ability of organisms to replace or restore damaged structures. 4) Reproduction, i.e., the fact that a detached part of the parent becomes a new organism.

4. Sound, Letters and the Power of Creation

1. At the practical level, the science of Indian yoga parallels the creative principles outlined here. Everything in the Universe is comprised of the 50 elementary principles represented by the Sanskrit letters, distributed among 36 concrete levels of unfoldment. It is important to realize that the Sanskrit letters were not arbitrarily assigned by anyone to the levels of creation. They represent the actual vibratory frequency of the energy of each creative level.

Pure Levels

At the 1st level of creation, the Shiva level, or pure Being, the subtlest level of vibration predominated by the shakti or power of supreme existence is expressed by the letter a, अ. The 2nd level, the Shakti level, predominated by the shakti of supreme contentment or bliss, is expressed by the 2nd vowel aa, आ. The 3rd level is predominated by the shakti of supreme will or desire: the will to create the objective aspect of the individual experience known as Iccha Shakti. This is the 1st stage of the motion or throb in the unfoldment of Consciousness and forms the vibration i, इ, the 3rd letter of the Sanskrit alphabet. Along with this, letters 7, 9, 4, 8 and 10 are manifested at the 3rd level, representing the various subtle vibrations in the process of the complete manifestation of the 3rd level. These are: (e)ri, ऋ, lri, ऌ, ee; ऎ; (e)rii ॠ;and lrii, ॡ. The 4th level is predominated by the shakti of perfect knowledge known as Jnana Shakti, and the objective side becomes more defined. This is the distinct blossoming of the plan of the Universe, where awareness of the Universe becomes clearer. Letters 5 and 6 come to express the vibrational sound aspect of the 4th level.

These are: *u*, उ, and *oo*, ऊ. Then the final 5th level of pure creation, *Kriya Shakti*, the shakti of supreme action, comes into being. At this level subjective and objective sides are equally balanced. Consciousness is now ready to split into two. Letters 11, 12, 13 and 14 are coming into being to represent the vibrational sound aspects of the 5th level. These are: *e*, ए; *ai*, ऐ; *o*, ओ; and *au*, औ (Singh, 1979a). The cornerstone of our physical universe, duality or *Maya*, is ready to manifest.

It is interesting to note here that vowels 15 and 16 do not appear in the levels of pure creation. The rest of the levels of creation are represented by consonants alone. The sounds of these vowels are *ah*, अः, for the 16th letter and *am*, अं for the 15th letter. *Aham* in Sanskrit means "I." One possible explanation might be that these 2 letters represent the transcendent nature of Paramashiva, the pure unmanifested Consciousness, and therefore are beyond any level of creation. They might represent the source of creation and not its process. It is interesting to note that in all 5 levels there is a predominant shakti, an aspect of the supreme Shakti. This clearly indicates that in all levels there exist all the shaktis, actually the vibrational aspects of all letters. Finally, in the culmination of the creative process, one of them comes forward and also manifests the appropriate letters. Jayaratha says in his commentary on the Shaivite philosophical text *Tantraloka* (Singh, 1979a): " 'A' resides in all the letters as their controller."

These vowels are said to form the inner nature of Shiva, his aspect before duality. It is very interesting that even at the pure level, Shiva does have the aspects of his outer nature, represented by the vibrational energies of consonants. At the first level, next to the first letter *a*, representing the inner nature of Shiva, the last letter of the alphabet, *ksha*, came to represent the outer nature of Shiva. One cannot help but notice that the first and last letters are coupled together to represent both aspects of Shiva: the inner and the outer. This might remind us of the general notion in Eastern thought that the beginning is the same as the end, as well as the statement attributed to Christ: "I am the Alpha and the Omega." Christ quite explicitly expressed the same principle, which is contained in the first and last letters of the Greek alphabet.

The outer nature of Shiva, in the 2nd level, is represented by the 49th letter, *ha*, ह, and so on until the 5th level, which is represented by the letter 46, *sha*, श. Right after the pure levels there is only manifestation of the outer nature of Shiva. Till then there is only the divine desire to manifest and the creation of the right conditions and tools at the level of a plan. There is no creation, yet, only a Thought in the Universal Mind.

Impure Levels

Following the pure levels, after the 5th level, *Maya* or the power of illusion arises. Here the sense of difference emerges. The ephemeral seems real and permanent, the non-eternal ever-lasting. The letter 45, *va*, व, relates to this level. From Maya emanate the 5 qualifying limitations or *kanchukas*, each limiting one of the universal conditions of Paramashiva. The *kala kanchuka* limits the omnipresence of Shiva-Shakti, gives rise to the notion of individuality and is represented by the letter 45, which is the same as Maya. The *vidya kanchuka* limits the power of omniscience of Shiva-Shakti, gives rise to the experience of limited knowledge and is represented by the letter 44, *la*, ळ. The *raga kanchuka* limits the wholeness of Shiva-Shakti and is represented again by the 44th letter. The *kaala kanchuka* limits the power of eternality of Shiva-Shakti, gives rise to limitations of time, gives rise to mortality and is represented by the letter 43, *ra*, र. The final kanchuka is the *niyati kanchuka*, which limits the omnipotence of Shiva-Shakti. It conditions us to fate, predestination and the round of life and is represented by the letter 42, *ya*, य. As the seed is covered with different layers of husk, so Paramashiva is covered by these 6 layers of restrictions. In this state it is called *purusha*, the Primordial Male Principle. It is represented by the letter 41, *ma*, म. At the same time Paramashiva, through the same limiting process of Maya and the kanchukas, becomes the objective side of individual experience, root cause of all the remaining levels of manifestation known as *prakriti*, the Primordial Female Principle, the embodiment of the active and creative qualities constituting the objective manifestation of nature. Prakriti is represented by the letter 40, *bha*, भ. It consists of three qualities, called *gunas: sattva,* the quality of radiance; *rajas*, the active, kinetic quality; and *tamas*, the quality of inertia (Khanna, 1979). As the process of unfoldment continues, the intellect, *buddhi*, comes into being, represented by the letter 39, *ba*, ब; the ego, *ahamkara*, develops and is represented by the letter 38, *pha*, फ; the mind, *manas*, evolves next and is represented by the letter 37, *pa*, प. The group of letters representing the levels of purusha, prakriti, buddhi, ahamkara and manas belong to the special group of labial letters of the Sanskrit language.

Then directly from ego emerge the five organs of senses, colored by the sattva quality of prakriti, represented by letters 36 to 32, the group of dental letters: *na*, न; *dha*, ध; *da*, द; *tha*, थ; *ta*, त; the 5 organs of actions, colored by the raja quality of prakriti, represented by letters 31 to 27, the group of retroflex letters: *na*, ण; *dha*, ढ; *da*, ड; *tha*, ठ; *ta*, ट; the 5 subtle elements, colored by the tamas quality of the prakriti, represented by letters 26 to 22, the group of palatal letters ña ञ; jha, झ; ja, ज; chha, छ; cha, च. Finally the last 5 gross elements evolve from the subtle elements. They are represented by letters 21 to 17, the group of velar letters ñam, ड; gha, घ; ga, ग; kha, ख; and ka, क.

According to Sanskrit scholars, not only do the vowels evolve from the letter a, but the consonants evolve from the vowels. Specifically, the group of the 5 vowels, a, i, ru, iru, and u, act as the powers which bring about the various groups of consonants and their corresponding principles, or levels of creation. Table 2 shows this correspondence (Coulson, 1976).

TABLE 2

Basic Vowels	Group of Consonants	Names of Letters	Levels
a	Velar	ka, kha, ga, gha, ṅa	5 gross elements
i	Palatal	cha, chha, ja, jha, ña	5 subtle elements
ṛ	Retroflex	ṭa, ṭha, ḍa, ḍha, ṇa	5 organs of actions
ḷ	Dental	ta, tha, da, dha, na	5 organs of senses
u	Labial	pa, pha, ba, bha, ma	manas, ahamkara, buddhi, prakriti, purusha

Since these 36 levels of creation represent universal principles in action, one can contemplate them in one's own being. In fact, the pure levels are beyond individual consciousness and represent Pure Being. Levels 6-11, Maya and the 5 limiting powers, represent the *causal body*, the root cause of limited experience. Levels 12-31 represent the constituent elements of the subtle or astral body (Yukteswar, 1984), the sum total of all our subtle experiences, while levels 32-36 are the constituent elements of the physical body: ether, air, fire, water and earth.

    2. The word *logos* does not translate as "word." The Greek word *lexis* does. *Logos* and *lexis* are two nouns deriving from the same root, the root of the verb *lego*, which means "to say." However, they do not mean the same thing. *Logos* is a statement; it is an account and not a single word. Its meaning includes reasoning; when one talks publicly, one gives a logos, a speech. In the ancient Greek language, however, words represented a spectrum of similar meanings that differ only slightly. We distinguish the meaning in an ancient text by the preposition used with the word and the case of the word. This is a well-known grammatical fact for ancient Greek. Each verb has a concrete set of prepositions that

go with it, and each preposition is used only with certain cases. Now the reader is in a position to appreciate not only the richness of the ancient Greek language but also its versatility and capacity to express subtle differences and shades of meanings. The first point, then, is that the translation of *logos* as "word" is not appropriate. We cannot find an English term to reflect correctly the meaning of *logos*, and this is apparently the reason that the term "word" was established as the official translation. We found it necessary to distinguish the meaning of "word" from that of *logos* in order to put into perspective the relation of the concept of mantra to the concept of the Word, as found in the translation of the Gospel according to St. John. A mantra can be a word, but, as we have seen, its power lies in its inherent frequency of vibratory energy. The reason that mantras have power is that their energy represents the energy of various levels of creation. If we were to translate *mantra* into Greek, we would use the word *lexis* and not *logos*.

The English translation of the Gospel according to St. John is as follows: "In the beginning was the Word, and the Word was with God, and the Word was God." In the original Greek text there is no word that would translate into "with." The original Greek text is as follows: 'Εν ἀρχῇ ἦν ὁ Λόγος, καί ὁ Λόγος ἦν πρός τόν Θεόν, καί Θεός ἦν ο Λόγος.

The preposition πρός with the accusative, τόν Θεόν, means "towards" and indicates movement. It does not mean "with," which is more passive. In the translation of the same passage in modern Greek, we find that the preposition πρός is translated into παρά and the dative case, which has the meaning of "near." One can then possibly extract the meaning "with." Neither modern Greek nor English translations exactly reflect the meaning of the original ancient text. The translation of the passage in modern Greek is: 'Εν ἀρχῇ ἦτο ὁ Λόγος, καί ὁ Λόγος ἦτο παρά τῷ Θεῷ, καί Θεός ἦτο ὁ Λόγος.

What does it mean that "the Word was with God"? How is this different from "the Word was towards God"? Who really understands what *Logos* is or even what "the Word" means? What does it mean for the Logos to "be God"? How can we understand this passage in the context of the language and linguistic rules of the Old and New Testaments?

This passage is fascinating in the explicit, brief and to-the-point way it puts forth the entire creation. Rather than attempting to discredit ancient authors and concepts, as John's mental state has been questioned (Teeple, 1974), we should recognize that often when great beings expressed and described Truth, they did it in a way that left scholars puzzled, perplexed and confused. This is definitely the case with the Gospel according to St. John.

Another concern of biblical scholars is the authorship of the gospel. This issue appears to be valid, since the only original document of the gospel we presently have is the Sinaitic code, which was written in the 4th century. St. John died at the beginning of the 2nd century. It is obvious that he could not possibly have been the gospel's author. The fact is that we simply do not know who wrote the 4th gospel or whether the author or authors were Jewish or Greek. We have no way of knowing for sure if the Sinaitic code was the mother tongue of the author(s), or if the gospel was originally written in Greek, which was the universal language in those times.

However, if we look at this particular passage in the light of what is known from other traditions, then it is extraordinarily descriptive of the initial throb of creation, or *spanda*. In one of the most widely accepted commentaries of the Gospel according to St. John, it is stated that the word "beginning" refers to the period before creation, since "creation" appears later in the verse: "Through him all things came into being, and apart from him not a thing came to be" (The Anchor Bible, 1966). If this is the case, then the first passage can be seen in a new way. According to Kashmir Shaivism, prior to the process of creation there are the pure levels where Shiva and Shakti are still one aspect. In the stillness of the infinite sea of Consciousness, Paramashiva or God, *spanda*, the creative pulsation, is manifested. This throb or pulsation, the desire of manifestation of the Universe, is the root of primordial unmanifest sound, which is the source and the basis of Logos. Now we can see that the translation of πρός τόν Θεόν as "towards God" rather than "with God," makes sense because the basic element in the creative pulsation, *spanda*, is movement, a concept expressed by "towards." So this passage, which at first appears quite incomprehensible, might imply much more than we had suspected. However, this is not the only biblical passage where reference is made to the involvement of sound in the process of creation. Also, according to the book of Genesis, "And God said: let there be light; and there was light." This is exactly analogous to what the Hindu sages said about the power of words. If one speaks from the level of the potential sound, then one has the power to manifest anything that is said.

5. Mind and Metamind

1. The absolutely unique concept the Eastern sages bring into the science of mind is that the mind itself is pure contracted

consciousness that performs three different functions: thinking, deciding and differentiating. However, the mind is not three different things. An appropriate analogy would be to consider different kinds of pots made of clay: each pot has a different function, although they are all made of the same stuff, clay. The ancient sages did not concern themselves with the physical brain. There is still a tendency in Western neuroscience to compartmentalize the brain based on its functions. Also, there is a widespread tendency among scientists and laymen to compare the brain to the computer (Lockwood, 1989). The irony is that not only is the analogy unfortunate for many reasons, but that the electronic computer itself does not function in a compartmental way. The same ferrite, for example, performs many functions, such as arithmetic operations, storing, controlling (Penrose, 1989).

6. *The Mystical Experience*

1. The golden number, Φ, can be found from the relation c/b = b/a, where c = a + b. Here c = Φ and b = 1. Then $\Phi = (\sqrt{5} + 1)/2$ = 1.61803 . . .

2. See *The Kybalion* (1908), a summary of the Hermetic philosophy including the seven universal Hermetic Principles: mentalism, correspondence, vibration, polarity, rhythm, cause and effect and gender.

3. We owe the discussion that follows to Rev. Lafayette Seymour.

4. See also Guillaumont, et al. (1959) for a description of the Kingdom of Heaven in the words of Jesus the Christ, found in *The Gospel According to Thomas.* Jesus called it the "mustard-seed" and the "light that lights the whole world." The terminology Jesus used, the tiny spark of light that is as small as a mustard seed, is almost identical with Meister Eckhart's "little spark" and with what the Hindus refer to as the "blue pearl."

5. The scriptures of Shaivism are divided in three categories: *Agama Shastra, Spanda Shastra,* and *Pratyabhijna Shastra.*

A. The *agamas,* revealed scriptures, form the foundation of the Shaivite philosophy and were handed down from teacher to pupil. Two important agamas are the *Shiva Sutras* and the *Vijnana Bhairava. The Shiva Sutras* (Singh, 1979a) are a collection of 77 aphorisms. In their profound simplicity they give the deepest meaning to spirituality by examining the nature of the Self and the means to reach it, the way to liberation from the bondage of limited understanding and ordinary experience. The *Vijnana Bhairava* (Singh, 1979b), a philosophical work of great practicality, is an exposition of 112 mental or contemplative practices through which the eternal Self can be directly experienced.

B. The *Spanda Shastras* delineate the principles found in the agamas. Two important *shastras* are *The Spanda Karikas* and *The Spandanirnaya* (Singh, 1980b). The *Spanda Karikas* are commentaries on the *Shiva Sutras*, emphasizing the Shakti or active aspect of Consciousness. This work emphasizes that *spanda*, the creative throb of Universal Consciousness, can be witnessed operating in everything.

C. The *Pratyabhijna Shastras* elaborate and interpret the basic premises of Shaivism in a philosophic manner. One of these works is the *Pratyabhijnahridayam* which means the "Secret of Self Recognition" (Singh, 1980a). It consists of 20 aphorisms which expound how Consciousness creates the Universe and how the individual can witness the universal processes within, to reach the highest state. The *Pratyabhijnahridayam* is a profound philosophical work, unparalleled in any tradition.

The Shaivite religion is probably one of the oldest religions in the world (Singh, 1980a). It appeared in different forms in different parts of the world. The particular form which appeared in Kashmir was imparted as a secret doctrine from teacher to disciple. The disciple would not use it as only intellectual knowledge, but as a tool to reach the Self within. Eventually the philosophical background was forgotten, and what remained were the rituals. In the brief time between the 8th and 10th centuries A.D. the lost knowledge was brought to light for the first time in written form. Many great sages lived in Kashmir at this time and imparted the philosophy of Shaivism from teacher to disciple. There is rarely a similar period of spiritual revival and enlightenment to be found anywhere. Some of the great sages of Kashmir were: Vasugupta, 8th-9th centuries, the author of *The Shiva Sutras* and *Spanda Karikas*; Kallata, 9th century, the main disciple of Vasugupta; Somananda, a 9th-century sage; Utpalacharya, 9th-10th centuries, disciple of Somananda and author of *Ishwarapratyabhijna*; Abhinavagupta, 10th century, disciple of Utpalacharya and author of many works including the great treatise *Tantraloka*; Kshemaraja, 10th-century sage and disciple of Abhinavagupta, who authored among other works the *Pratyabhijnahridayam*. These sages were not just great philosophers; they brought out in the open a complete path of transformation for humanity. As in other parts of India at other times, the Shaivite sages were extremely practical and did not live in the clouds. Abhinavagupta, for example, wrote a voluminous work on esthetics that is considered to be one of the most authoritative works on this subject in the world. Today one can study their teachings and extract the jewel of the science of recognizing the Self. We can truly call Kashmir Shaivism the "science of revelation," because in a practical, methodical way which can be learned, it provides the means to reach the inner Self.

7. Undivided Wholeness

1. For example, 1 was the Beginning, the One, and also the Mind; inherent in this identification is the belief that there is really only one mind; 2 was Strife or the first moving away from unity; 3 represented the Idea and also Completeness or Wholeness —the beginning, the middle and the end; 3 signifies God in most religious traditions; 4 was Form or Application; 5 represented Understanding and also Marriage consisting of 2 + 3, an even number regarded as female and an odd number regarded as male. The numbers 6 to 10 were regarded as deriving from the first 5 numbers, each representing a different creative principle. Number 6 represented the balance of Ideas (3 + 3); 7 the Actualization resulting from the coming together of the Idea (3) and the Form (4); 8 the balance of Forms (4 + 4); 9 the perfecting of the Ideas (3 + 3 + 3). For the Pythagoreans 10 was particularly important since 10 = 1 + 2 + 3 + 4; it represented the Eternal Cycle.

8. The Physics of Consciousness

1. For a unique description of the marvelous inner world of Consciousness, see Swami Muktananda's spiritual autobiography, *Play of Consciousness* (1978).

Bibliography

Anchor Bible, The, 1966. Gospel According to John. New York: Doubleday.

Arp, H. 1980a. "Analysis of Quasars Found in the CTIO Curtis Schmidt Survey in the -40° Zone." *Astrophysical Journal* 239:463.

———. 1980b. "High-Redshift Objects Near the Companion Galaxies to NGC 2859." *Astrophysical Journal* 240:415.

Aspect, A., Dalibard, J., and Gerard, R. 1982. "Experimental Test of Bell's Inequalities Using Time-Varying Analyzers." *Physical Review Letters* 49:1804.

Avalon, A. 1974. *The Serpent Power.* New York: Dover.

Bahadur, K. P. 1979. *Upanishads.* New Delhi: Heritage Publishers.

Barrow, J. D., and Tipler, F. J. 1986. *The Anthropic Cosmological Principle.* New York: Oxford Press.

Bell, J. S. 1964. "On the Einstein Podolsky Rosen Paradox." *Physics* 1:195.

Bible, Agia Graphe, The, 1953 (in Greek). Athens: Vivlike Etairea.

Blair, L. 1976. *Rhythms of Vision.* New York: Schocken Books.

Blakemore, C. 1977. *Mechanics of the Mind.* Cambridge: Cambridge Univ. Press.

Bohm, D. 1952. "A Suggested Interpretation of the Quantum Theory in Terms of 'Hidden Variables'. " *Physical Review* 85:166.

———. 1980. *Causality and Chance in Modern Physics.* Philadelphia: Univ. of Pennsylvania Press.

———. 1981. *Wholeness and the Implicate Order.* London: Routledge and Kegan Paul.

Bohr, N. 1928. "The Quantum Postulate and the Recent Development of Atomic Theory." *Nature* 121:580.

———. 1949. "Discussion with Einstein on Epistemological Problems in Atomic Physics." In *Albert Einstein, Philosopher-Scientist.* P. A. Schilpp, ed. New York: Library of Living Philosophers.

———. 1958. *Atomic Physics and Human Knowledge.* New York: John Wiley and Sons.

Briggs, J. P., and Peat, F. D. 1984. *Looking Glass Universe: The Emerging Science of Wholeness.* New York: Simon and Schuster.

Burnet, J. 1930. *Early Greek Philosophy.* New York: Macmillan.

Burtt, E. A. 1954. *The Metaphysical Foundation of Modern Science.* Garden City, NY: Doubleday Anchor Books.

Campbell, J. 1971. *The Portable Jung.* New York: The Viking Press.

Capra, F. 1975. *The Tao of Physics.* Boulder, CO: Shambhala.

Cline, B. L. 1987. *Men Who Made a New Physics.* Chicago: Univ. of Chicago Press.

Cocke, W. J., and Tifft, W. G. 1983. "Redshift Quantization in Compact Groups of Galaxies." *Astrophysical Journal* 268:56.

Coulson, M. 1976. *Sanskrit.* New York: Hodder and Stoughton.

Crombie, A. C. et al. 1961. *Turning Points in Physics.* New York: Harper Torchbook.

Davies, P. C. W. 1984. *Superforce.* New York: Simon & Schuster.

d'Espagnat, B. 1979. "The Quantum Theory and Reality." *Scientific American* 241:158.

de Lubicz, S. R. A. 1977. *The Temple in Man: The Secrets of Ancient Egypt.* Brookline, MA: Autumn Press.

Dirac, P. A. M. 1937. "The Cosmological Constants." *Nature* 139:323.

Drake, S. 1957. *Discoveries and Opinions of Galileo.* Garden City, NY: Doubleday Anchor Books.

———. 1970. *Galileo Studies.* Ann Arbor: Univ. of Michigan Press.

Dummelow, J. R., ed. 1960. *One Volume Bible Commentary.* New York: Macmillan.

Durham, F., and Purrington, R. D. 1983. *Frame of the Universe.* New York: Columbia Univ. Press.

Dyczkowski, M. S. G. 1987. *The Doctrine of Liberation.* Albany, NY: State Univ. of New York Press.

Eddington, A. 1929. *Science and the Unseen World.* New York: Macmillan.

Einstein, A., Podolsky, B., and Rosen, W. 1935. "Can Quantum Mechanical Description of Physical Reality be Considered Complete?" *Physical Review* 47:777.

Eliade, M. 1959. *The Sacred and the Profane.* New York: Harcourt.

———. 1969. *Yoga, Immortality and Freedom.* Princeton: Princeton Univ. Press.

Fang, L. Z., Kiang, T., Cheng, F. H., and Hu, F. X. 1982. "Determination of the Deceleration Parameter q_o." *Quarterly Journal Royal Astronomical Society* 23:363.

Feynman, R. P. 1988. *QED. The Strange Theory of Light and Matter.* Princeton: Princeton Univ. Press.

Folse, H. J. 1985. *The Philosophy of Niels Bohr.* Amsterdam: North Holland Press.

Gaillard, M. K. 1982. "Toward a Unified Picture of Elementary Particle Interactions." *American Scientist* 70:506.

Gambhirananda, Swami. 1977. *Eight Upanishads*. Calcutta: Advaita Ashrama.

Gibbons, G. W., Hawking, S. W., and Siklos, S. T. C., eds. 1983. *The Very Early Universe*. Cambridge: Cambridge Univ. Press.

Gleick, J. 1988. *Chaos: Making a New Science*. New York: Viking.

Goleman, D., and Davidson, R., 1979, eds. *Consciousness: Brain, States of Awareness, and Mysticism*. New York: Harper & Row.

Graviger, P., ed. 1982. *Pythagoras and the Mystical Teachings of Pythagorism* (in Greek). Athens: Sphynx.

Gregory, R., ed. 1987. *The Oxford Companion to the Mind*. Oxford: Oxford Univ. Press.

Gribbin, J. 1984. *In Search of Schrödinger's Cat*. New York: Bantam Books.

Griffin, D. R., ed. 1986. *Physics and the Ultimate Significance of Time*. Albany, NY: State Univ. of New York Press.

Grof, S. 1985. *Beyond the Brain*. Albany, NY: State Univ. of New York Press.

Guillaumont, A., Puech, H.-Ch., Quispel, G., Till, W., and Al Masih, Y. A., translators. 1959. *The Gospel According to Thomas*. New York: Harper & Row.

Guth, A. H. 1982. "Phase Transitions in the Very Early Universe." In *The Very Early Universe*, G. W. Gibbons, S. W. Hawking and S. T. C. Siklos, eds. Cambridge: Cambridge Univ. Press.

Gyatso, T. 1989. *Kindness, Clarity, and Insight, 14th Dalai Lama*. J. Hopkins, tr. and ed. Ithaca, NY: Snow Lion Publication.

Hariharananda, Swami. 1983. *Yoga Philosophy of Patanjali*. Albany, NY: State Univ. of New York Press.

Harris, E. E. 1991. *Cosmos and Anthropos*. London: Humanities Press International.

Harrison, E. R. 1981. *Cosmology*. Cambridge: Cambridge Univ. Press.

Hawking, S. W. 1976. "Black Holes and Thermodynamics." *Physical Review D* 13:191.

———. 1989. *A Brief History of Time, from the Big Bang to Black Holes*. New York: Bantam Books.

Heisenberg, W. 1971. *Physics and Beyond*. London: George Allen and Unwin.

Herbert, N. 1987. *Quantum Reality: Beyond the New Physics*. New York: Anchor Press.

Holton, G., and Brush, S. G. 1985. *Introduction to Concepts and Theories in Physical Science*. Princeton: Princeton Univ. Press.

Hooker, C. A. 1972. *Paradigms and Paradoxes: The Philosophical Challenge of the Quantum Domain.* Pittsburgh: Univ. of Pittsburgh Press.

Howard, D. 1989. In *Philosophical Consequences of Quantum Theory,* J. T. Cushing and E. McMullin, eds. Notre Dame, IN: Univ. of Notre Dame Press.

Ishwarananda, Swami, 1987. "Practice is Enlightenment: The Life and Teaching of Zen Master Dogen." *Darshan* 6:47.

Jampolsky, G. 1979. *Love is Letting Go of Fear.* Berkeley, CA: Celestial Arts.

Jammer, M. 1966. *The Conceptual Development of Quantum Mechanics.* New York: McGraw Hill.

Jeans, J. 1931. *The Mysterious Universe.* Cambridge: Cambridge Univ. Press.

Kafatos, M. 1985. "The Universal Diagrams and Life in the Universe." In *The Search for Extraterrestrial Life: Recent Developments,* IAU Symposium No. 112. M. D. Papagiannis, ed. Dordrecht: D. Reidel.

———. 1986. "The Position of Brown Dwarfs on the Universal Diagrams." In *Astrophysics of Brown Dwarfs.* M. Kafatos, R. S. Harrington, S. P. Maran, eds. Cambridge: Cambridge Univ. Press.

———, ed. 1989. *Bell's Theorem, Quantum Theory and Conceptions of the Universe.* Dordrecht: Kluwer Academic Press.

——— and Nadeau, R. 1990. *The Conscious Universe: Part and Whole in Modern Physical Theory.* New York: Springer-Verlag.

Khanna, M. 1979. *Yantra.* London: Thames & Hudson.

Kuhn, T. 1962. *The Structure of Scientific Revolutions.* Chicago: Univ. of Chicago Press.

Kybalion: A Study of the Hermetic Philosophy of Ancient Egypt and Greece, The. 1908. Chicago: The Yogi Publication Society.

Lamy, L. 1981. *Egyptian Mysteries: New Light on Ancient Spiritual Knowledge.* New York: Crossroads.

LaViolette, P. A. 1986. "Is the Universe Really Expanding?" *Astrophysical Journal* 301:544.

Linde, A. D. 1982. "The New Inflationary Universe Scenario." In *The Very Early Universe,* G. W. Gibbons, S. W. Hawking and S. T. C. Siklos, eds. Cambridge: Cambridge Univ. Press.

Lockwood, M. 1989. *Mind, Brain and the Quantum: The Compound "I."* Oxford: Basil Blackwell, Ltd.

Lovelock, J. E. 1979. *Gaia: A New Look at Life on Earth.* London: Oxford Univ. Press.

Margenau, H. 1984. *The Miracle of Existence.* Woodbridge, CT: Ox Bow Press.

McLean, P. 1973. *A Triune Concept of the Brain and Behavior.* Toronto: University of Toronto Press.

Mermin, N. D. 1985. "Is the Moon There When Nobody Looks? Reality and the Quantum Theory." *Physics Today* Apr. 1985:38.

Meyendorff, J. 1962. *The Orthodox Church*. New York: Pantheon Books.

Misner, C. W., Thorne, K. S., and Wheeler, J. A. 1973. *Gravitation*. San Francisco: W. H. Freeman and Co.

Mookerjee, A. 1986. *Kundalini: The Arousal of the Inner Energy*. Rochester, VT: Destiny Books.

Muktananda, Swami. 1976. *A Book for the Mind*. South Fallsburg, NY: SYDA Foundation.

———. 1978. *Play of Consciousness*. New York: Harper & Row.

———. 1979. *Kundalini: The Secret of Life*. South Fallsburg, NY: SYDA Foundation.

———. 1980. *Understanding Siddha Yoga*, Vols. 1 & 2. South Fallsburg, NY: SYDA Foundation.

———. 1981. *Mystery of the Mind*. South Fallsburg, NY: SYDA Foundation.

Nikhilananda, Swami. 1975. *Upanishads*, Vol. III. New York: Ramakrishna-Vivekananda Center.

———. 1978. *Bhagavad Gita*. New York: Ramakrishna-Vivekananda Center.

Ott, E. 1981. "Strange Attractors and Chaotic Motions of Dynamical Systems." *Review of Modern Physics* 53:655.

Pagels, H. R. 1982. *The Cosmic Code*. New York: Bantam New Age.

Pais, A. 1981. In *Some Strangeness in the Proportion*, H. Woolf, ed. New York: Addison Wesley.

Palmer, E. H. 1974. *Oriental Mysticism: A Treatise on Sufistic and Unitarian Theosophy of the Persians*. London: The Octagon Press.

Pandit, B. N. 1977. *Aspects of Kashmir Shaivism*. Boulder, CO: Utpal Publications/Santarasa Books.

Pearce, J. C. 1985. *Magical Child Matures*. New York: E. P. Dutton.

———. 1987. "The Vision of Meister Eckhart." *Darshan* 3:48.

Peat, F. D. 1988. *Superstrings and the Search for the Theory of Everything*. Chicago: Contemporary Books.

Penrose, R. 1989. *The Emperor's New Mind*. New York: Oxford.

Philokalia, 1957 (in Greek). Athens: Astir.

Polkinghorne, J. C. 1984. *The Quantum World*. Princeton: Princeton Univ. Press.

Ponce, C. 1973. *The Kabbalah: An Introduction and Illumination for the World Today*. San Francisco: Straight Arrow Books. Wheaton, IL: Theosophical Publishing House, Quest Books, 1978.

Prabhavananda, Swami, and Isherwood, G. 1953. *How to Know God: The Yoga Aphorisms of Patanjali*. Hollywood: Vedanta Press.

Prigogine, I., and Stengers, I. 1984. *Order Out of Chaos*. Toronto: Bantam Books.

Radha, S. 1978. *Kundalini Yoga for the West*. Boston: Shambhala.

Ranade, R. D. 1983. *Mysticism in India: The Poet-Saints of Maharashtra*. Albany, NY: State Univ. of New York Press.

Rucker, R. 1982. *Infinity and the Mind*. Boston: Birkhauser.

Rudrappa, 1969. *Kashmir Shaivism*. Prasaranga: Univ. Mysore.

Rutherford, E. 1940. *Background in Modern Science*. New York: Macmillan.

Schimmel, A. 1975. *Mystical Dimensions of Islam*. Chapel Hill: The Univ. of North Carolina Press.

Schramm, D. N. 1983. "The Early Universe and High-Energy Physics." *Physics Today* Apr. 1983:27.

Sheldrake, R. 1981. *A New Science of Life*. Los Angeles: J. P. Tarcher.

Shimony, A. 1988. "The Reality of the Quantum World." *Scientific American* 258:46.

Singh, J. 1979a. *Shiva Sutras*. Delhi: Motilal Banarsidas.

———. 1979b. *Vijnanabhairava*. Delhi: Motilal Banarsidas.

———. 1980a. *Pratyabhijnahridayam*. Delhi: Motilal Banarsidas.

———. 1980b. *Spanda Karikas*. Delhi: Motilal Banarsidas.

Stapp, H. 1975. "Bell's Theorem and World Process." *Il Nuovo Cimento* 29B:271.

———. 1988. In *The World View of Contemporary Physics*, R. Kitchener, ed. Albany, NY: State Univ. of New York Press.

———. 1989. In *Philosophical Consequences of Quantum Theory*, J. T. Cushing and E. McMullin, eds. Notre Dame, IN: Univ. of Notre Dame Press.

Sulentic, J. W. 1983. "Confirmation of the Luminous Connection Between NGC 4319 and Markarian 205." *Astrophysical Journal Letters* 265:L49.

Taylor, C. 1981. *The Natural History of the Mind*. England: Penguin Books Ltd.

Teeple, H. 1974. *The Literary Origin of the Gospel of John*. Evanston, IL: Religion and Ethics Institute, Inc.

Trefil, J. 1983. *The Moment of Creation*. New York: Macmillan.

Underhill, E. 1957. *Mysticism: A Study in the Nature and Development of Man's Spiritual Consciousness*. New York: Meridian Books.

Venkatesananda, Swami, 1984. *The Concise Yoga Vasistha*. Albany, NY: State Univ. of New York Press.

Wald, G. 1984. "Life and Mind in the Universe." *International Journal of Quantum Chemistry* 11:1.

Walker, K. 1961. *The Extra-Sensory Mind*. New York: Harper & Row.

Warner, R. 1958. *The Greek Philosophers*. New York: New York American Library.

Waters, F. 1969. *The Book of the Hopis*. New York: Ballantine.

Weinberg, S. 1972. *Gravitation and Cosmology*. New York: John Wiley and Sons.

Weizenbaum, J. 1976. *Computer Power and Human Reason.* San Francisco: W. H. Freeman and Co.

Westcott, W. W., ed. 1960. *Sepher Yetzirah.* New York: Occult Research Press.

Weyl, H. 1949. *Philosophy of Mathematics and Natural Science.* Princeton: Princeton Univ. Press.

Wheeler, J. A. 1981. In *Some Strangeness in the Proportion,* H. Woolf, ed. New York: Addison-Wesley.

———. 1983. In *Quantum Theory and Measurement,* J. A. Wheeler and W. H. Zurek, eds. Princeton: Princeton Univ. Press.

White, John, ed. 1979. *Kundalini, Evolution and Enlightenment.* Garden City, NY: Anchor Press.

Whitehead, A. N. 1929. *Process and Reality.* New York: Macmillan.

Wigner, E. 1983. In *Quantum Theory and Measurement.* J. A. Wheeler and W. H. Zurek, eds. Princeton: Princeton Univ. Press.

Wilber, K., ed. 1982. *The Holographic Paradigm.* Boulder: Shambhala.

———, ed. 1984. *Quantum Questions.* Boston: New Science Library, Shambhala.

Wilkins, W. J. 1990. *Hindu Mythology.* Calcutta: Rupa & Co.

Wright, R. 1988. *Three Scientists and their Gods.* New York: Times Books.

Yogananda, Swami. 1952. *The Autobiography of a Yogi.* Los Angeles: Self-Realization Fellowship.

———. 1982. *Metaphysical Meditations.* Los Angeles: Self-Realization Fellowship.

Yukteswar, S. 1984. *The Holy Science.* Los Angeles: Self-Realization Fellowship.

Zee, A. 1986. *Fearful Symmetry.* New York: Macmillan.

Zukav, G. 1979. *The Dancing Wu-Li Masters.* New York: Morrow.

Index

NOTES

NOTES

NOTES

NOTES